TRUTH IN MANY TONGUES

TRUTH IN MANY TONGUES

Religious Conversion and the Languages of the Early Spanish Empire

Daniel I. Wasserman-Soler

THE PENNSYLVANIA STATE UNIVERSITY PRESS
UNIVERSITY PARK, PENNSYLVANIA

Library of Congress Cataloging-in-Publication Data

Names: Wasserman-Soler, Daniel I. (Daniel Isaac), 1984– author.
Title: Truth in many tongues : religious conversion and the languages of the early Spanish Empire / Daniel I. Wasserman-Soler.
Description: University Park, Pennsylvania : The Pennsylvania State University Press, [2020] | Includes bibliographical references and index.
Summary: "Examines how the Spanish monarchy managed an empire of unprecedented linguistic diversity, making only sporadic efforts to propagate Spanish during the sixteenth century. Challenges the assumption that the pervasiveness of the Spanish language resulted from deliberate linguistic colonization"—Provided by publisher.
Identifiers: LCCN 2019058401 | ISBN 9780271085999 (cloth)
Subjects: LCSH: Conversion—Catholic Church—History—16th century. | Spain—Languages—History—16th century. | New Spain—Languages—History—16th century. | Spain—History—Philip II, 1556–1598.
Classification: LCC P381.S6 W37 2020 | DDC 409.171/246—dc23
LC record available at https://lccn.loc.gov/2019058401

Printed in the United States of America
Published by The Pennsylvania State University Press,
University Park, PA 16802-1003

The Pennsylvania State University Press is a member of the Association of University Presses.
It is the policy of The Pennsylvania State University Press to use acid-free paper. Publications on uncoated stock satisfy the minimum requirements of American National Standard for Information Sciences—Permanence of Paper for Printed Library Material, ANSI Z39.48-1992.

To Katie

CONTENTS

List of Illustrations | viii
Acknowledgments | ix
Note on the Text | xii

Introduction | 1

1. The Spanish Language and the Inquisition, ca. 1550–1600 | 13

2. Arabic and Spanish in Granada, ca. 1492–1570 | 39

3. Arabic and *Romance* in Valencia, ca. 1540–1600 | 69

4. Native Tongues and Spanish in New Spain, ca. 1520–85 | 98

5. Creating a Multilingual New Spain, ca. 1550–1600 | 131

Conclusion | 157

Appendix: Linguistic Abilities of Franciscan Friars in Sixteenth-Century New Spain | 168
Notes | 172
Bibliography | 203
Index | 223

ILLUSTRATIONS

1. Philip II of Spain | 2

2. Martin Pérez de Ayala, *Doctrina christiana* | 49

3. Martin Pérez de Ayala, *Doctrina christiana* | 75

4. Philip II letter | 137

5. Alonso de Molina, *Confessionario breue en lengua mexicana y castellana* | 147

6. Maturino Gilberti, *Diálogo de doctrina christiana* | 149

7. Juan de la Anunciación, *Sermonario en lengua mexicana* | 153

TABLE 1. Language practices advocated by Valencian archbishops | 77

ACKNOWLEDGMENTS

In my time as a student of the early modern world, I have received generous support from many people. Any value in this project is due in large part to their help; the shortcomings or errors in the pages that follow remain mine. I will not be able to thank adequately the many individuals who graciously have given me their time and support, but I would like to try.

I am indebted especially to the institutions that provided me with long-term support for my research: the Andrew W. Mellon Foundation (especially the Mellon Mays program), the Fulbright Commission, the Newberry Library, and the University of Virginia, where this project began. For additional financial support, I would like to thank the Woodrow Wilson Foundation, the John Carter Brown Library, the Princeton University Library, the Harvard University Atlantic History Seminar, Oberlin College, the Renaissance Society of America, the Social Science Research Council, the American Historical Association, the University of California at Berkeley's Bancroft Library, the Huntington Library, the American Philosophical Society, Penn State University, the Program for Cultural Cooperation between Spain's Ministry of Culture and United States Universities, and the Center for Reformation Research.

My first individual thanks go to H. C. Erik Midelfort, who—even before I was his student—showed interest in my work, though it is outside his own field. He has challenged my points of view, put my work on the right path at several points, and continues to be a source of good humor and invaluable advice. I also am deeply grateful to Alison P. Weber, who so graciously and skillfully manages to be both critical and encouraging; working with her and continuing to count on her guidance and friendship has been a privilege and a pleasure. I owe many thanks to Lu Ann Homza, who has generously given her time, wisdom, and support to someone for whom she had no obligation. I am grateful to Kim Lynn as well for her mentorship and support of this project.

I also would like to thank my teachers from the University of Chicago: Constantin Fasolt, Hanna Holborn Gray, and Katy O'Brien Weintraub; without them, I would not have developed a deep interest in Renaissance Europe, the Reformation, and the study of history, in general. Each of them continues to serve as a model for me of teaching at its best. I also am grateful to Nadine O'Connor Di Vito, whose enthusiasm for language study I could not help but absorb; Elise LaRose, for her support and encouragement as I developed an interest in academic research; and Dan Riches, for his guidance as I began to navigate the history of the Reformation. I am very grateful, too, for the Institute for Recruitment of Teachers at Phillips Academy Andover, especially for guidance from Kelly Wise and Chera Reid at a crucial juncture of my career.

At the University of Virginia, I learned a great deal from Brian Owensby, who introduced me to the fascinating history of Latin America, and from Erin Rowe, who provided truly insightful commentary on my work. At UVA, I benefited from a wonderfully collegial, supportive, and stimulating environment. I am grateful to classmates and professors as well as to Molly Angevine and Tally Sanford.

Since 2013, I have been fortunate to work in a collegial and rewarding environment like Alma College. I would like to thank Jeff Abernathy, Dana Aspinall, Kate Blanchard, Liping Bu, Patrick Furlong, Ed Lorenz, Kristin Olbertson, Michael Selmon, and Keith Wise for their support of my work. I also appreciate the support of the Alma College Library, particularly for help with interlibrary loan materials, and the Alma Public Library, where I spent much time working on revisions.

In Madrid, I am grateful to Jim Amelang and Virgilio Pinto Crespo for their support of my work, especially at an early stage, and also to Laura Bass, Mercedes García-Arenal, María José del Río Barredo, María Ángeles Gallego, María Tausiet, and Ari Zighelboim. Equally crucial to my time in Madrid was the friendship of Blanca Ampudia de Haro, Ricardo Calleja, Juan Pedro Carrera, Adolfo Cazorla, Fernando Fragoso, José Foronda and Adela Perea, Víctor Moreno, and Sergio Moreno.

I am indebted to colleagues outside of my home institutions for their interest in and support of my work: Jodi Bilinkoff, David Boruchoff, Andrew Devereux, Bernard Ducharme, Randy Head, Ronnie Hsia, Michael Lansing, Ann Moyer, Sally Nalle, Martin Nesvig, Carla Phillips, Beth Plummer, Adina Ruiu, Scott Taylor, Zeb Tortorici, and Betsy Wright. I also am thankful to Penn State University Press for taking up this project, to Ellie Goodman for her interest and support, and to two anonymous readers for their insightful comments.

I would like to thank the staff of the institutions where I conducted research, especially Sensi Molero, Blanca Marina Díaz Garcia, and the staff of the Archivo Histórico Nacional in Madrid; Fr. Robert Danieluk, Fr. Francisco de Borja Medina, Mauro Brunello and the staff of the Archivum Romanum Societatis Iesu; Roy Goodman and the staff of the American Philosophical Society; Peter Hanff and the staff of the Bancroft Library; Jim Muldoon, Margot Nishimura, Rosa Paiva, Elaine Tucci, Ken Ward, and the staff of the John Carter Brown Library; Diane Dillon, Scott Stevens, Ron Thomas, and the staff of Newberry Library.

Though academic research can be isolating, I am deeply grateful to have formed many friendships in the course of my work. I am especially grateful to Paolo and Cecilia Aranha, Dan and Cason Cheely, Matt Gaetano, Claire Gilbert, Patricia Giménez-Eguibar and Javier Casaseca, Verónica Gutiérrez, Michael Kelly, Will and Erin Kurtz, Margaret Lewis, Bronwen McShea, Harold and Brandie Mock, and Jared and Michelle Staller. For many years now, Pat and Dan Cheely and their family have enriched my life in countless ways. Last, but certainly not least, I thank my beloved family: Stephi, Joey, Alex, and my parents, Henry and Maria del Carmen Wasserman, who believed in me and encouraged me at every stage. Finally, I am grateful to James, Patsy, Zélie, and Peter, who bring joy to me every day, and to Katie, who reminds me of my true purpose and to whom I dedicate this book.

NOTE ON THE TEXT

Wherever possible, I have combined the notes for each paragraph: when a quotation lacks an immediate note, the reader usually will find it near the end of the paragraph.

Unless otherwise noted, all translations are mine. Should the reader wish to consult the text from the original documents, I have provided them when possible as an appendix on my personal webpage.

INTRODUCTION

In the sixteenth century, Spanish monarchs ruled over perhaps the most linguistically diverse kingdoms in the world. Inhabitants of Iberia spoke Arabic, Basque, Castilian, Catalan, Ladino, or another Romance language. Iberians lived in a land of many tongues, but they still were astonished by the number of languages that they encountered in the Americas. No short list could do justice to the immense range of both languages and language families in the "New World." And the Spanish Empire extended well beyond America and into the Pacific islands. How Spanish authorities dealt with a dizzying range of languages is the subject of this book.

One example will help explain. In 1567 King Philip II (fig. 1) prohibited Granada's Islamic community from speaking Arabic. He and leading churchmen thought that the language prevented conversions to Christianity. One might assume that Philip took similar action across his kingdoms, pushing his native Castilian and restricting the languages of other peoples.[1]

Philip, however, never issued a comparable ban of Native American languages. In fact, he seems to have done the opposite. Throughout his reign, he urged churchmen in the Americas to devote themselves to learning native tongues. He did not even enact the same restriction of Arabic throughout Castile; that initial decree applied only to Granada. To the modern reader, this way of thinking may appear contradictory. This book argues that

FIG. 1 | Philip II of Spain. Library of Congress, Washington, DC, LC-USZ62-100317.

Philip's mode of thought actually was common among churchmen in the sixteenth-century Spanish kingdoms.[2]

This anecdote points to three surprising aspects of sixteenth-century Spanish thought and practice regarding languages in both Iberia and the Americas. First, sixteenth-century Spanish authorities demonstrated less interest in propagating Castilian than we might think. Although that language eventually became widespread, Spanish officials had no unified policy aiming to promote Castilian during the first century of expansion. Spanish monarchs and leading churchmen put much more effort into encouraging the use of American indigenous languages. Some influential clerics also called for and used Arabic, though they were far fewer in number. Within this general framework, there existed many variations.[3]

Second, just as Philip and his leading churchmen had no uniform approach with Castilian, they also had no set policy for the use of other languages. One might assume that they would have taken one of two routes in governing this multilingual body of subjects.[4] On the one hand, they might have accommodated the people's linguistic differences, allowing everyone to speak the language of their choice. On the other hand, they might have forced everyone to assimilate to Castilian. They did neither one exclusively. They restricted Arabic in some contexts and not in others; they advocated the use of Amerindian languages but not in all cases. Sixteenth-century Spanish churchmen thought about language in ways that modern categories cannot explain: they were neither liberal nor conservative, neither tolerant nor intolerant. In fact, they did not think only or even predominantly in terms of accommodation or assimilation—categories that remain common in much contemporary scholarship on missions. Rather, their actions reveal a highly practical mentality, in which they considered each context on its own terms before deciding what language practices would help bring more souls into the Catholic Church.

In several cases, Spanish religious leaders called for and implemented multilingual methods to foster religious conversion. Even when a language seemed useful for one context, it was not necessarily appropriate elsewhere. Thus in spite of heterogeneous and often polyglot methods, the Spanish Empire was no multilingual utopia. Churchmen often restricted the vernaculars to certain contexts, and religious leaders did, on some occasions, actively lobby against particular ways of using a language. The Spanish Crown and its churchmen, therefore, did not accommodate all languages at all times. Still, throughout the sixteenth century, they never adopted a firm policy of eliminating all foreign cultural markers. As a whole, early modern Church leaders thought about language in a situation-specific way. They viewed some vernaculars as appropriate for certain contexts but not for others. They did not demonstrate a firm commitment to propagating one language above all others.

Finally, in the minds of many sixteenth-century Spanish officials, the languages of the people were somewhat less central to effective religious instruction than we might expect. For the modern reader, it may seem obvious that the vernaculars would serve as the sine qua non of successful catechesis. Without dismissing the obvious utility of the people's languages, several churchmen troubled the notion that the vernaculars stood at the center of conversion efforts. Chapter 1 demonstrates that several churchmen, such as the Dominican friar Melchior Cano, thought that the increasing availability of Castilian prayer books could, in fact, hinder proper religious instruction rather than help it. Chapters 2 and 3 indicate that churchmen who lacked Arabic still made important contributions to the evangelization of Islamic communities while speaking only in Castilian or Valencian. While the Jesuit Juan de Albotodo preached in Arabic, most of the Jesuit priests and brothers in Granada worked only or primarily in Castilian. Despite their linguistic limitations, both their contemporaries and modern historians agree that they had some success in their efforts to convert Granada's Islamic community. The last two chapters show, similarly, that even those men who struggled to learn Amerindian languages still could participate meaningfully in the instruction of native peoples. While the Franciscan friar Alonso de Molina demanded that every cleric know an indigenous language and know it well, others—such as his fellow Franciscan Maturino Gilberti—apparently considered this standard impractical. Gilberti and others appear to have accepted that some churchmen would not learn the local languages very well, so they produced lengthy collections of sermons and reflections. With these aids, even the less linguistically adept missionaries could simply learn to read the text aloud to their indigenous flock.

In general, Spanish churchmen did consider the vernaculars very useful. In some situations, however, it was not always possible or appropriate to use the language of the people. For virtually all the churchmen examined here, the best means for teaching Christian doctrine consisted of living virtuously and encouraging—by their example—participation in the sacraments and the life of the Church. The fact that they often did not use the languages of the people did not—in their minds—lead necessarily to failure. Instead, it meant that they saw the vernacular languages as highly useful tools but not as the only method of religious conversion.

THE DIVERSITY OF THE SPANISH EMPIRE

In the sixteenth-century Spanish kingdoms, Catholic clerics worked with a wide range of people, who had varying levels of knowledge regarding Christian doctrine. Most residents of Castile and Aragón had been Christian for centuries, yet they often lacked religious instruction. For this reason, many churchmen used the term "Indies" to underline the need for basic religious instruction in Europe.[5] Muslims in Europe had been aware of Christianity for centuries and—for the most part—had rejected it. The indigenous peoples of America had no exposure to Christianity prior to 1492. Each group was diverse and presented distinct challenges.

Before addressing the peoples studied in this book, it is important to explain the absence here of two major groups within the Spanish kingdoms: African and Jewish communities. Both appear only briefly because little documentation exists regarding the place of language in the religious instruction of Africans and Jews. When the bishops of Mexico discussed the conversion of Africans at the Third Provincial Council of Mexico (1585), they recommended that ministers use the Castilian language. The choice of Castilian probably was a practical one: slave traders brought Africans to the Americas without regard for preserving their linguistic communities.[6] Thus Africans who lived in a particular area in the Americas did not necessarily share a language. Churchmen faced another challenge with Africans: they spent relatively little time with African slaves, because the latter belonged to Spanish masters. Theoretically, the masters had the duty of providing them with religious instruction.[7]

While clerics' relative lack of contact with Africans may explain the paucity of sources addressing language practices for their evangelization, no substantial linguistic barrier existed for the instruction of Jewish communities. Because Jews and *conversos* (Christians of Jewish descent) spoke Ladino, a Romance language bearing strong similarities to Castilian, Church authorities in sixteenth-century Spain generally did not face a linguistic obstacle in communication with them. By the end of the *Reconquista* in 1492 and afterward, Jews increasingly spoke Romance languages, except in religious practice and literary culture, both of which utilized Hebrew as the language of choice. That said, the study of Hebrew scripture by Christian scholars did provoke a significant controversy in sixteenth-century Spain. It posed a particular problem for scripture scholars who found themselves suspected of heresy.[8] The chapters that follow focus on a different problem: how to use language to instruct a broader populace who lacked formal training in theology.

For priests who instructed the people, each situation required a different set of languages. Most of the traditionally Christian (or "Old Christian") peoples spoke Castilian or another Iberian Romance language (e.g., Catalan, Galician, or Valencian). Some relied on Basque, a linguistic isolate, unrelated to any Indo-European language. Churchmen also could instruct others through religious writing, but much of it remained limited to those people who knew Latin well.

Spanish Muslims, similarly, used a variety of languages. In 1492 the Muslims of Granada had just become subjects of a Christian monarchy for the first time. At that moment, they spoke Arabic and had limited knowledge of Castilian. The Muslims of Valencia, however, had been under Christian rule for over two hundred years. While Arabic remained an important language in sixteenth-century Valencia, many Muslims there spoke the local Romance language (Valencian). For centuries, Muslim writers had translated works from Arabic into Spanish and also into *aljamiado* (Spanish written with Arabic script).[9]

In the Americas, indigenous peoples spoke hundreds of languages. Linguists in the twentieth century have identified over three hundred languages in Mexico and Central America and well over a dozen linguistic families in the same area. In fact, just one portion of Mexico had a degree of linguistic diversity that surpassed entire continents of the "Old World." Altogether, no sixteenth-century community across the globe had a wider range of languages than the Spanish Crown.[10]

According to established accounts, Spanish churchmen initially responded with flexibility to these heterogeneous circumstances. In mid-sixteenth-century Spain, churchmen such as John of Ávila, Francis Borgia, Bartolomé Carranza, and Louis of Granada published vernacular Castilian books of prayer and doctrine. In doing so, they aimed to expand the traditionally Latin corpus of Christian writing and engage a wider audience. Their attempts came under suspicion in 1559, when the Spanish Inquisition prohibited several vernacular books of prayer and doctrine.

Interest in Arabic, similarly, appears to have risen and fallen. For instance, Hernando de Talavera, archbishop of Granada (1492–1507), encouraged Muslims to pray in Arabic. Around the turn of the century, Granada's Muslims faced the unattractive choice of conversion to Christianity or departure from Iberia. Those who stayed accepted baptism and became known as Moriscos, or "New Christians" of Islamic descent. By the mid-sixteenth century, virtually all Moriscos in the city would have known some Castilian, at least enough to put together a few broken sentences. Still, many continued to use Arabic, especially the inhabitants of rural areas. In 1565 the bishops of Granada agreed that Moriscos should be discouraged from using Arabic, and King Philip II agreed. He issued a royal order to prohibit Granada's Moriscos from using Arabic.[11]

In America, the Church's interest in indigenous languages took on a much more profound and long-lasting nature, compared to Arabic. Dozens and dozens of churchmen learned a native language, and many learned more than one.[12] But by the late eighteenth century, the archbishop of Mexico City and King Charles III agreed to suppress indigenous languages. Altogether, the Church and Crown eventually favored the propagation of Castilian Spanish and the restriction or elimination of Arabic in Spain and of native tongues in America.[13]

CONTRIBUTIONS TO CURRENT SCHOLARSHIP

From this general view, sixteenth-century Spain became increasingly homogeneous, rejecting dissident beliefs and cultures. The flexibility of early generations seems to have given way to a more rigid dogmatism. Much evidence corroborates this outlook, given that Spanish kings and churchmen clearly have a record of attempting to restrict if not prohibit certain languages. This emphasis within existing scholarship tends to oversimplify the story. It suggests that, beginning around midcentury—more or less during the Council of Trent (1545–63)—churchmen became either more closed or intransigent, as it were, or they eventually lost out to men who espoused such perspectives.[14]

This book aims to modify that story. It demonstrates that these churchmen thought about language in subtler ways, largely ignored until now. The many variations in their thoughts and practices regarding language reveal themselves in a wide range of documents—inquisition reports and letters; royal and ecclesiastical correspondence; records of Church assemblies, councils, and synods; and printed books in a variety of genres and languages—scattered across more than thirty archives and libraries in Spain, Italy, England, the United States, and Mexico. Church and Crown officials thus had no single, unified conversation or debate regarding language and religious conversion in the sixteenth-century Spanish territories. Rather, their discussions usually addressed specific problems, taking place in particular circumstances. Altogether, in the second half of the sixteenth century, Spanish churchmen shared much in common with earlier generations. They operated with a surprising degree of flexibility not only in the early 1500s but throughout that century.

This book contributes to three related fields of study within early modern history (ca. 1450–1800). First, this project enhances a well-established body of scholarship that has revised traditional views of early modern Spain and its place within Reformation Europe. Leading historians now generally agree that the Church, the Crown, and the ill-famed Inquisition did not have a tight grip on the religious practices of the common people. These scholars have, therefore, dismantled the stereotypical view of Catholic authorities successfully enforcing adherence to orthodox doctrine and suppressing all dissent in the Spanish world.[15] Scholars of early modern Europe more generally have demonstrated that—far from conforming to a strict body of doctrine—a spectrum of religious beliefs and practices existed among the common people during the Reformation era.[16]

In a similar vein, this book seeks to complement the work done by scholars of colonial Latin America who have provided new assessments of the relationships between Europeans and Amerindians. Anthropologists, art historians, linguists, literary critics, and historians have overturned the now outdated notion that powerful European conquerors dominated weak indigenous communities. While not denying the existence of unequal power relationships among Europeans and Native Americans, scholars have found much continuity across the pre- and postconquest periods in Latin America. They have argued that even after the European arrival, members of indigenous communities persevered in communicating their religious, governmental, legal, and cultural traditions to younger generations. Rather than characterize Native Americans as individuals who passively received European culture, current scholars increasingly have depicted Native Americans as interlocutors with Europeans in forming a New World society.[17]

Scholars of both early modern Europe and colonial Latin America thus have revised old notions of powerful Catholic authorities and submissive, homogeneous peoples. Instead, we are now learning more about the rich diversity of belief and practice in the lives of early modern peoples. Scholars have provided a more nuanced view of the *impact* of Church and Crown authorities on the common people. We still know little, however, about the agenda of bishops, inquisitors, and the other Catholic officials who attempted to delineate and enforce religious doctrine in the Spanish world. Our knowledge of many individuals who served in leadership roles—such as the Dominican friar Louis of Granada and the archbishop Martín Pérez de Ayala—remains limited.[18] The chapters that follow attempt to address that gap.

This book also contributes to the comparative study of early modern Spain and its overseas territories. For some time, scholars have pointed to the conquest and evangelization of Islamic Granada as a model for similar developments in America.[19] Many reasons make this comparison a compelling one. The "Catholic kings," Ferdinand and Isabella, achieved the conquest of Islamic Granada in 1491, just a short time before Christopher Columbus would claim new overseas territories in the name of the Crown. In both Granada and the Americas, churchmen attempted to propagate the Christian faith. Both areas coupled Christian evangelization with efforts to inculcate European civility. Recent scholarship taking this comparative angle has focused especially on the Society of Jesus. It has emphasized that the Jesuits developed a universal strategy for evangelization across the globe.[20] Some of this work has offered insight with regard to the language practices of the Spanish Church and Crown.[21] No study, however, has focused on this topic systematically and in a transatlantic context.[22]

While this research has underlined common phenomena across the Spanish kingdoms, scholars know less about the differences between these simultaneous attempts to evangelize. Methods of religious instruction and general attitudes toward Islamic and Amerindian communities differed substantially, especially concerning the use of language.[23] When compared to the Church's use of Arabic in Spain, the New World witnessed a significantly larger degree of support for indigenous languages. The differences become especially salient when examining the positions taken by Charles I and Philip II, the long-reigning monarchs of the sixteenth-century Spanish kingdoms. While both attempted to enact wide-ranging restrictions of Arabic, neither monarch tried to replicate that approach with Amerindian languages.[24]

RELIGIOUS CONVERSION AND LANGUAGES IN THE MIDDLE AGES

Conversations about the vernacular were by no means a novelty of the sixteenth century. Long before the Renaissance and Reformation, Christian authorities had contemplated how to use the vernacular to communicate doctrine. In the fourth and fifth centuries, St. Jerome carried out his famous effort to translate Hebrew and Christian scripture into Latin, the vernacular of the Romans.[25]

Centuries later, the Fourth Lateran Council (1215) commanded that "the bishops of these cities and dioceses provide suitable men who will, according to the different rites and languages, celebrate the divine offices for them, administer the sacraments of the Church and instruct them by word and example." While this decree enabled the inclusion of diverse languages and rites within the Catholic Church, the ideal did not always translate into practice. In thirteenth- and fourteenth-century Aragon, for example, leaders of the Order of Friars Preachers (Dominicans), sought to establish programs of study for both Arabic and Hebrew. At least a few Dominicans did learn one or both languages, but on the whole, these campaigns of language study seem to have produced only informal and temporary initiatives. Beyond Iberia, the Council of Vienne (1311–12) also called for language study, particularly Hebrew, Arabic, Chaldean, and Syriac/Aramaic, in order to facilitate preaching throughout the Mediterranean world. Such programs of language study were to take place at Europe's leading centers of learning—Oxford, Paris, Bologna, and Salamanca. The council's plans, however, appear to have produced no tangible results.[26]

More than two centuries later, Catholic authorities met at the Council of Trent, in response to Martin Luther and to decades of internal calls for reform. Together with discussions on the nature of salvation and the sacraments, Catholic clerics also thought about how the vernaculars would fit into the future of the Roman Church. Replying to criticism by Luther and others,[27] the Roman Church affirmed the Latin Vulgate Bible as authoritative. One might assume, therefore, that the Catholic Church championed Latin and disdained the languages of the people. Catholic leaders, however, proved surprisingly adaptable.

While they confirmed the authority of the Latin Vulgate Bible, they still permitted the translation of scripture into the vernaculars.[28] Local authorities would determine whether to translate into the vernacular; accordingly, rules and practices varied widely.[29] In discussing the vernaculars, the delegates at Trent addressed more than just scripture. They encouraged bishops to produce vernacular catechisms, books that enumerated the basic prayers and teachings of Catholicism, such as the Ten Commandments and the works of mercy. Leaders at Trent also sought to ensure that local priests would preach in the languages of the people.[30] Though many Catholic authorities associated the vernacular with Luther and thus with dissent, the same individuals often considered the vernacular an eminently useful tool within certain contexts.

Though Spanish churchmen did discuss using the vernaculars for sacred scripture,[31] they spent more time thinking about language use in other contexts. The following chapters explore how churchmen thought about and used the vernaculars for basic religious instruction, preaching, and religious books (e.g., catechisms and books of prayer). In sixteenth-century Europe, Luther and other Protestant reformers raised one set of questions about the vernaculars. Catholic leaders dealt with a wider set of challenges.

THE STRUCTURE OF THIS BOOK

Between approximately 1470 and 1540, the Spanish kingdoms experienced several major events, each of which had a linguistic component. By 1480, eight Spanish towns had printing presses.[32] The innovation of the printing press and the Protestant Reformation brought to a new level the demand for education through the text, notably the more accessible, vernacular book. Iberia was no exception to this rule: chapter 1 discusses authors like Bartolomé Carranza (d. 1576) and Louis of Granada (d. 1588), who saw vernacular, Castilian books as a new opportunity to provide religious instruction to the reading populace.

Just a few decades earlier, the completion of the *Reconquista* in 1492 brought all of Iberia under Christian rule. With Spanish Islamic communities now in a subordinate position, Spanish churchmen—such as Hernando de Talavera (d. 1507), Martín Pérez de Ayala (d. 1566), and Juan de Ribera (d. 1611)—made efforts to convert Islamic communities and considered whether Arabic could facilitate conversions to Catholicism.

Finally, this period also witnessed the exploration of lands previously unknown to continental Europeans. Chapters 4 and 5 shift to New Spain, examining how the Americas raised a plethora of questions related to religion and governance, not least of which concerned how to spread the Gospel to people who spoke different languages. At once, the leaders of the Spanish Church considered how to approach some very different populations. The subject of vernacular usage, long considered a distinctly Protestant rallying cry, took on many forms in Catholic lands.

As a whole, this book shows that language practices could differ significantly from one context to another and even within one setting. Regardless of location, most churchmen seem to have shared a common conviction: they often believed that the knowledge of local languages would help foster religious conversion. Nonetheless, by no means did they consider the spoken or written word as the *only* key to communicating the meaning of Christianity.

Examining efforts to Christianize both Spain and its empire, this book shows that the Church and the Crown experimented with a multiplicity of approaches to facilitate communication among its people. Aware that a single policy would not serve the entire Spanish monarchy, religious authorities carefully considered each context and developed situation-specific language practices. As a whole, this book illuminates the thought processes of Spanish royal officials and churchmen, reconsidering them as they would have seen themselves: as educational reformers and administrators aiming to develop practical and effective modes of instruction for their charges.

CHAPTER 1

THE SPANISH LANGUAGE AND THE INQUISITION, CA. 1550–1600

In 1558 the Spanish Inquisition initiated perhaps the most infamous individual prosecution in its history: the arrest of the highest-ranking bishop in Spain, Bartolomé Carranza. Inquisitor General Fernando de Valdés prohibited Carranza's *Comentarios sobre el catechismo christiano* (Commentaries on the Christian Catechism) as well as the "best-selling" book of the Spanish Golden Age, the *Libro de la oración y meditación* (The Book of Prayer and Meditation), written by Louis of Granada. Valdés also banned all vernacular books of doctrine printed outside of Spain after 1550, claiming that those texts divulged complex religious teachings to common men and women. Throughout the second half of the sixteenth century, authors who wrote in the vernacular made their work suspicious of heresy.[1]

Leading scholarship contends that the Inquisition's concern with the vernacular served merely as a front for a long-standing vendetta between Carranza and Melchior Cano, a censor and theologian of the Inquisition. Inquisitor Valdés, who had his own history with Carranza, sided with Cano. This chapter complements recent work by acknowledging that not only personal histories *but also* pastoral concerns played a role in the suspicion accorded toward vernacular books, like those of Carranza and Granada. To the modern reader, the vernacular may seem an obvious aid to understanding religious teaching. This chapter's purpose lies in exploring the reasoning behind a widely shared concern—namely, that vernacular texts could cause confusion and error. The evidence demonstrates that churchmen recognized writing in the vernacular as a controversial issue. In response to that challenge, they developed a range of pastoral solutions.

Not all vernacular religious books posed a problem. Basic catechisms and books of hours (containing prayers to be recited at specific times of day), for instance, remained acceptable. Inquisitor Valdés banned vernacular texts that included more than standard prayers and basic teachings. His concern lay with books that included elaborate expositions of doctrine. For Valdés, these vernacular books led to a misguided freedom, allowing common people to bypass priestly authority and study doctrine on their own. Some Inquisition officials linked this popularization of doctrine to the dissent and variety of opinion that characterized the Protestant Reformation. Accordingly, Valdés's prohibition of vernacular texts followed the discovery of Protestant communities in the major cities of Valladolid and Seville.[2]

In prohibiting these Castilian-language books, Valdés identified the works of some apparently orthodox writers. One churchman responded by saying, "The faint-hearted have reacted by becoming more faint-hearted and those dedicated to virtue are in dismay, seeing that the Inquisitor General has published an edict forbidding almost all the books in Spanish that have been used up to now by those who try to serve God."[3] Besides Carranza and Granada, Valdés's Index also included work by future saints, such as John of Ávila and Francis Borgia. Carranza, as the archbishop of Toledo, occupied the highest episcopal see in Spain and the second highest in all Christendom after the Holy See in Rome. Granada, his student from the Colegio de San Gregorio in Valladolid, did not trail him by far. He served as the provincial of the Dominican friars in Portugal and enjoyed fame as a preacher throughout the Iberian peninsula. Granada's *Libro de la oración* went through an astounding twenty-three editions in just the first five years after its publication.[4]

Although Inquisitor Valdés prohibited Granada's popular prayer book and Carranza's *Comentarios sobre el catechismo christiano*, Pope Pius IV later stated that both books contained sound doctrine. The support of the pope and of other prominent Catholic clerics highlights the peculiar situation in which Carranza, Granada, and others found themselves. While many of their contemporaries within the Catholic Church admired them and their work, these clerics fell on the wrong side of the Inquisition's campaigns against heresy.[5]

For the Inquisition, the orthodoxy of the texts did not constitute the entire or even the primary problem. In addition to summarizing relevant personal histories, this chapter highlights the Inquisition's concern with a book's medium of expression. By using the Castilian language, Carranza and Granada provided common men and women with unmediated access to complex ideas. Moving beyond the Latinate circles of the educated elite to the world of vernacular readership, these texts became available to a substantially greater population. Indeed, historians of early modern Europe have shown that even individuals of negligible social status, with little or no formal education, still had access to books.[6] Inquisition authorities feared that the common populace, owing to a lack of education, could all too easily misinterpret these texts.

CONTRIBUTIONS TO CURRENT SCHOLARSHIP

Scholars in recent decades have challenged long-standing views of the Inquisition and early modern Spain. In general, they have demonstrated that earlier research exaggerated the Inquisition's influence over Spanish society. Scholars now largely agree that the Inquisition neither produced a uniform, doctrinally orthodox society nor stifled all creative and intellectual developments.[7] This chapter aims, in a similar way, to trouble long-standing views of the Spanish Inquisition. While research on the Inquisition has bourgeoned in recent decades, studies on the officials of the Spanish Inquisition remain few and far between.[8] While the subject of Inquisition book censorship has attracted no shortage of scholarly attention, previous studies have tended to focus on the institutional function of censorship rather than on the textual ideas that authorities considered dangerous. Discussing censorship in sixteenth-century Spain, a respected survey of the Inquisition focuses on the ineffectiveness of that institution in controlling the circulation of heretical texts. While previous generations of scholars maintained that the Index of Prohibited Books suppressed literary creativity, more recent work maintains that the Index was imposing in theory but less so in practice.[9]

Related work has distanced the study of Spanish censorship from the polemics of previous scholars who bickered over whether the Inquisition had inhibited Spain's intellectual progress. Looking instead to censorship as an institutional practice, we learn that the Inquisition's apparatus for the control of books developed gradually, becoming efficient and systematic around 1550 to 1560. The consolidation of the Spanish monarchy required an ideologically uniform program, and thus the Inquisition's system of censorship grew along with the monarchy over the course of the sixteenth century.[10]

Moving from the institutional function of censorship to the Inquisition's reasons for prohibiting books, recent scholarship has challenged the notion of the Inquisition as a monolith, unified in its prosecution of heresy. Instead, this work has highlighted tensions between different individuals, as well as the personal agenda that Inquisition officials harbored against certain authors. This revisionist work has provided a valuable service in underscoring the human, bureaucratic side of the Inquisition. I contend, however, that the same work has tacitly dismissed theological and ecclesiological concerns as factors that fueled the agenda of Inquisition officials.[11] Before examining these concerns, we will survey the social and political context that crucially informed the cases of Carranza and Granada.

HISTORICAL CONTEXT

Born in 1504, Louis of Granada came from a poor family in southern Spain. One of his biographers suggests that his humble origins influenced his devotion to the impoverished people of Spain and Portugal.[12] Through the patronage of a wealthy family, he attended the prestigious Colegio de San Gregorio de Valladolid, eventually becoming a renowned preacher and the prior provincial of the Dominican friars in Portugal in 1556. In 1554 Granada published the "best-seller" of the Spanish Golden Age, his *Libro de la oración*. In 1559, however, Inquisitor General Valdés banned the popular book because it used the vernacular to popularize a complex program of spirituality. Valdés and his theological adviser believed that uneducated readers might confuse Granada's ideas with alumbradismo, a heresy addressed by Spanish inquisitors throughout the sixteenth century.

An understanding of what the alumbrados actually believed remains difficult to ascertain. As far as historians know, they never produced any written document demonstrating a common creed. What we do know comes from Inquisition sources. In 1525 Inquisitor General Alonso Manrique issued an edict regarding the alumbrados of Toledo, in which he stated forty-seven propositions that the Inquisition associated with these individuals. In general, alumbrados seem to have disdained the traditional Catholic ceremonies and acted upon divine promptings that they claimed to receive from the Holy Spirit. Aside from the initial accusations of alumbradismo beginning in the early 1500s, another round of accusations arose in the 1570s in western Spain and again in the 1620s in Seville. Although varying practices characterized the alumbrados during these periods, they apparently emphasized silent, interior prayer and an unmediated relationship with God.[13]

A number of high-ranking Catholics—Archbishop Carlo Borromeo of Milan, King John III of Portugal, and Pope Pius IV—affirmed Granada's orthodoxy. Consequently, one may wonder if Inquisition leaders had some other motivation to target him, using alumbradismo merely as an excuse for censuring his work. Another reason for the Inquisition's prohibition of his book may lie in his enthusiasm for the Jesuits, known rivals of many clerics within the Dominican Order and within Spain in general. In fact, historians have credited Granada with introducing the Society of Jesus into Portugal, a position that probably did not endear him to Melchior Cano, a prominent theologian and censor for Valdés's Inquisition. A Dominican friar, Cano played a leading part in a larger movement aiming to discredit the Society of Jesus.[14]

The ulterior motives of Melchior Cano played a key role in the prohibition of Granada's book, according to Álvaro Huerga, the most assiduous scholar of Granada. Huerga argues that absent of Cano, Granada's work would not have found a place on the Index of Prohibited Books. He maintains that if King Philip II had not been traveling outside of Spain at the time, the censure of the *Libro de la oración* would never have happened. One biographer of Philip notes that the king read Granada's works devoutly—so much so that on his deathbed, he chose to have passages from Granada's writings read to him. With Philip absent, however, Cano took the opportunity, in Huerga's words, to make impassioned claims of limited substance, misrepresenting Granada's words. In general, scholarship on this episode has focused on personal and political factors to explain book censorship.[15]

Social networks and personal enmity have an even more important place in the history of Carranza's *Comentarios sobre el catechismo christiano*. Bartolomé Carranza had served as one of Spain's delegates to the early sessions of the Council of Trent (1545–47, 1551–52), the Catholic Church's official response to the Protestant Reformation. He also played a leading part in Spanish efforts to reinstitute Catholicism in England during the reign of Mary Tudor. In the mid-sixteenth century, he repeatedly received offers of prestigious positions within the Church. In 1542 King Charles V offered him the bishopric of Cuzco, in the recently conquered Andean highlands. Carranza declined the position and did the same six years later when Philip II recommended him for the bishopric of the Canary Islands and for the position of royal confessor. By 1550, however, he accepted Philip's offer of royal confessor, as well as the position of prior provincial of the Dominicans in Castile.[16]

Though he gained the good favor of the royal family and worked on behalf of Catholic renewal in Europe, Carranza's opinions did not endear him to everyone. During his time as a delegate to Trent, Carranza published four disputes, one of which advocated the principle of episcopal residence, arguing that bishops had a responsibility to their faithful to remain in residence and preach. This particular position probably did not sit well with Inquisitor Valdés, who occupied the archbishopric of Seville in absentia. In the records of Carranza's trial with the Spanish Inquisition, he mentioned the many disapproving comments he had made in the past regarding Valdés as an absentee archbishop. For his part, Valdés affirmed that he knew of Carranza's criticism, but he denied the claim that he had complained about Carranza and held him as an enemy. Carranza disapproved not only of Valdés's absenteeism. Just before leaving for England, Carranza also penned a document against Valdés's management of the Inquisition, requesting a visitation of the institution. Specifically, Carranza pointed to the increasing influence of jurists within the Inquisition's ranks. In his opinion, jurists lacked the theological formation necessary to judge cases of heresy.[17]

The following years gave Carranza's peers more reasons for animosity. In 1557 Philip II appointed Carranza to the archbishopric of Toledo, an office entailing primacy over all Spanish churches since a papal bull of Urban II in 1088. Shortly after his appointment, Carranza again targeted the Inquisition, this time denouncing its approach to dealing with heresy. Although Carranza himself had worked for the Inquisition as a censor of books, he believed that the Holy Office had gone too far, having latched onto the concept of alumbradismo and extended suspicion to every person with spiritual inclinations. Carranza attempted to discredit the Inquisition's campaign against alumbradismo, for he believed that Inquisition efforts had caused more damage than that which they prevented.[18]

Besides Valdés, Carranza incurred the hostility of other prominent Spanish clerics, such as Melchior Cano. As with Valdés, Cano and Carranza had a history before the prohibition of Carranza's *Comentarios* by the Inquisition. They had been enemies since the 1530s, when both taught at the Colegio de San Gregorio de Valladolid. Both clerics had earned the respect of their peers and had large student followings. Although Cano may have superseded Carranza intellectually, Carranza repeatedly received nominations over Cano for various positions. Carranza, rather than Cano, became the secondary regent, and eventually the primary regent, of the Colegio de San Gregorio. Cano eventually accepted the position of bishop of the Canary Islands but not before Carranza received and turned down the same offer. Cano's censure of Carranza's book marked perhaps the final step in their rivalry, as Cano died shortly afterward.[19]

In his Inquisition trial, Carranza argued that the enmity between Cano and himself colored Cano's censure of the *Comentarios*. According to Carranza, Inquisitor General Valdés accepted Cano's opinion even though "the said Lord Archbishop knew that Melchior Cano was my notorious enemy." Carranza added that the inquisitor general refused to accept the opinions of other churchmen who approved of Carranza's work: Francisco Blanco, bishop of Orense; two professors of theology at the renowned University of Salamanca (Pedro de Sotomayor and Ambrosio de Salazar); and two bishops esteemed by Carranza—Andrés de la Cuesta, bishop of León, and Pedro Guerrero, the archbishop of Granada. Besides seeking high-ranking churchmen to endorse his book, Carranza offered to revise any problematic sections but claimed that Valdés offered no response. For his part, Valdés explained that he could do nothing regarding Carranza's *Comentarios* because the book already circulated at the time Carranza approached the inquisitor general. Valdés denied, furthermore, the claim that he and Cano had conspired together against Carranza, as well as the contention that he refused the judgments of other theologians.[20]

Besides the personal motives that Inquisition officials harbored toward Granada and Carranza, historians question whether Valdés exaggerated the threat of heresy infiltrating Spain in order to recover the good standing he had lost with the royal court. Philip II had favored Inquisitor Valdés, who held the wealthy archbishopric of Seville, for his financial support of various military feats. In the later 1550s, however, Valdés fell from his esteemed position with the royal family, as adverse reports about him reached Philip during a visit to the Low Countries. Valdés apparently sought an opportunity to redeem himself before the king and found it with the discovery of Protestant communities in Seville and Valladolid. Valdés wanted to convince Philip that he could trust the Inquisition to take control. The king agreed with Valdés on the need for swift action and gave the inquisitor general authority to take any measures necessary.[21]

Besides the personal motivation against Carranza and Granada, jurisdictional conflict between the papacy and the Spanish Inquisition also loomed large in the case of Carranza. Beginning in Spain, his inquisition trial lasted seventeen years before ending in Rome. To arrest Carranza, the leaders of the Spanish Inquisition needed the permission of Pope Paul IV, the only person with jurisdiction over the primate of Spain. Conflict over exactly who had final authority continued throughout the trial. Accordingly, historians attribute the extraordinary length of Carranza's trial to the conflict between the Spanish Inquisition and the papacy, which changed hands multiple times during the seventeen-year case. The conflict began when Philip II and the Spanish Inquisition refused to recognize the Council of Trent's 1563 approval of Carranza's work. Although Philip had held Carranza in high enough esteem to appoint him to the archbishopric of Toledo, the Inquisition's reputation remained Philip's priority. Consequently, Philip did little to help Carranza and accepted the opinion of those who linked him with heresy. In the end, Rome and Spain reached a compromise. Instead of denouncing Carranza as a heretic, the Roman Inquisition forced him to abjure a list of errors so as to not discredit the Spanish Inquisition. The controversial Dominican—over seventy years old by then—died just eighteen days after his release from imprisonment.[22]

Having discussed the personal and political circumstances surrounding these cases, we now proceed to the less-emphasized theological and ecclesiological concerns. Because Carranza and Granada had written in the vernacular, their ideas had the potential to reach many individuals. Owing to high rates of literacy in sixteenth-century Castile, Cano and Valdés had reason to believe that the ideas of Carranza and Granada would circulate widely. According to one study, literate men accounted for more than 50 percent of the male population in Madrid, Ávila, Toledo, and Cuenca. Books and pamphlets—mostly religious—circulated widely outside large towns to villages, where the ability to read was not rare. Religious literature affordable to the common populace certainly existed, and people from all levels of Castilian society read it. Since the works of both Granada and Carranza could reach a broad audience, their books represented a threat for Inquisition authorities, especially given the contemporary fear of heterodox ideas entering Spain from northern Europe.[23]

While personal and political considerations remain essential to understanding the Inquisition's leaders, we now turn to the texts of Carranza and Granada in order to underline what Inquisition authorities identified as problematic.

CARRANZA'S *COMENTARIOS SOBRE EL CATECHISMO CHRISTIANO*

The vast majority of Carranza's book seems in line with sixteenth-century Catholic doctrine. Concerning some central points on which Martin Luther departed from the Roman Church, Carranza clearly remained on Rome's side. He maintained, for instance, that faith cannot survive without works, that priests mediate between men and God, that Christ instituted all seven sacraments (each with its own effects and dignity), that the Church ought to preserve and defend the ceremonies of each sacrament, that those who mocked Church ceremonies mocked Christ and the apostles, and that "perfect" Christians kept both the spirit *and* the letter of the law.[24]

In addition to affirming the Catholic Church's position on several points that Luther contested, Carranza maintained that during the mid-sixteenth century, the Christian religion found itself in a most dangerous position. In the dedicatory letter of his *Comentarios*, addressed to Philip II, he wrote, "Heresies never came to what [they are] now [. . .]. Never was religion so cornered as [it is] in these times. Because if we look with attention, we find that only Spain has lifted itself, fleeing from the impieties and errors that reign in the majority of the other lands. Your Majesty has the great obligation to sustain that tranquility that we have enjoyed for so many years in

Spain." In order to assist in keeping Spain free from heresy, Carranza wrote his *Comentarios*, which he believed contained all the things Christians needed to know.[25]

Because Carranza's text contains so much material attesting to its orthodoxy, one might conclude that its prohibition came about because of an overzealous Inquisition. Inquisition leaders, however, had reasons for subjecting his book to close scrutiny. Primary was Carranza's choice to write in Castilian. Carranza believed that his book would help contemporary Christians because damaged catechisms and books of false doctrine—in both Latin and the vernacular—had done much harm to the Church. Bishops at the Council of Trent had debated whether to produce vernacular Bibles. While they affirmed the authority of the Latin Vulgate Bible, they did not explicitly prohibit or endorse vernacular translations of it, thus leaving the decision to local authorities.[26]

Although Carranza knew the delicate nature of the debate over vernacular scripture, he declared, "a middle way could be taken with this conflict." He proposed to produce not a Castilian-language Bible but another text with "glosses and prudent interpretations" as a resource for laypeople who could not read the authoritative Latin Bible. While he believed that common men and women should not have access to the entire Bible without clerical guidance, he still included some translations of scriptural passages in his *Comentarios*. In deciding to publish his lengthy vernacular text, Carranza took a bold step, especially considering his knowledge of the controversy surrounding the translation of scripture. In fact, the Inquisition censor Melchior Cano identified a similar issue in his censure of Carranza's text. In Cano's mind, the book used the Castilian language to "provide the common populace with difficult and perplexing concepts from theology and sacred scripture that they cannot understand because of their ignorance."[27]

Related to his use of the vernacular, Carranza stated the following in his introductory letter to the reader: "There are some individuals of such good mind, and of such calm judgment, and so good and devout, that one would do just as well or even better to give all the Scriptures to them instead of to many who know Latin and are well-educated." While Carranza stated here that only *some* laypersons could read scripture, his point still clashed with Cano's belief that commoners could not properly understand scripture without a priest providing guidance. Carranza's support of scripture reading by lay people—even if limited to certain individuals—challenged the teaching authority of clerics.[28]

Carranza viewed the issue differently. From his perspective, he did not subvert clerical interpretation of scripture. Rather, he believed that his text would provide the necessary guidance to help Christians to distinguish between good doctrine and the ideas of heretics. Thus in his mind, he merely put into textual form the clerical guidance that he deemed necessary to avoid heresy. If clerical interpretation of doctrine protected against heresy, why not provide such guidance in the form of a permanent text and not only through sermons and personal contact?[29]

Melchior Cano took issue not only with Carranza's use of the vernacular but more generally with the notion that common laymen could handle knowledge appropriate for educated churchmen. Cano believed that Carranza gave Christians greater discretion of what is good and bad: "The principal intent of the author, as he himself says, was to take the instruction of the public away from the priests and other appropriate persons and give the knowledge of priests, judges, and prelates of the Church to common men and women." Cano maintained that Carranza's approach intruded upon the domain of educated clerics, dealing a blow to the priest as a teacher and as a mediator between God and the congregation. Cano noted, furthermore, that Carranza "disrespects and divulges" (*profana y haze públicos*) the mysteries of the Christian faith by trying to explain complex concepts to common laypeople. In doing so, Carranza diminished the distinction between the spiritual capabilities of the laity and clergy.[30]

Carranza, however, sometimes did emphasize personal clerical guidance. In fact, in order to determine which individuals had a "good mind" and "calm judgment" he maintained the following: "Everything is left to the discretion of the pastors and spiritual doctors. They are the ones who have to know the sheep of Christ, our Lord . . . in order to concede that they can or cannot have the Holy Scripture in the vernacular." Carranza further emphasized that he did not make the same recommendations to all Christians, underscoring the direction that he gave them:

> On my advice, some people have read all the Holy Scripture [. . .] and they took great profit for their consolation and correction of life. Among these were some women [and] neither Paula nor Eustochium, the noble Roman women at whose request Saint Jerome

> translated Scripture according to the Hebrew truth, could have read it more worthily [. . .]. On the other hand, I counseled many to not read [Scripture] but books of devotion because I saw that they did not have that tranquility that I would like with regard to judgment and understanding [. . .]. Just as all precious things are very rare, so are these people of whom I speak; it is necessary to have great care and experience of some years to give them this confidence.

Carranza emphasized that only "pastors and spiritual doctors" could allow individuals to read scripture independently and that just a few "very rare" Christians should have this privilege. This qualification did not suffice for Cano. He saw concessions, such as vernacular Bibles and other vernacular religious texts, as closely associated with the origins of Protestant heresies in northern Europe. He argued as follows: "Experience has shown that [. . .] the liberty of reading sacred scripture in the vernacular in part or in its entirety has done much harm to women and the uneducated." For Cano, a formal education served as a prerequisite to engaging complex theology and spirituality.[31]

Altogether, Cano took issue with two fundamental aspects of Carranza's work: the language in which he wrote and his assumption that uneducated men and women should deal with the more intricate aspects of Christian doctrine. Cano's concerns were by no means unique to Carranza. Many contemporaries shared his anxiety about the religious practices of "women and the uneducated." The Inquisition also extended its suspicion to *any* book printed abroad in Castilian.[32]

GRANADA'S *LIBRO DE LA ORACIÓN Y MEDITACIÓN*

As in the case of Carranza, Granada's book also appears in line with official Catholic teachings from the Council of Trent. His text on prayer and meditation had the support of respected leaders. In Spain, however, Granada ran into Inquisitor Valdés, who—according to recent scholarship—used heresy as a tool to recuperate his good standing with the Spanish Crown. Considering the support of Granada's book by notable Catholics, together with its prohibition by an ambitious inquisitor, one might conclude that the book became a victim of Church politics. A closer look at the content of Granada's book, however, forces a revision of this view.[33]

Similar to the case of Carranza, the censor Melchior Cano identified Granada's attempt "to teach the people in Castilian" as a primary problem.[34] Having written in the vernacular, Granada made a body of complex doctrine accessible to a populace significantly larger than the Latin-reading elite. In doing so, he allowed the reader to bypass the vigilance afforded by an individual spiritual director.

Cano also criticized Granada for discussing ideas that many readers could not understand, putting them in danger because of their "lack of strength and capacity." Compounding the choice to publish his text in the vernacular, Granada gave his readers the freedom to choose their own methods of prayer. In the prologue to the first version of his book, Granada said that Christians could choose from various meditations, and they need not use them all. Rather, he believed that one should "choose that which best suits one's purpose." While clearly not problematic per se, Granada's support of individual choice in prayer had *potentially* dangerous consequences. According to the fourteenth-century work of Nicolau Eimeric—seminal reading for Spanish inquisitors—the act of choice itself lay at the heart of heresy.[35]

Besides emphasizing individual choice in prayer, Granada did not believe in specifying the words that one should employ in prayer. Rather, he advocated praying with words that came from the Holy Spirit: "The prayer made by the person who prays is often more beneficial, with the words that the Holy Spirit teaches him, than the one that is ordered and composed with foreign words." Granada's recommendation that readers use their own words in prayer must be understood in the context of the Inquisition's fear of alumbradismo (and Protestantism). Inquisitors had expressed concern with laypersons independently developing their own devotional practices. For instance, in the Inquisition's 1525 Edict concerning the alumbrados of Toledo, then-Inquisitor General Manrique attributed the origins and proliferation of alumbradismo to secret meeting groups of laypersons. Considering longstanding suspicion of alumbrados, we can see how the Inquisition might have read Granada's allowance of choice in prayer as an opportunity to depart from the regular rules and practices of the Church (e.g., to neglect the recitation of vocal prayer).[36]

A similar danger appears in Granada's recommendation that his reader study "the sacred books" in addition to books of prayer and spirituality: "For this same protection and purity of the heart, devout reading of spiritual books also helps[. . . . I]t is fitting to occupy it (our heart) many times with reading the sacred books, because when it must think about something, it thinks about that with which we keep it occupied." The danger in this passage lay in Granada's lack of specificity. He advocated reading "sacred books," but he neither offered guidance concerning their truth nor recommended seeking direction from a priest. The very idea of Christians acting independently of the Church's guiding hand resembled alumbradismo. In fact, Melchior Cano stated that Granada's book contained a number of "grave errors that had a certain resemblance to the heresy of the alumbrados." Furthermore, in view of the many heterodox interpretations that Protestants gleaned from Christian scripture, the Inquisition's leaders felt especially uneasy with the idea of unguided study.[37]

Another potential problem in Granada's original text resided in the central role that he ascribed to mental or silent prayer. He wrote, "Because those who pray with their mouth, reading for a few hours, or praying as a group, often easily pass very quickly through the things that they are praying, and thus they neither understand nor reach their substance or quality. But those who pray or meditate with the heart often dwell more in consideration of things, which without doubt is of great benefit." Because of Granada's effort to "make all individuals contemplative and perfect," Cano believed that the Church could "gravely reprimand him." Readers might have interpreted the importance that Granada attributed to mental prayer as excluding other important means of obtaining grace, like the sacraments. The Inquisition most certainly feared individuals who infringed on the Church's authority by making mental prayer a central part of religious life—to the exclusion of other Church-administered practices, like the Mass. Cano found this central emphasis on mental prayer highly suspect because it reminded him of the alumbrados. Although not heretical in itself, mental prayer possibly signified heterodox affiliation.[38]

Granada's emphasis on prayer also raised problems because he gave a substantial (perhaps disproportionate) amount of power to laymen and women, regardless of status and rank. In fact, the Inquisition took issue precisely with Granada's implication that one could reach a kind of spiritual "perfection" through prayer. For Granada, prayer helped Christians to change their lives and become new people. He said that Christ wished to make apparent "the virtue that prayer has for transfiguring souls, which is to make them lose the customs of the old man and clothe themselves anew." Granada wrote that prayer provides the principal medium for reaching all good, also noting the benefit of asking for grace and other virtues from God through prayer. For example, "We can try speaking internally with God, saying these things or other similar words: 'Lord, give me grace so that I might love you with all my heart and soul [. . .].' In this way, you can ask for fear of God and for humility and some other virtues." Granada continued this discussion in another section when he wrote, "Here we are discussing the perfect prayer through which one reaches union with God." By describing prayer as a method to attain spiritual perfection, Granada might have inadvertently led readers to believe that they could be good Christians without the guidance of the Church. By writing in the vernacular and addressing himself to a broad audience, he essentially "democratized" mental prayer. As in the case of Carranza, theologians like Cano ascribed such practices to learned theologians or ascetic monks but certainly not to humble laymen and women.[39]

MELCHIOR CANO AND THE PEOPLE

The two preceding sections have outlined the basic concerns that Inquisition authorities identified in the vernacular works of Carranza and Granada. Scholarship on the same matter, however, expresses skepticism at the authenticity of this Inquisition initiative against vernacular texts. Historian José Luis González Novalín has argued that the effort to prevent the circulation of vernacular texts served as a mere front for the pursuit of Carranza. Indeed, Inquisition sources appear to suggest as much: "It is appropriate to confiscate all copies of the *Comentarios sobre el catechismo christiano*, written in the vernacular by the archbishop of Toledo. So that we do not appear to make this effort solely for that book, it would be good to publish edicts that order the confiscation of all vernacular books that address Christian doctrine and were printed outside of these kingdoms starting from 1550 until now." González Novalín adds that the edict against vernacular books of doctrine provided an impetus for the entire 1559 Index of Prohibited Books. In this line of thought, the Index would have obscured the ban on Carranza's work, making it appear as just one small part of a larger campaign against heretical books.[40]

In the section that follows, however, I argue that this campaign against vernacular religious texts did not have clear origins as a response to Carranza. In fact, the Inquisition goal of restricting theology and spirituality as the domain of the Latin-reading elite relates closely to themes in Cano's earlier work, written long before the publication of Carranza's *Comentarios*. In his magnum opus, *De locis theologicis*, and elsewhere, Cano identified the dangers inherent in allowing common people to have unmediated interpretation of the Bible, as well as direct access to complex Catholic doctrine.[41]

In his *De locis theologicis* (the bulk of which he had completed several years prior to the Carranza affair), Cano discussed the Lutheran position that Christians should make judgments directly from the Bible itself. In his view, Lutherans found evidence for this claim in the first letter of John, which says, "You have no need for someone else to teach you." For Cano, this position clearly aimed at dismantling the Catholic Church's traditional practice of having priests interpret sacred scripture for the people.[42]

Responding to the call for unmediated access to scripture, Cano implied that Lutherans had not read the aforementioned passage from John's letter with sufficient care. He could not deny that John had recorded Jesus Christ as dismissing the need for teachers. Yet Cano still had an answer: "One could easily respond that the Apostle there preached not to the unlearned but to the learned. For he said: I did not write to you as to those ignorant of the truth but as those learned [in the truth] (1 John 2:21). For the wise teachers of the Church, therefore, the inner blessing suffices to refute those things that oppose the faith. But for the unlearned, external instruction is still useful. God placed ministers and teachers in the Church especially for them." From Cano's perspective, his Lutheran opponents had read John's letter in an overly general way. They had taken a message intended for a specific group of people (the Apostles) and applied it to a much larger audience that, for Cano, still needed instruction.[43]

Cano was not alone in thinking that laypeople needed clerical guidance in reading sacred scripture. As we have already seen, Carranza himself took a similar position on the subject of lay reading of scripture, bypassing the project of a vernacular Bible in favor of a vernacular book of doctrine. One could argue that upon the publication of Carranza's work, Cano conveniently expanded his position to disapprove not only of vernacular scripture but also of vernacular religious writing more generally. In his censure of Carranza's work, his second point criticizes "giving the knowledge of priests, judges, and prelates of the Church to women and common men." But again, in work from earlier years, Cano already had made clear his more general belief that common people had no business taking part in the interpretation of doctrine. In his commentaries on Aquinas, Cano wrote that Church councils provided the only appropriate context in which to resolve disagreements concerning the Catholic faith: "The entire Church could not come together, and even if it could, it would be an intolerable confusion. What else could occur when the ignorant people, the old charlatan, the delirious old man, and the capricious, imprudent youth meet to discuss matters of faith? At what conclusion would they arrive? What would be the value of a decision reached by the ignorant people? Thus, such matters are best left to councils and not to the universal Church." For Cano, bringing the common people into theological discussions only opened the door to problems.[44]

At a later point in his commentaries on Aquinas, Cano underlined again his belief that only the Church elite should handle sophisticated questions related to faith. He wrote, "It would be idiocy to think any other way, for the whole Church could not come together. And even if all the faithful could assemble, it is not appropriate nonetheless. It would be absurd. In the Acts of the Apostles, it says that when Paul and Barnabas came, they were received by the Church, and by the elders and Apostles. *But when the question was proposed, the most illustrious men assembled—not the women, not the youth, not the laity, but rather the elders and the Apostles.*" Before closing, Cano condemned "the new heretics" as insolent men because they presumed to include the whole Church as part of the body qualified to interpret doctrine.[45]

According to Cano, the idea of Church teaching as a complement to scripture dated back to the time of the apostles: "Christ gave judgment to the Apostles so that they might understand scripture. He did so not so much for them but much more so for the Church. From which we understand that Christ opened his designated book to his Church in perpetuity. The Apostles bequeathed to the Church the knowledge of scripture." Cano added, "In the name of the Church, doctrine cannot be understood by all the faithful but rather by pastors and teachers of the Church, especially when assembled in a council." Cano read Christ's commissioning of the Apostles as a specific act. He assigned teaching authority to a select few for the benefit of the Church as a whole.[46]

Because of the controversial nature of Cano's position (especially with regard to Carranza), scholars have considered him one of the more intransigent churchmen of sixteenth-century Spain. Yet his position against lay access to scripture and complex theology was by no means a unique stance. Before concluding, we will draw comparisons to other individuals who served as Inquisition censors after Cano's death.

THE 1583 INDEX OF PROHIBITED BOOKS

Inquisition efforts to combat heresy went far beyond the 1559 prohibition of the works by Carranza and Granada. In the same year, the Inquisition took action against the Protestants of Valladolid and Seville. Several *autos de fe* (public "acts of faith" proclaiming the penances of Inquisition defendants) took place from 1559 through the 1560s. In 1563 Philip II ordered all bishops to guard against Protestant efforts to spread their heresies in the Spanish kingdoms. Inquisitor General Valdés died in 1566, but the vigilance of Protestants continued into the 1570s. In 1572 the Inquisition received a report that the princess of Béarn in southwest France sought to send Lutherans into Spain as missionaries. By 1578 Inquisition officials had learned that Protestants had printed heretical copies of the New Testament in Castilian, with intentions to circulate the texts in Iberia.[47]

As a part of ongoing efforts to eliminate threats of Protestantism, the Inquisition commissioned another Index of Prohibited Books. The process of compiling it appears to have been long, beginning at least in 1572. By 1583 Inquisitor General Gaspar de Quiroga released the new Index of Prohibited Books. While it banned three times as many volumes as its 1559 predecessor, the 1583 Index may have been less aggressive than it appears. In one view, the newer Index did not significantly change Spaniards' reading habits because the new entries largely referred to texts from foreign lands.[48]

The 1583 Index seems to have espoused a change in attitude toward vernacular religious literature. Inquisitor Quiroga clarified that a place on the Index did not mean that an author had deviated from the Church, thus seeming to clear several revered men of heterodox associations.

> When books of great Christians known throughout the world are found in this Catalog (such as . . . Thomas More, Francis Borgia, Louis of Granada, John of Ávila and other similar individuals) it is not because the authors have deviated from the holy Roman church . . . rather, it is because either the books have been falsely attributed to them, or because spurious words or sentences were found . . . , or because it was not appropriate for them to circulate in the vulgar tongue, or because, despite the piety and learning of the author, the texts included things that were expressed in a plain way . . . such that the enemies of the Faith can distort them for the purposes of their malicious intentions.[49]

This passage from Quiroga seems to indicate a departure from Valdés's Inquisition. Indeed, recent scholarship on the Inquisition confirms this observation, with one author arguing that Inquisition censors made "completely arbitrary decisions" and "frequently contradicted each other."[50] Bearing these apparent changes or contradictions in mind, we examine the writings of Inquisition censors during the last quarter of the sixteenth century.

Did other Inquisition officials take Cano's lead and view vernacular religious texts as problematic? In 1584 the Dominican friar Alonso de la Fuente noted that "many books in the vernacular" transmit the heresies of his fellow Dominican from Germany, Johann Tauler (ca. 1300–1361), whom Fuente called a licentious, ecstatic mystic, who propagated "pesilential" doctrine. Fuente's primary problem with Tauler lay in his doctrine, rather than in the German Dominican's language of choice (Latin). But Fuente had another concern—namely, that Tauler's work had begun to circulate in the vernacular, presenting "a most grave danger to the Christian republic." For Fuente, a bad situation became worse with the translation of Tauler's sermons into the vernacular, propagating heretical ideas to an audience beyond the Latin-educated elite.[51]

Others besides Fuente expressed similar concerns with the vernacular. Fray Hierónymo Guzmán, the Inquisition censor who read Fuente's letter, actually disagreed regarding the orthodoxy of Tauler's work. Guzmán did not consider Tauler heretical, but he still appreciated Fuente's rigorous reading of Tauler's sermons. Given that Luther himself had expressed interest in Tauler and that his sermons circulated in the vernacular, Guzmán believed that any Catholic should approach Tauler's work with caution. He supported the restriction of his writings to a Latin-trained audience, emphasizing that *learned* men might take advantage of the German Dominican's work. Though Guzmán departed from Fuente's judgment of Tauler's doctrine, Guzmán still did note that Tauler's sermons should incur the reader's suspicion simply for having circulated in the vernacular. For Fuente, then, the vernacular aggravated an already existing doctrinal problem in Tauler's work, and for Guzmán, the vernacular served as a sign of potentially dangerous content.

The year before Fuente's 1585 letter to the Inquisition, Juan de Angulo addressed himself to King Philip II. Writing from Hispaniola, he informed the monarch that just a few years earlier, "certain books printed in *romance* had been appropriated and [among them was] one [written] as [a Book of] Hours, entitled Prayer and Spiritual Exercise [*oratorio y exercicio espiritual*] and reading one of them, it seemed to have some things that were superfluous and, in a way, ill-sounding and dangerous, especially among ignorant people, who for the most part, are the readers." Rather than prohibit this vernacular book altogether, Inquisition officials confiscated the texts and cut out "the things that engendered suspicion," deciding to "return the corrected books to their owners so that they might use them to pray while a final decision was made." In this case, we see an alternative to a general prohibition of the book.[52]

In his letter, Angulo justified the decision in Hispaniola by pointing to precedent in Mexico. He noted that a man had come recently to Hispaniola from Mexico, bringing a copy of the same book, *Oratorio y exercicio espiritual.* Angulo related that the Inquisition tribunal of Mexico had corrected the book, having identified and removed the same sections as suspicious. Shortly afterward, New World printers produced the same work without the troublesome passages. Angulo decided to write to His Majesty about whether to prohibit the book altogether or permit the corrected versions. The final word from Spain indicated a decision to prohibit the book. According to the peninsular authorities, the 1583 Index included a very similar Latin book in its entirety. If a similar book in Latin deserved prohibition, then a Castilian version justified prohibition with all the more reason.

Back in Spain, suspicion of vernacular texts continued. In 1585 a *licenciado* named Montoya identified another language-associated problem, pointing to "a significant hurdle for priests who preach from books in *romance.*" Montoya had become aware of a troublesome passage in the

Discourses on the Creed, by Don Esteban de Salazar, a Carthusian priest. Salazar had written that the three divine persons, Father, Son, and Holy Spirit, are three *substances*. Montoya cited Thomas Aquinas in explaining the danger in this passage. By saying that the Father, Son, and Holy Spirit were three substances, Salazar had contradicted the Church teaching that the Trinity constituted three persons of the *same substance*. Though he identified this problem in Salazar's text, Montoya by no means intended to denounce Salazar as a heretic. Rather, he described Salazar as "a pious, Catholic cleric of very sound doctrine." Upon receiving Montoya's letter, the Inquisition censor agreed that the passage was problematic, "especially since it is circulating in *romance*," and he proceeded to order its correction, from "three substances" to "three persons."[53]

The notion of the vernacular as an aggravating factor underlies these censures and the suspicion surrounding the works of Carranza and Granada. For many Inquisition officials, the vernacular made an already dangerous passage worse by amplifying the number of people whom it might reach. Indeed, others expressed similar concerns, as in the case of the fray Hernando de Castillo, who stated that a text written by Fray Hernando de Santiago contained "passages that should be erased, especially because they are circulating in *Romance*." In the case of Salazar's *Discourses*, furthermore, Montoya mentioned that the passage describing the Trinity as three substances served as a hurdle for *priests*. We know, therefore, that Inquisition censors expressed concern for the religious integrity of not only lay readers but also clergy.[54]

A few years later, in April 1592, the Hieronymite friar Francisco de Cavañas asked for permission to purchase a book called *Readings Against Calvin*, stating that the book was sold publicly and citing some authorities who found no problem with owning the book. Cavañas, nonetheless, expressed concern over the book's status as a vernacular (Italian) dispute against heresy and acknowledged that he might need official permission to purchase it. The following month, Cavañas received an answer to his petition. Acknowledging that the book contained "sound and catholic" doctrine, the response emphasized that the book still contained the errors of heretics, and thus no one should own it without official permission. Cavañas, recognized as "such a religious and learned person," received approval to purchase the book. While individuals such as Cavañas obtained permission to own such texts, the inquisitor general overruled the decision just a few months later, ordering the confiscation of the book from Cavañas and that no one read the book under any conditions.[55]

In the Cavañas case, we see a common concern that books in the vernacular pose danger. But sometimes respected clerics could acquire these books with official permission. Why, then, did the inquisitor general revoke the permission granted to Cavañas? The documentation does not provide further clues, but contemporary events may suggest an answer. Highly learned men, such as Benito Arias de Montano and Francisco Sánchez, had obtained permission to examine heretical texts at approximately the same time. But accusations against them may have led the Inquisition's highest tribunal (the Suprema) to become wary of granting such authorizations.

Such permissions as the one granted temporarily to Francisco de Cavañas were not rare. In 1593, the year following the Cavañas case, Juan Alonso del Curiel stated that Fray Luis de León's work on the book of Job was "very much in keeping with the doctrine of the Church and of great importance for understanding the Book of Job." For these reasons, Curiel wished that León's commentaries would not "remain hidden in the hands of just a few." Instead, he recommended printing them for the universal benefit of the Church. He also believed that the book would benefit those who did not know Latin. Curiel's position seems to mark a substantial departure from the Inquisition's previously hostile stance toward the work of León, who had endured time in the Inquisition's jails for suspicion regarding his biblical scholarship.[56]

Curiel did not, however, advocate the completely free circulation of León's work. Rather, he qualified his call for access to León's text, noting that because the volume was written in the vernacular and contained the entire text of Job, those individuals interested in reading it would need to seek official permission from the Inquisition. He added that those individuals who had opposed the translation of scripture into the vernacular had done so more out of a concern for the Gospels and Epistles, "in which there is more difficulty as a result of containing more of the mysteries of our holy faith." The book of Job, however, "could circulate free of danger in the vernacular because it contains plain history and moral doctrine."

We have seen a range of concerns expressed in these censures. First, vernacular texts sometimes served as the conduit of heresy; second, texts in the vernacular should arouse the suspicion of good Christians; and third, doctrinally complex or dangerous passages became worse in the vernacular, which offered a broader readership than did Latin texts. While the Inquisition censors sometimes disagreed with their informants over the danger of a particular passage or book, they did not necessarily contradict each other. Rather, they seem to have shared a belief in proceeding cautiously when dealing with vernacular religious texts. From that common premise, they chose from a range of solutions that demonstrated different degrees of suspicion.

CONCLUSION

Even in what is perhaps the most well-known trial of the Spanish Inquisition, there remains room for examining attitudes toward the vernacular with more subtlety. The efforts by Bartolomé Carranza and Louis of Granada to use Castilian as a tool for instructing the Catholic faithful through print ran against Melchior Cano and the Spanish Inquisition. In using Castilian, Carranza and Granada appear as relatively progressive, reform-minded Catholics attempting to make religion more accessible to the common people. Cano's call to prohibit their works, however, seems characteristic of a regressive Inquisition and its supporters, seeking to keep the masses in ignorance. The stances taken by the three Dominican friars, however, do not fit into neatly oppositional categories.

Carranza did not insist on unmediated access to scripture in the vernacular. Introducing his work, he emphasized that the question of translating the Bible into the vernacular had provoked a substantial debate. He therefore bypassed the project of a vernacular Bible and chose a different medium: a vernacular catechetical (instructional) text. In doing so, he provided the reader with access to doctrine and some scriptural passages while still offering the guidance of a priest through his own words. Carranza explicitly underscored the importance and validity of the Church's guidance, stating that "we can understand how [vernacular] scripture has become prohibited [in Spain] and the authority that the Church and its ministers have to do so."[57]

Cano's stance, similarly, reveals more subtlety than meets the eye. Amid his opposition to the ways that Carranza and Granada used the vernacular, he still revealed a pedagogical philosophy. Cano opposed the publication of theology and scripture in the vernacular, taking what appears as an authoritarian, elitist position, highlighting his own advanced comprehension of theology in contrast to the ineptitude of the common people. His stance, however, still reveals an understanding of differing needs among the Catholic faithful, for distinct levels of catechesis. In Cano's mind, individuals with a university education in theology possessed the credentials for dealing with sacred scripture and large tomes of Catholic doctrine. Most Catholics—possessing only the rudiments of a formal education (if that)—had no business delving into complicated theological inquiry. In keeping with their lack of a formal education, they required a greater degree of clerical guidance than their educated Catholic elite.

Both Cano and Carranza, therefore, had philosophies of instruction. Their personal clashes over a variety of issues obscure the fact that they had important common ground. Though they differed on the question of using the vernacular for books of prayer or spirituality, neither one would have contested the use of the vernacular for sermons during the Mass, for instance. Both, furthermore, agreed on the potential danger of publishing scripture in the local languages. More generally, each friar sought solutions to the challenges that heretical sects posed to the Roman Church; in doing so, both upheld the central role of the clergy in interpreting and teaching doctrine.

Established in 1478, the Spanish Inquisition officially existed to prosecute heresy. Inquisition authorities sometimes acted upon less lofty goals, such as personal vendettas. The arrest and trial of Spain's highest-ranking priest and the prohibition of his work and that of esteemed colleagues have long served as evidence for the Inquisition's abuse of power. Even authorities within the infamous institution recognized the potential for using the tribunal as a medium for taking vengeance upon one's enemies.[58] Recognizing the weight of personal politics in the Inquisition offers one way to explain how its leaders prosecuted revered and apparently orthodox individuals, such as Carranza and Granada.

However, a larger range of concerns affected inquisitorial proceedings. Inquisition authorities concerned themselves not only with *responding* to heretical ideas but also with *preventing* them from gaining traction. To keep heretical ideas from developing, therefore, Inquisition officials often identified areas of potential concern. From the perspective of Melchior Cano and other Inquisition censors, authors who used the vernacular to write about theologically complex topics were treading on dangerous ground. Though authors may not have made explicitly heretical statements, they could still deserve the tribunal's attention for other reasons, such as presenting complex ideas to people who might misunderstand them.

Concerns over the vernacular did not arise for the first time in response to Carranza and Granada, and they remained present long after the death of Cano and Inquisitor Valdés. Though Inquisitor General Quiroga seems to have departed from the position of Valdés, the positions taken by the two men actually do not differ radically. When Quiroga exonerated authors like Louis of Granada, he explained that they remained "great Christians" in communion with the Church, despite the presence of their works on the Index.[59] Valdés, similarly, indicated that the Index of Prohibited Books might include a text for a range of reasons. The work could be heretical or written by a heretical author, but it also could be "suspicious," "contain some error," or "cause a scandal or a problem."[60] Valdés thus acknowledged that the inclusion of a book on the Index did not mean that the author was a heretic. Rather, a number of reasons—besides heresy—could justify including a book on the Index.

Scholarship suggests that the mid-sixteenth century witnessed a uniquely repressive era in the history of the Spanish Inquisition.[61] But in characterizing this period as the height of Spanish campaigns against heresy, we have sometimes presumed that leaders of the Inquisition went further than necessary, that they had overstepped their boundaries by bringing accusations against individuals whom they should have recognized as orthodox Catholics. How we can prove that inquisitors overreacted to the circumstances they faced remains unclear, if not methodologically dubious.

Recent work on the Inquisition has emphasized its human side, as it were. Our knowledge of the personal conflicts among Inquisition officials and other ecclesiastical authorities calls into question the authenticity of inquisitorial concerns regarding heresy. I argue here, however, for a more integrated approach in studying the Inquisition. While personal histories must enter into the story, we also should take the words of Inquisition officials seriously, studying their concerns with the same attention that we have given to censured authors. Inquisition authorities like Melchior Cano had pastoral concerns; accordingly, ulterior motives or grudges should not diminish the validity of theological or ecclesiological convictions. In fact, the real ideological differences between Carranza and Cano suggest that their personal tensions may well have resulted—at least in part—from their different pastoral convictions.

The conflict between Cano, on the one hand, and Carranza and Granada, on the other, has been explained as one of intransigent churchmen attempting to silence their more flexible or progressive colleagues. This view misses the fact that they all shared two significant convictions. First, both Carranza and Cano recognized the possible danger of translating the Bible into the vernacular. Second, they shared a recognition that the Catholic faithful needed priestly guidance; widespread, independent scripture reading would not do. Crucially, well after Cano's death in 1560, several other officials continued to view the vernacular as a reason for suspicion. Rather than become increasingly inflexible, churchmen found multiple ways to tackle the intersection between religious orthodoxy and the vernacular.

CHAPTER 2

ARABIC AND SPANISH IN GRANADA, CA. 1492–1570

Just a few years after the Inquisition's prohibition of several vernacular books, the Spanish Crown found itself with another problem of language and religion. In January 1567, Philip II prohibited Granada's Moriscos from writing and speaking in Arabic, citing the language as an impediment to their conversion. In the same legislation, he also banned Muslim religious ceremonies as well as the traditional dress and baths of Islamic Granada.

To enforce the decrees, Philip appointed Pedro de Deza as the president of Granada's royal appellate court. Deza ordered the restrictions to be read publicly in Granada's streets and plazas. The following two years witnessed the start of the Revolt of the Alpujarras, a bloody war between mostly rural Moriscos and Spanish authorities. The Moriscos' defeat led to significant demographic changes in the Spanish kingdoms, leaving Granada with three to four thousand Moriscos, down from fifteen to twenty thousand in the years leading up to the revolt. Altogether, the Crown dispersed approximately 80 percent of Granada's Moriscos throughout Castile. Scholars have often identified this moment as a watershed, foreshadowing the eventual expulsion of Spain's Moriscos (1609–14). The Alpujarras revolt thus marked a major turning point in the history of Spain's Islamic presence.[1]

This chapter considers the relationship between Philip's 1567 decree, particularly his orders regarding language, and the 1569 expulsion of the vast majority of Granada's Moriscos. The Crown's restriction of Arabic appears to mark a shift in linguistic strategies and methods of catechesis, more generally. In the Middle Ages and into the early modern period, some churchmen advocated the use of Arabic for preaching to Islamic communities. The 1567 ban seems to denote the end of the earlier, so-called idealistic approaches to catechesis and the onset of increased repression, eventually ending in rebellion and expulsion.[2]

The infamous decree might have sparked a war and, indirectly, the massive relocation of Granada's Moriscos. I argue, however, that it did not mark as crucial a shift as previously thought in the history of Spanish Islamic communities. Rather than signal a sharp departure in methods of catechesis, the 1567 restriction of Arabic actually resonated with previous modes of instruction, including approaches that incorporated Arabic. This chapter argues that the restriction of Arabic did not exist at loggerheads with the religious instruction of Moriscos. In some cases, the two impulses actually proceeded hand-in-hand.

THE FIRST YEARS

The capture of Granada in 1492 by the Catholic monarchs Ferdinand of Aragón and Isabella of Castile marked the end of the last Islamic stronghold in Spain and thus the completion of the *Reconquista*. The Capitulations of Granada stated the terms by which Granada would pass from Islamic to Christian rule. The capitulations allowed Granada's Muslims to continue to live in their homes and to practice their religion, and Christians who had converted to Islam under Islamic rule would not have to return to their original faith.[3]

Given the task of evangelizing the city's Islamic population, Hernando de Talavera, a Hieronymite friar, was named archbishop of Granada. He came from Ávila, where he had served as bishop since 1485. Not long after his arrival there, he had published *Catholica impugnación* (Catholic debate), where he argued in favor of using persuasion rather than force in evangelization efforts. It has been suggested that he adopted this position, in some part, because of his converso origins, but scholars have disagreed regarding his lineage.[4]

When he arrived in Granada, he oversaw the creation of a virtually new Christian kingdom. The Christian diocese of Granada actually had existed as early as the third century and had bishops prior to Talavera. But when Talavera took the position, things were different. Granada was in the midst of a transition from Muslim to Christian governance, and it was also elevated from a diocese to an archdiocese. Talavera thus was tasked with building a new, Christian foundation for Granada. Because Granada had been under Muslim rule between 711 and 1492, one might suggest that Talavera's position carried interesting similarities with the tasks of those churchmen who went to the Americas.[5]

In order to encourage conversion from Islam to Christianity, Talavera advocated preaching in Arabic and the continued use of certain practices of Granada's "native" Muslims that did not contradict Christian teaching. Decades after Talavera's death, one of his pages—Francisco Núñez de Muley—would recall that Granada's first archbishop permitted the *zambra* (festive popular music of Granada's natives) as part of a Corpus Christi procession, to give honor to the sacraments. Talavera found nothing in it contrary to Catholicism. The archbishop's "instruction" for the religious life of Granada's Islamic communities is known for allowing the literate "to have books of prayers and psalms in Arabic," intended for use in church. According to Núñez Muley, Talavera encouraged the Moriscos to pray in Arabic, and he allowed Arabic responses in Mass; he would say, "Dominus vobiscum," and the people would respond in Arabic. Talavera also sought the services of Arabic-speaking priests as well as converts from Islam who could serve as interpreters.[6]

Although Talavera allowed these particular uses of Arabic, he seems to have viewed Arabic as a temporary tool, aiming for the eventual assimilation of the Islamic population into a Spanish Christian society.[7] The first point raised by Talavera in his "instruction" indicates that the members of Granada's Islamic communities must "forget all ceremonies and all Moorish things in prayers, in fasting, in [Ramadan], on feasts, on birthdays, for weddings, for baths, for funeral rites and in all other things." He added, furthermore, that parents should "send their children to the churches to learn to read and sing, or at least [to learn] the aforementioned prayers."[8] To this end, Talavera oversaw the production of *cartillas* (elementary grammar books) to help children learn Christian doctrine and to read Castilian.[9] While Talavera allowed adults some continued use of their native language within a liturgical context, he encouraged the immediate instruction of their children in Castilian and the abandonment of all religious customs related to Islam.

He also made more general injunctions against native customs. As early as 1498, he forbade Granada's Christian residents from bathing in Muslim bathhouses, from eating poultry prepared by Muslim butchers, and from walking in public wearing "Moorish" dress. He also oversaw the construction of a new cathedral on the site of Granada's mosque.[10] It is true that Talavera advocated more use of Arabic than some later bishops would.[11] But it is perhaps a little acknowledged fact that when Núñez Muley wrote about Talavera's permissive attitude with regard to the *zambra* and Arabic, he described Talavera's visits to the Alpujarras, not his activity in the city of Granada itself. It is possible, therefore, that Talavera adopted a different attitude toward the use of Arabic in provincial parts of Granada, which had a significantly higher Islamic population than the capital city. Altogether, the evidence suggests that Talavera looked toward the religious and cultural assimilation of Spain's Islamic community.

Talavera's fellow Hieronymite and personal confessor, Pedro de Alcalá, took a similar position. Talavera commissioned Alcalá to produce an Arabic-language dictionary and grammar, which ideally would facilitate the acquisition of Arabic by preachers ministering to Spain's Islamic communities. In the prologue to his text, Alcalá indicated that he studied Arabic not out of an interest in preserving the language, but as an explicit means to achieve the conversion of Spain's Islamic communities. For Alcalá, the time had arrived to remove "these newly converted people from the darkness and the many errors into which that malicious man, unworthy of being a human, the dirty and wretched Mohammed [led them]. His master, the devil, vomited upon him all the errors and heresies that he had planted in all the heretics of the past." While some scholars have attributed a certain idealism to individuals like Talavera, Alcalá, and the rest of the churchmen who advocated some use of Arabic, we would do well to recognize that in their minds, the language served as an instrument of catechesis, not as an expression of value ascribed to Islam. Considering the Arabic language a useful tool did not necessarily make Islam less repulsive.[12]

In 1499, midway through Talavera's time as archbishop, Ferdinand and Isabella visited Granada, accompanied by Francisco Jiménez de Cisneros, the recently appointed archbishop of Toledo and primate of Spain. Rather than advocate the original capitulations, Cisneros recommended that the city's Muslims be given the unattractive choice of baptism or exile, and Queen Isabella backed his approach. Those Muslims who remained in Spain received baptism under duress and came to be known as Moriscos. They and their descendants would take the same name. Scholars agree that this moment witnessed the beginning of crypto-Islam in Granada.[13]

Throughout the sixteenth and early seventeenth centuries, some Spanish clerics carried on efforts to evangelize the Moriscos, with scholarship on early modern Spain often taking Talavera and Cisneros as representing two basic approaches to catechesis. Those clerics who advocated instruction in Arabic and/or concessions in favor of retaining Islamic customs seem like Talavera; those individuals calling for an ostensibly more rigid approach appear to act in the line of Cisneros. Individual attitudes toward Arabic thus are often explained in binary terms (i.e., either support of or opposition to the language). At least one author has noted that these two groups did not adopt completely opposed positions. But even while acknowledging subtlety, the general tendency remains to divide early modern churchmen according to "soft" and "hard" methods, or more generally, as either "open" or "intransigent."[14]

But even in the years immediately following Cisneros's visit to Granada and the first Alpujarras rebellion, the picture seems far less "black-and-white" than one may think. For instance, it would be wrong to see Cisneros's visit as marking the end of Arabic usage in Granada. In the final six years of Talavera's episcopate (1502–7), the use of Arabic remained licit. When Talavera permitted Alpujarras residents to respond in Arabic during the Mass, he did so in 1502; in 1506 or 1507, according to Núñez Muley, he encouraged others to pray in Arabic for rain. Alcalá, furthermore, released four editions of his *Arte para saber la lengua araviga* (Grammar for learning the Arabic language) between 1501 and 1505, published in Granada by Juan Varela.[15]

Categorizing individuals as either for or against the use of Arabic or as either progressive or regressive can distort their respective approaches to catechesis. Rather, ecclesiastical and royal attitudes toward the Arabic language developed along more complex lines. Some Spanish Church and

Crown officials supported *particular* uses of Arabic, never blanket statements favoring the general use of the language. Similarly, the notion of the entire prohibition of Arabic is a myth. The Crown did attempt wide-ranging restrictions in Granada, but those same decrees applied only in Granada.

The present chapter examines a range of attitudes toward Arabic, as espoused by churchmen and the monarchy in Spain. We will devote substantial attention to the linguistic strategies of Bishop Martín Pérez de Ayala and the methods utilized by the Society of Jesus in Granada, comparing them to the 1567 restriction of Arabic. Specifically, this chapter will demonstrate that the 1567 royal decree did not mark an abrupt transformation of catechesis, as previously thought. While eminent Moriscos such as Francisco Núñez Muley argued against the royal decrees, the ordinances may not have come as a surprise. There exists abundant evidence to suggest that such a moment had been in the works for decades, proceeding—to some degree—in tandem with the religious instruction of Moriscos.[16]

USING ARABIC IN GRANADA

By the time of Talavera's death in 1507, the city's demographics had shifted. Around 1492, about fifty thousand Muslims called Granada their home. Between 1492 and 1494, a few thousand Muslims departed, but only the wealthy who had the means to leave Iberia did so. At first, many of Granada's Muslims stayed, fearing financial loss and probably taking some consolation in the protections afforded them by the Capitulations of Granada. By 1499 many protections had evaporated, and local authorities had attempted to segregate the city into Christian and Muslim zones. Cisneros's interventions in local affairs and ensuing rebellion and mass conversions led thousands of Muslims to leave, now willing to take on the financial difficulties involved. After 1502, Granada in theory no longer had Muslims, only Moriscos.[17]

For many years after Talavera, Granada lacked effective leadership from its archbishops. From 1507 to 1524, Granada had a largely absentee archbishop, Antonio de Rojas Manrique. As president of the Royal Council of Castile, he had duties that seem to have distracted him from his obligation to Granada. Between 1524 and 1529, Granada had three archbishops: Francisco Herrera Ruesta, Pedro Portocarrero, and Pedro Ramírez de Alba.

Herrera and Portocarrero both died within one year of their appointments and Ramírez within two years.[18]

Despite the dearth of Church leadership in the 1520s, that decade witnessed significant legal pronouncements concerning the Moriscos. In June 1526, the emperor Charles V began his first and only visit to Granada. Shortly after his arrival, he received several complaints from local Morisco leaders, who decried abuses at the hands of civil and Church authorities. Charles put together a team—including Gaspar de Ávalos de la Cueva, bishop of Guadix (1524–29) and future archbishop of Granada (1529–42)—to investigate the charges. They concluded that the abuses were true, but they also emphasized that many of Granada's Moriscos continued to practice Islam in secret. In response, Charles convened another group, the assembly of the Royal Chapel of Granada, which also included the future archbishop Ávalos. Charles charged them with two goals: first, determining what did and did not constitute the secret practice of Islam, and second, how to remedy the abuses directed at Moriscos. The assembly called for a reform both of local administrative practices and of Morisco traditions.[19]

In a list of twenty-five mandates, the 1526 Edict of Granada dedicated significant space to the Arabic language. They called on Moriscos to speak and write in Castilian rather than Arabic:

> Furthermore to prevent and remedy the damages and problems which arise from the continued use of Arabic among the newly converted, we order that from now on none of them, nor their children, nor any other person of theirs, speak in Arabic or write anything in Arabic, and that they all speak the Castilian language. We also order that those who buy and sell and hire in the marketplace and outside of it do not ask or demand any price, or speak while buying or selling, in Arabic, but rather in Castilian, to be punished with three days of imprisonment for the first violation, and double punishment for the second time.

The text of the edict calls for a prohibition of written and spoken Arabic among Moriscos, yet it contains punishments only for those individuals who broke the law's guidelines regarding commercial practices. Thus while Arabic was used in many different spheres of everyday life, the 1526 decree emphasized the Arabic language's influence in commerce.[20]

Besides addressing written and spoken uses of the Arabic language, the assembly's decrees also forbade the use of Islamic names: "In addition, we are aware that some of the recently converted have Moorish names and nicknames; we order that from here onward they not be named as such, and if any of them now have a name or nickname which sounds Moorish, that they discard it and must no longer be named as such and that they take another Christian name." Despite these restrictions, the Morisco community raised approximately ninety thousand ducats in an effort to persuade Emperor Charles V to revoke the edict, which he agreed to suspend. Philip II would revisit this legislation several decades later.[21]

Though Charles V suspended the edict, he evidently appreciated the work done by one of its authors, Gaspar de Ávalos, promoting him from the bishopric of Guadix to the archbishopric of Granada in 1529. Ávalos seems to have been the most active archbishop stationed in Granada in many years. As a member of the 1526 Royal Chapel Congregation, he had witnessed corruption among local administrators as well as crypto-Islam among Moriscos. He attempted to take a strong stance against both, though he appears to have faced much resistance and thus experienced limited success.[22]

When Charles left Granada after his 1526 visit, he recommended that the archdiocese hold a synod. Granada and two suffragan dioceses (i.e., under the jurisdiction of the archbishop of Granada), Almería and Guadix, were the only dioceses in Spain that lacked approved synodal constitutions. Ávalos attempted to provide them for Granada, but in the process of writing them, he sought little or no input from local clergy. Although a synod technically required only the vote of the bishop, it was customary to undertake the synod together with an assembly of local churchmen. Ávalos, however, broke with custom in this regard. Thus when he tried to gain approval for his synodal constitutions, he failed, given the opposition from many of Granada's churchmen.[23]

In his draft constitutions, Ávalos attempted to enact a number of measures that reflected the conditions of Granada and its high population of New Christians. For instance, he ordered priests in parishes that consisted predominantly of New Christians (of both Jewish and Muslim backgrounds) to identify and discourage specific Jewish and Muslim practices. He also called on priests to take time during the Mass to explain the basic tenets of Christianity (e.g., the Ten Commandments, the Our Father and other prayers, the mortal sins, the sacrament of confession). Ávalos specified that the priest should speak slowly and plainly, in unadorned vernacular Castilian, taking care to avoid any potentially pedantic theological language. By favoring Castilian as the language of religious instruction, Ávalos seems to have remained in line with the general sentiment of the 1526 Edict of Granada.[24]

MARTÍN PÉREZ DE AYALA AND ARABIC IN GUADIX

While Ávalos favored Castilian for religious instruction, some churchmen pushed Castilian while also calling for the instruction of the Moriscos in Arabic. One such individual was Martín Pérez de Ayala, bishop of Guadix, a suffragan diocese of Granada. When Charles I nominated Ayala for the bishopric in 1548, he apparently tried to deny the appointment, citing his ignorance of Arabic. After eventually accepting the position, he attempted to overcome this shortcoming by working closely with an Arabic-speaking priest, Bartolomé Dorador, who had learned Arabic while living in Melilla, a Spanish stronghold in North Africa. In Guadix, Dorador collaborated closely with Ayala, serving as his interpreter when the bishop preached to the Moriscos; Dorador also translated a catechism into Arabic for Ayala in 1554.[25]

Though Guadix formed a part of the former kingdom of Granada, it featured a substantially different demographic makeup than the city of Granada. A 1561 royal census revealed the city of Granada as having approximately 45,000 residents, with about one-third identified as Moriscos. In Guadix, a much smaller city, Moriscos made up almost half of the population, with about 1,000 Moriscos out of a total of 2,200 residents around 1571. In the diocese of Guadix, including both the city and its surrounding area, Moriscos outnumbered Old Christians by more than a three-to-one ratio: 4,758 Morisco residents compared to 1,476 Old Christians. The relatively high percentage of Moriscos in Guadix may help explain why its bishop, Martín Pérez de Ayala, would advocate Arabic as a language of religious instruction to a greater degree than Avalos did in Granada.[26]

Before becoming involved with the catechesis of the Moriscos, Ayala, a priest of the Order of Santiago, had a scholarly reputation. He taught at the University of Alcalá and produced a number of works, including *De divinis, apostolicis, atque ecclesiasticis traditionibus* (On sacred, apostolic, and ecclesiastical traditions), published in at least eight editions between 1549 and 1562, with several more in the eighteenth century. Ayala attended all three periods of the Council of Trent, where he advocated the authority of prelates and Church councils and opposed the movement to affirm the increased power of the papacy.

While the decrees of the Council of Trent do not explicitly mention the Spanish Moriscos, many of Ayala's plans for the Morisco-dense diocese of Guadix originate in the decrees of Trent. In the prolegomena to the decrees of his 1554 synod of Guadix, he notes that everything implemented at Trent shall be upheld in Guadix. The first decree from Guadix, a partial description of the duties of priests, indicates that beneficed priests ought to know Arabic: "Because souls do not remain safely in the path of Our Lord without spiritual food, which is the teaching of the Gospel, we order, with the approval of the holy Synod, that in the places or parishes where there is no priest, that the beneficed priest[s] be present on a weekly basis, have a curate's payment and sufficient means, and know Arabic. They ought to proclaim the holy gospel, focusing on one of its important points so that the listeners might profit [from it]." This record from Guadix draws upon the conclusions made at Trent, where delegates affirmed that priests should be able to explain basic doctrine in the language of the people.[27]

Besides ordering that beneficed priests know Arabic, Ayala also published a bilingual, Arabic-Castilian catechism in 1566, as archbishop of Valencia (fig. 2). Ayala commissioned the translation "into the common Arabic language of this kingdom so that those [. . .] who did not understand the Spanish language would not fail to take advantage of instruction in the Christian faith and religion."[28]

Though Ayala clearly found Arabic useful, a full examination of the 1554 synod's decrees does not reveal a unilaterally "pro-Arabic" stance on his part.

> We order, in these cities of Guadix and Baza, that all new Christians come together, on Sundays of Advent and Lent or during some feasts that occur during the week, in a church well-accommodated so that they all may come together and have a sermon in Arabic on the doctrine and the Gospel of that day, since not every parish has learned men who know Arabic and can teach the people.

FIG. 2 | Martin Pérez de Ayala, *Doctrina christiana*. Biblioteca Valenciana Nicolau Primitiu. Photo: BIVALDI.

> Prelates can [preach] with an interpreter or they can appoint someone [to preach]. [The new Christians] have not had this until our time, and it is a great danger to the souls of the new converts to not have it.[29]

While Ayala previously had indicated that beneficed priests ought to know Arabic, this requirement did not mean that they had to use Arabic in all their ecclesiastical duties. Ayala focused, rather, on using Arabic for sermons. Even within this particular usage of the language, he circumscribed the space for its use, recommending the delivery of Arabic sermons during important seasons of the liturgical year, not on every Sunday. Ayala's recommendation of preaching on special occasions imitated the decrees from Trent, where delegates emphasized the duty of priests to "explain, in the said vulgar tongue, *on all festivals, or solemnities*, the sacred oracles, and the maxims of salvation."[30] Delivering a sermon on each Sunday of the year would not have been the norm in mid-sixteenth-century Spain; the weekly Sunday sermon that churchgoers eventually would expect did not yet comprise a part of regular worship for many Catholics. In fact, Ayala's proposals would have represented an improvement upon earlier expectations in Spain. But in other parts of the Spanish territories, such as Mexico, many churchmen set an expectation of weekly sermons.[31]

The wording of Ayala's decree above also confirms that most priests did not know Arabic and that Ayala knew and expected as much, since he allowed priests to employ Arabic interpreters, either to translate sermons or to give Arabic sermons themselves. On this point, too, he overlapped with the Tridentine record, which recommended priestly explanations of the sacraments "in the vernacular tongue, if need be, and it can be conveniently done." In both cases, the councils *recommended* the use of the vernacular but left a loophole if a priest with the necessary linguistic preparation were not available.[32]

Similar to the provisions for sermons, Ayala also recognized the need to provide the sacrament of confession in Arabic: "Very often, the curates that we assign are not sufficiently proficient in Arabic to hear the confessions of the newly converted [. . .]. We order that confessors proficient in Arabic be available during Lent if they can be had." Here once again Ayala recognized that priests proficient in Arabic would provide an important service to the Moriscos. Yet we also see that Ayala called for their service on particular occasions, rather than as a regular resource. Furthermore, in specifying that confessors proficient in Arabic should be available *if possible*, the decree provided another loophole should Arabists not be available.[33]

The record from Ayala's synod in Guadix reiterated, on multiple occasions, the need for clerics or assistants with competence in the Arabic language.[34] But again, the synod called for the use of Arabic only in particular contexts. Accordingly, the support of Arabic did not extend to Islamic naming practices:

> In the times that we have administered the holy sacrament of confirmation, we have seen that many of the newly converted who come to be baptized have and give themselves names (and it seems that they seek them out purposely) that are not of saints that the Holy Mother Church honors and celebrates, such as Garcia, Rodrigo, Brianda, Guiomar, and names of this sort, and even beyond this, we have been informed that, secretly, in their houses, they call their children by typical names of Moors, explaining to us that these [names] are [only] surnames, inherited from their ancestors, and not proper names, [although] they allow themselves to be named in this way outside of their houses.

After opposing the use of Islamic names and indicating that Moriscos purposely deceived Christian authorities, the synod record states that Moriscos must use Christian names: "All of the above is a suspicious behavior of the new Christians. Desiring to remedy it, we order, in keeping with our obligation, that no one who is baptised or confirmed take a name that is not of a saint or honored and celebrated by the Holy Mother Church." The synod record continues, furthermore, to recommend that anyone who maliciously corrupted his or her baptismal name with an Islamic one should be punished: "And if a new Christian is found to have maliciously corrupted his baptismal name with a name that signifies something from the Mohammedan sect, he incurs a punishment of ten days in jail."[35]

In addition to punishing the use of Muslim names, Ayala's synod also recommended that Moriscos demonstrate their knowledge of the Castilian language: "Those who are to be married are to come before us, or before one of our ecclesiastical judges or visitors, so that they may be examined in [Catholic] doctrine (which they have to know in the Castilian language) in order to receive the license to marry." Thus while Ayala's synod at Guadix recognized the importance of using the Arabic language in particular ecclesiastical contexts, it also favored the use of Castilian in some cases at the expense of Arabic. The sources thus indicate that Ayala recommended the use of Arabic specifically when it could help Moriscos to understand Christian doctrine. He stood against other usages of Arabic that—in his mind—impeded Christian catechesis.[36]

For Ayala, the effective catechesis of the Moriscos involved advocating some usages of Arabic and prohibiting others. His limited support of Arabic, along with his requirement that individuals pursuing marriage recite Catholic doctrine in Castilian, suggests that he viewed Arabic as a temporary measure, to be superseded eventually by the use of Castilian among Moriscos.

THE SOCIETY OF JESUS AND THE ARABIC LANGUAGE

Ayala's time as bishop of Guadix (1548–60) coincided with the early years of Pedro Guerrero as archbishop of Granada (1546–76). Guerrero received the position despite having no previous experience as a bishop and little knowledge of the city of Granada and its Morisco population. As a student at the University of Alcalá in the 1520s, however, Guerrero had befriended John of Ávila, who—by the 1540s—had become an immensely popular preacher, known as the "apostle of Andalusía." Guerrero thus received Ávila's recommendation and became archbishop and perhaps the most significant figure in Granada at midcentury.[37]

As an inexperienced archbishop, Guerrero "epitomized a spirit of cooperative effort," trying hard to avoid the controversy that had plagued the reform attempts of Gaspar de Ávalos. Though his ideas mirrored those of Ávalos, he seems to have enjoyed more success, perhaps because he did not call a synod in those early years. Instead, he gave reform mandates through visitations, which did not require official promulgation. After his installation, Guerrero collaborated closely with his old friend, Ávila, who served as a constant adviser, encouraging him to take special care in selecting virtuous men for the priesthood. To this end, Guerrero invested in the Colegio de Santa Catalina—a school established by Ávalos and Ávila to train future priests—and the Colegio Eclesiástico de San Cecilio—an institution started by Talavera, also for the formation of future priests. Additionally, rather than wait years for these schools to produce virtuous, young churchmen, Guerrero invited members of the Society of Jesus to Granada to bolster the city's preaching efforts.[38]

Both Guerrero and the leadership of the Society hoped that the Jesuit presence in Granada might help foster the conversion of the Moriscos. When they arrived in 1554, Granada's Jesuits consisted of just father Pedro Navarro and three novices. Within only a couple of years, and with the support of Archbishop Guerrero, the Granada contingent had grown to include eight priests and twenty Jesuits in training. Letters from the mid-sixteenth century indicate both theoretical and practical support for Arabic; the Jesuits had an Arabic-language preacher, Juan de Albotodo, whom they viewed as a positive force in the catechesis of the Moriscos.[39]

The Jesuit college in Granada apparently had a number of well-liked preachers, among them Juan de Albotodo, the Arabic-language preacher of the Albaicín: "Father Albotodo preached to the Moriscos in their own Arabic language on Sundays and feast days, and they established a school to teach the Moriscos' children how to read and write [in Castilian], as well the mysteries of the faith and good customs. A great number of children attended, as well as some children of Old Christians." This passage encapsulates a guiding principle of the linguistic practice adopted by the Jesuits in Granada: Albotodo regularly preached in Arabic at the same time as other Jesuits worked for the propagation of Castilian, teaching the Morisco children to read and write in Castilian. These apparently divergent approaches, however, seem to have worked toward a common goal of religious conversion. Similar to the approach taken by Martín Pérez de Ayala in Guadix, most Jesuits seem to have viewed Arabic sermons as very valuable but not as the only or even the primary component of their apostolate to the Moriscos.[40]

Contemporary letters attest to the ongoing presence of Arabic-language sermons in the Albaicín. In August 1557, the Jesuit Alfonso Ruiz wrote to Superior General Laínez, explaining that one of their preachers "continued giving sermons in Arabic in the Albaicín, which is the place where the Moriscos are very fervent." While Ruiz describes the Moriscos as "generally, a very hardened people," both he and a fellow Jesuit, Francisco de la Torre, acknowledged the notable, positive effects of the sermons given by Albotodo.[41]

> Father Albotodo preaches thus on all feast days in the Albaicin and the fruit that the Lord produces from his sermons is greatly felt. An old, wealthy Morisco has come to speak to Father Albotodo and brought to him another man, who wanted to donate his entire estate for the construction of a hospital in the Albaicín, and he wanted to be present to care for the poor and die there in their service. A young Morisca, whose own mother incited her to offend God, went to the archbishop [Pedro Guerrero], asking him to separate her from [her mother] and to place her among the *arrepentidas* [penitent religious women], a request approved by the lord archbishop.[42]

Another letter written to Laínez in the summer of 1559 indicated that "Father Albotodo preaches in Arabic to the Moriscos on feast days [*fiestas*] in the Albaicín. In him, our Lord certainly has given them a good minister of His Word."[43] Another Jesuit writing a year or two earlier acknowledged the fruit of Albotodo's Arabic language efforts in prisons: "The priest who preaches to the Moriscos in vernacular Arabic has produced some fruit, especially in those who are in prison, where he goes to give them confession. They love him very much and come to him, saying that they want to die as good Christians."[44]

Was Albotodo the only Arabic-language preacher in the Albaicín, or even in all of Granada? While his name seems to appear in connection with Arabic more than any other Jesuit at the time, the Society did have additional men who studied Arabic. Whether they had success similar to Albotodo remains unclear (and probably unlikely, given the lack of references in the sources). In a 1561 letter to Laínez, Pedro Navarro wrote, "For the newly converted Moors detained in prison, instruction in Christian doctrine has begun in their vernacular." He added, "It is said of one among the brothers who study the Arabic language that he portends to explain Christian doctrine in Arabic fashion."[45] Navarro's letter confirms that in addition to Albotodo, the Society did have other men studying the Arabic language. How many of them acquired a level of proficiency sufficient to preach remains unclear. The letter suggests that some may have had sufficient abilities to convey basic doctrine in Arabic even if they did not have the preparation necessary for the more advanced task of preaching.[46]

While Albotodo's preaching produced the kind of devotion that the Jesuits desired among the Moriscos, other members of the Society maintained active and successful roles in the apostolate to the Moriscos while preaching in Castilian. Arabic preaching did not constitute the cornerstone of the Jesuit apostolate to the Moriscos; instead, contemporary sources indicate that the Society enjoyed success with the Moriscos even when not engaged in Arabic-language preaching. Indeed, Jesuit sources seem to attribute at least equal—if not greater—importance to aspects of catechesis carried out in Castilian.

A 1557 letter from the Jesuit Alfonso Ruiz explained that "Father Ramírez gives [the Moriscos] some talks in our language, because most of them understand it, and they listen with great attention." Compared to his description of Albotodo's sermons, Ruiz ascribed similar results to Ramírez's efforts in Baza, a part of the neighboring diocese of Guadix, which—as noted previously—had a significant population of Moriscos. Ruiz wrote, "At the beginning of these four months, Father Ramírez went with another priest to a city of this kingdom, called Baza, at the request of the Duke of Gandia, son of our own Father Francis Borgia. They spent fifteen days there, with one [Ramírez] preaching and the other teaching doctrine and both giving confession. The reaction produced in the city was notable, with many people coming to the sermons, and the effect was so great that the abbot there endowed a school." Besides giving notice of Ramírez's well-attended sermons, Ruiz also noted that the people "made frequent use of confession and communion." Another letter addressed to Laínez approximately two years later also attributed positive results to a Jesuit who preached in Castilian: "Father Baptista delivers some sermons in parishes and plazas with his characteristic zeal, and he is well followed and loved in this city." In general, the Jesuits in the archdiocese of Granada seem to have preached frequently and vigorously, even if they did not speak Arabic.[47]

In 1559 the Granada Jesuits established a school in the local Morisco neighborhood, the Albaicín, "for the benefit of the newly converted natives." The school combined the efforts of the Arabic-speaking Albotodo along with several other Jesuits who would teach children to read and write in Castilian. This initiative had the support of Archbishop Guerrero and the Jesuit superior general, Diego Laínez. After procuring a house for the school, four Jesuit priests and five brothers took up residence that same year.[48]

The Jesuits in the Albaicín taught local boys "to write and to read in the Spanish language and, above all, Christian doctrine." Father Francisco de la Torre taught the boys how to write, and they received reading lessons from Father Juan García, two other Jesuit brothers, and another assistant. Juan de Albotodo would preach to them in Arabic. Besides wishing to "to endear [the children] to the Catholic religion," the Jesuits also hoped that their work would have a broader effect, "to lead their parents to knowledge and perseverance in the faith." The children who studied Christian doctrine with the Jesuits then became teachers themselves: "Having learned very well the things of our faith, they would teach them in the streets and plazas of the Albaicín in their vernacular language. They also went to the jails of the city, where there were many prisoners of their nation, and there they would teach them doctrine with much edification." The apostolate in the Albaicín thus relied on Castilian-speaking Jesuits in addition to the efforts of bilingual Morisco children and the bilingual Jesuit Albotodo.[49]

According to a roughly contemporary Jesuit history, Torre earned the students' goodwill "with the fervor and love that he put into such a humble position." García, likewise, won the "admiration and respect of the moriscos, who saw the wisdom of such a venerable priest . . . taking his time in teaching children to read."[50] One may suspect hagiographical intentions on the part of Martín de Roa (1559–1637), the Jesuit author of this chronicle, who might have painted a purposely optimistic picture of his predecessors, Torre and Díaz. That said, other scholarship has corroborated that the Jesuits' efforts in the Albaicín did enjoy "at least modest success among certain sectors of the local Morisco community."[51] Other contemporary sources corroborate the popularity of the Jesuits in the Albaicín. A 1563 letter from Pedro Navarro to Laínez highlighted the enrollment of Morisco children in the Jesuit school: "The children in the school number about 300 and each day children of both natives [Moriscos] and others [Old Christians] come again, and many of the natives have come to plead that their children be accepted for schooling in the Jesuit house with the other children so that they might be taught about the law of God. They have done so with enthusiasm. Others of the same group have offered their virgin daughters to become nuns, which is something that has been unheard until now." Besides the account of children brought to the Jesuit school, the same letter related detailed stories—though perhaps isolated instances—of grown men and women coming eagerly to confession and of others asking for baptism.[52]

Altogether, Roa's claim that many Moriscos admired the Castilian-speaking Torre and Díaz seems plausible.

Roa did not offer a uniformly positive reception for each of the Albaicín Jesuits. When he described the work of Albotodo, who "preached to them in their language," Roa gave a somewhat mixed assessment. On the one hand, many Moriscos "loved him and heard his sermons eagerly and devoutly received confession and communion from him regularly." On the other hand, "many hated him since he was of their nation yet rejected their customs." Albotodo certainly made a fundamental contribution to Jesuit efforts in the Albaicín, through his Arabic preaching. His brothers—Torre, Díaz, and others—who lacked Arabic also offered substantial help in evangelizing the Moriscos. It appears that their lack of Muslim ancestry may even have helped them.[53]

The Jesuits thus seem to have enjoyed success among the Moriscos for multiple reasons. Even in Albotodo's case, Arabic sermons represented only one aspect of his work in Granada. After his death in 1578, his contemporaries remembered him as a saintly man. A eulogy, written by a fellow Jesuit, says, "God plucked him as a rose among thorns." The document emphasizes Albotodo's efforts to encourage his fellow Moriscos' increased devotion to the Christian faith: "As a religious, he lived as an apostle, and he worked so hard to convert the people of his nation in spite of their attempts to take his life. But God, in his providence, preserved his life so that he might give it to others by the help he gave them in times of need, by saving them from their errors, by reforming them in their customs. He worked wonders of charity in Granada, Córdoba, and Sevilla, things that were celebrated as miracles." The eulogy adds that the greatest among his qualities was his "most profound humility, treating himself in word and deed as a lowly Morisco among clerics and laymen; consequently, the great men of our time revered him as a saint." The eulogy notes further that "some of the most influential men of Granada and Seville—judges, governors, and other men of rank—entrusted their consciences to him." Notably absent, however, in Albotodo's eulogy is his ability to preach in Arabic. Though other Jesuits certainly remembered him for his preaching in Arabic, the letters cited above do not link his success explicitly to his use of Arabic.[54]

As a whole, the Jesuits in Granada utilized both Castilian and Arabic as languages of preaching. Though Castilian served as the brothers' primary language, Albotodo was an important exception (and perhaps others, too, but to a limited degree). In other forms of catechesis, such as the instruction of children, the Jesuits also used Castilian as their main language. A June 1559 letter to Laínez indicated that "The principal means for the instruction of the young ones and the conversion of adults is to teach them to read and write Christian doctrine and all virtue." Absent any reference to another language, this instruction presumably would be carried out in Castilian.[55]

Even if most Jesuits did not know Arabic, they still found ways to incorporate it into their teaching. Children played an important role in the instruction of Moriscos: "If [the children] emerge from here as lettered men and preachers, then we will find it easier to reform all these people of Granada [. . .]. Our men who go there will take care to instruct the children in Castilian and to learn their language of Arabic as a necessary means for the end at which they aim." According to the letter above, the successful instruction of the Morisco population of Granada depended not only on the priests themselves but also on the proper catechesis of the children who would serve as key instruments in the instruction of the adult population. The children even might—it was hoped—succeed in teaching some Arabic to the Jesuits.[56]

A 1561 letter from the Jesuit Pedro Navarro similarly emphasizes the importance of children in the Jesuit apostolate to the Moriscos: "The Lord Archbishop [. . .] ordered that we look for Morisco boys who do not have a father or mother and bring them to our house in the Albaicin so that our men can instruct them in doctrine and customs, and those who prove themselves competent can help those from their nation." Children would learn Castilian (thus propagating the language), and they would help the Jesuits not only by teaching them Arabic but also by serving as instructional assistants. The Morisco children who attended Jesuit schools included both orphans and children whose parents wanted them to obtain a Jesuit education, complete with instruction in Castilian and in Catholic doctrine.[57]

Other correspondence indicates that the Jesuits had some success in utilizing Morisco children as linguistic collaborators in the catechesis of their broader communities. Describing the tasks that Jesuits entrusted to the Morisco children, one letter underlines the enthusiasm of the young Moriscos and the positive reception of their efforts among adults: "The native children, whom we wrote about in the last letter, take advantage of the customs and doctrine [taught to them] and demonstrate that they ought to be instruments for the assistance of the Lord and his servants. They regularly go on Sundays to parishes of the natives and teach them doctrine in Arabic, which the same natives admire and enjoy in a special way. In the [Jesuit] house, they are given a lesson in vernacular Arabic on the articles of the faith, and they speak about it among themselves."[58]

That the Jesuits ascribed importance to the use of Arabic is significant, given that they did so at the same time that they contributed to the propagation of Castilian. If indeed the use of Castilian was increasing among Granada's Moriscos, as contemporary authorities suggest, then why did the Jesuits not direct their time and efforts away from Arabic and instead toward more fully propagating the Iberian Romance languages among Islamic communities, thus facilitating religious instruction? The attention—however limited—given by the Jesuits to the use of Arabic points to two things: first, a belief in the urgent need to communicate doctrine to those individuals who knew only Arabic. While the use of Castilian had increased among Granada's Moriscos, those authorities who advocated the use of Arabic believed that catechesis could not wait until Castilian had become the primary language of all Moriscos. Second, they may have insisted on using Arabic because they believed in the symbolic importance of studying that language as a gesture of goodwill toward the Moriscos.

The fact that some Jesuits ascribed importance to the use of Arabic in catechesis seems to indicate a sort of idealism. Yet we must bear in mind that they advocated *some* Arabic use at the same time that they contributed to the propagation of Castilian. Although Jesuit contemporaries ascribed much success to Albotodo, they also praised his Jesuit brothers who preached only in Castilian. Furthermore, while Jesuits employed Morisco children to provide their parents with doctrinal instruction in Arabic, the children themselves received instruction in Castilian. The Jesuits' combination of Castilian and Arabic mirrors the practices espoused by their predecessor, Martín Pérez de Ayala. While Ayala supported sermons and confession in Arabic, he required Moriscos to recite Catholic doctrine *in Castilian* before matrimony. He required them to take Christian names only, to the exclusion of Arabic ones. The evidence above, indicating limited usage of Arabic combined with the propagation of Castilian, casts the Crown's 1567 restriction of Arabic in a different light. It appears less as a major shift in methods of catechesis and more as a step in line with previous initiatives.

THE PROHIBITION OF ARABIC (1565–67)

The idea to implement a wide-ranging ban on Arabic came not from Philip II but from the bishops of Granada. At the 1565 Provincial Council of Granada, Bishop Melchior Álvarez de Vozmediano (Ayala's successor in Guadix) joined Archbishop Pedro Guerrero (Granada) and Bishop Antonio Corrionero de Babilafuente (Almería). Together, they recommended the prohibition of the Arabic language among Moriscos in the archdiocese of Granada. One may wonder why they chose to do so, given that the Jesuits seemed to be enjoying success with their combined usage of Arabic and Castilian. To answer that question, it will help to examine Archbishop Guerrero's actions during the 1560s.[59]

In 1563 Guerrero completed his active role as the leader of the Spanish bishops at the Council of Trent. At the last meeting of the council (1562–63), delegates furiously debated the nature of the bishop's authority. Some argued that the pope delegated authority to bishops. Archbishop Guerrero and the Spaniards, however, maintained that Jesus Christ himself had instituted the office of the bishop, entrusting it to the apostles. Accordingly, Guerrero and the Spanish contingent desired to see the bishop's authority enhanced. They argued that bishops possessed their office by divine ordinance (*ius divinum*) and not through the pope. Among that council's many outcomes, bishops emerged as the primary figures responsible for enacting reform in their dioceses.[60]

Perhaps returning from Trent with an enhanced sense of his authority in Granada, Guerrero called the Provincial Council of Granada. When he met with the bishops and his local cathedral chapter, he indicated that only the bishops would have a formal vote. The clerics of the cathedral chapter, however, would not have it. Guerrero and the bishops would have their council and make their recommendations, but the cathedral chapter prevented the successful publication and enactment of the decrees as official statutes. It is thought that in leading the council, Guerrero pursued "rigorous and inflexible policies" that contributed to the Morisco Alpujarras Revolt.[61]

Despite failing to make the decrees official, the bishops' recommendations remain worthy of study given their direct impact on legislation by Philip II. When the bishops revisited the Moriscos' situation, they first called for the prohibition of Moorish dress. Then they took a similar action on the linguistic front:

> Secondly, Arabic should be taken from them. A ruling by the assembly of the Royal Chapel exists on this issue / the seventh chapter orders that neither the Moriscos nor their children speak Arabic [. . .] but it lacks the provision that all Moriscos have their children of five years and above learn to read and write in Romance [Castilian] and, for this purpose, there should be teachers everywhere. It seems that if all the Morisco children learned to read and write in Castilian that they would learn *alxamia* [Castilian as used by Moriscos, often written with Arabic letters] and if it were ordered that none learned to read and write Arabic and that those Moriscos who know *alxamia* were put in charge of teaching it to their wives and children, that with this, in a few years vernacular Arabic could be eliminated and it would be even better if it were ordered that within four or six years all those of forty years or less had to learn [Romance] and after this they would not, under very harsh penalties, speak or write Arabic.

In restricting Arabic, the bishops invoked precedent, specifically noting the 1526 Edict of Granada. This earlier legislation, however, prioritized only the Crown's commercial interests. In 1565, however, Guerrero, Babilafuente, and Vozmediano emphasized the more general prohibition of written and spoken Arabic among the Moriscos. The three bishops also recommended specific steps to facilitate the eventual elimination of Arabic in Granada: first, procuring instructors to teach Morisco children how to read and write in Castilian; second, recommending that none of the children learn to read or write in Arabic; and third, calling for adult Moriscos who knew Castilian to teach it to their wives and children. The legislation proposed in 1565 thus indicates a more assiduous attempt to restrict Arabic.[62]

The churchmen present at the council addressed linguistic practices not only for Moriscos but also for the priests who would instruct them in Catholic doctrine: "Pastors of our archbishopric and province shall be obliged to read Christian doctrine aloud in Castilian devoutly to the people during the high Mass at the time of the offertory on the Sundays of

Advent [. . .], Sundays of Lent, and other feast days that they deem important. This shall be done in the towns and parishes of Old Christians and in those of the natives on all Sundays of the year when there is no sermon." The linguistic guidelines for clergy mirrored those for the Moriscos, once again favoring the propagation of Castilian.[63]

The steps recommended by the bishops point toward the elimination of Arabic among Granada's Moriscos. The document also obliges churchmen to read Christian doctrine in Castilian. While the bishops clearly prioritized Castilian, it is worth noting that an Arabic-speaking churchman, like Albotodo, could continue to use Arabic as long as he also taught doctrine in Castilian. In fact, it is plausible that Albotodo made no less use of Arabic, given that the Jesuit college in the Albaicín remained open, with Guerrero's support. The position taken by Guerrero and his fellow bishops undoubtedly signals a change: they prioritized Castilian to a higher degree than in the past, and they did not explicitly recommend that churchmen use Arabic.

Nonetheless, the continuity with earlier ideas also bears emphasizing. Like the bishops, both the Jesuits and Ayala aimed to propagate Castilian, pointing to an eventual assimilation of the Moriscos into a Castilian-speaking, Christian society. While Ayala had not gone so far as to recommend wide-ranging restrictions of Arabic, he did—as we have seen—desire that Moriscos learn Christian doctrine in Castilian before they married and that they not use Islamic names. The council in Granada confirmed both measures, one implicitly and the other explicitly. Ayala's position suggests that he also intended Arabic to fall out of use, indicating a general agreement with the bishops' main goal and disagreement in the time frame and method.[64]

It bears emphasizing that Guerrero and his bishops from Guadix and Almería did not view the elimination of Arabic as a radical break from previous attempts to evangelize the Moriscos or as a solution taken out of desperation. Their intention appears to have been different: "The first and greatest priority that we consider under the guardianship of Your Majesty is that which concerns these New Christians, ensuring the removal of the occasions that they have for being Moors so that there may be some hope that they will be Christians. Although this matter has been addressed many times as one of utmost importance, it has never been carried out appropriately." The recommendations thus were conceived neither as punishments for Moriscos nor as marking a definitive turn toward their expulsion. While the sources do reveal some frustration of the bishops with the failure of earlier catechesis, they remained open to other solutions and hopeful for a better outcome.[65]

In recommending the restriction of Arabic, Guerrero and the other bishops appear to stand opposite the Jesuits, many of whom prided themselves on the Arabic sermons of Juan de Albotodo. Guerrero's position, however, eludes easy categorization. The Jesuits' efforts in Granada had impressed Guerrero, so much so that he "always paid the rent" for the Society's growing college in the Albaicín. After providing significant financial support to the Jesuits, why would Guerrero apparently take a step against them, by attempting to restrict Arabic?[66]

At least two possible explanations help us to understand Guerrero's position better. First, although several Jesuits lauded Albotodo's preaching in Arabic, Guerrero apparently did not view Arabic sermons as the cornerstone of Jesuit efforts in the Albaicín. Jesuits themselves appear to have praised Castilian-language preachers as often if not more than Albotodo. Thus even for the men of the Society, Albotodo's Arabic-language sermons formed a valuable part of Jesuit efforts in Granada but not necessarily the foundation. Second, Guerrero's simultaneous support of the Jesuits in the Albaicín while calling for the restriction of Arabic seems to indicate that he supported Arabic preaching as a useful *temporary* tool but not as a long-term measure. Similarly, the Jesuit letters noted in the previous section highlight the fact that at least some members of the Society advocated the propagation of Castilian while praising Albotodo's sermons. Many Jesuits thus helped expand the usage of Castilian among Moriscos, and in doing so, they implicitly looked forward to a time when Arabic would no longer be necessary. Neither for Guerrero nor for many Jesuits did restricting Arabic necessarily reflect a downgrade or regression in catechesis efforts but rather a step forward. It seems clear that Guerrero had not lost hope. He continued to ask the Jesuits to staff the Colegio del Albaicín, and he opposed the Crown's decision to expel Granada's Moriscos. Similarly, it has been suggested that for members of the Society, the prohibition of Arabic served as an opportunity for continued work rather than as a lost chance.[67]

After the recommendation of Granada's bishops regarding Arabic, Philip II issued a royal decree in 1566 (published in 1567) prohibiting all written and spoken use of the Arabic language in Granada. Similar to the claims of

Granada's bishops, Philip's decree identified one of the chief impediments to the true conversion of the Moriscos as "the use of the Arabic language, which the aforementioned newly converted, not only men but women and children as well, used in speaking and writing, and reading in the aforementioned tongue and producing their writings as they had, contracts and wills, and other dealings among themselves: through this language, they retain and conserve the memory of their ancient and dangerous sect and life. And by this same medium of the aforementioned language, they have dealt with each other freely and secretly." Besides providing a medium through which the Moriscos could communicate "freely and secretly," thereby conserving the memory and traditions of their faith and culture, the Arabic language, according to Philip's decree, served as an impediment to Catholic catechesis:

> Most of them, especially women and children, did not understand our language, and could not be instructed or indoctrinated in the holy Catholic faith and Christian religion, and few ministers knew the aforementioned language, through which they [the Moriscos] could listen and understand the aforementioned Christian doctrine, and according to current knowledge, if this decree were not put into practice, and were they allowed to continue to use their language, readings, and writing in Arabic, there is little hope that the other aforementioned mediums and remedies would work, in addition to the other efforts that have been made until now and could be done in the future.

Philip's goal in banning Arabic among Granada's Moriscos thus followed the position taken by Granada's bishops, viewing the elimination of the language not as a step toward expulsion but as one that ideally would facilitate the religious conversion of the Moriscos by removing its chief impediment.[68]

Given that Philip had few clerics with proficiency in Arabic, he viewed the continued use of the Moriscos' language as perpetuating a bad situation, one in which the Church lacked the necessary manpower to minister to the Morisco community. The best solution, therefore, seemed to lay in enforcing the use of the Castilian language and creating severe punishments for any use of Arabic among the Moriscos:

> We decree and order that after three years, starting from the day in which our letter is published and promulgated in the aforementioned city of Granada, a period of time given to them so that they may learn to speak and write in our Castilian language, which they call Aljamia, none of the aforementioned newly converted of the kingdom of Granada, either man or woman, can speak, read, or write in the aforementioned Arabic language, either in their house, outside, in public, or in secret. Rather, they will speak, write, read, and interact in our Castilian language, under the penalty that the person who speaks, writes, or reads in the said Arabic language, will, for the first offense, be put in jail for thirty days, exiled from the said kingdom [Granada] for two years, and pay six thousand maravedís, with one third given to the denouncer, another third to the judge, and the final third to our chamber. For the second offense, the penalty will be doubled, and for the third, still more and he will fall into permanent punishment and exile from the said kingdom of Granada.

In Philip's view, allowing the Moriscos to continue to use Arabic would only delay their conversion indefinitely. Aiming instead to accelerate their evangelization, he ordered that they learn Castilian within three years. Neither Ayala in Guadix nor the Jesuits in the Albaicín had called for this kind of time frame. Still, they agreed with Philip on the more general need to propagate Castilian among the Moriscos.[69]

While Philip, the bishops of Granada, and others viewed the Moriscos' use of Arabic as an impediment to their conversion, not all agreed. In a famous memorandum addressed to the president of Granada's *audiencia* (court), Francisco Núñez de Muley, a Morisco loyal to the Spanish Crown, expressed his disapproval of the new legislation. In part, Núñez Muley considered it impossible to enforce Castilian among the Moriscos. In his view, even if the monarch gave them twenty years and the Moriscos wished to do it, they could not: it would be too hard to leave a language that they had spoken for so long. If, he argued, the Crown enforced its penalty of exile for failing to speak Castilian, it would mean the loss of thousands of Moriscos. He also criticized the attempt to confiscate all Arabic documents (e.g., land titles, books), wondering how the Crown would provide the translators to achieve the task of inspecting all the documents. Noting the limited number of translators, he feared that documents like land titles would be held for too long and eventually become worthless. Finally, he cited several silk brokers, agents, and other economic producers that needed to write in Arabic in order to maintain their business. All told, he warned of the loss of important contributors to Granada's economy and thus the destruction of Granada.

Aside from his pragmatic and economic arguments, Núñez Muley also made a more theoretical point, one that has made him famous. He argued, "The Arabic language has no direct relation whatsoever to the Muslim faith." Substantiating his point, he reminded his readers that Christians in Jerusalem, Malta, and elsewhere spoke Arabic and used it in the Mass and in official documentation. Though he wrote as a loyal subject of the Crown, his critique gives the distinct impression that both Philip and his leading churchmen had misled themselves. From Núñez Muley's vantage point, they worried excessively about Arabic and other cultural markers, wrongly considering them as tainted by Islam. Some modern scholarship has taken its lead from Núnez Muley, claiming that Arabic was, in fact, not a religious language. Altogether, his argument suggests that Church and Crown officials need not concern themselves about the use of Arabic among Moriscos.[70]

Recently uncovered evidence, however, suggests that Spanish officials actually had tangible evidence to support their suspicion of Arabic. A 1554 record from the diocese of Guadix reveals that for one influential Morisco, the desire to learn Arabic also suggested an affinity for Islam. In this case, a Morisco named Diego Çaybon had engaged in conversations with Bartolomé Dorador, the Arabic-speaking priest who worked with Martín Pérez de Ayala. Çaybon had begun to visit Dorador's house, perhaps in the hope that he could convert the Arabic-speaking priest to Islam. During one of their conversations, Çaybon relayed that he suspected Bishop Ayala of crypto-Islam. He had asked Dorador whether "the bishop still was becoming an expert in writing Arabic." When Dorador told him that Ayala continued to work hard toward that goal, Çaybon replied that Dorador should "test him to see if he is a Muslim since he has such an affinity for writing in Arabic. . . . Truly, there's something Muslim about him." After that initial conversation, Dorador said that if he were to test the bishop regarding Islam, he would need someone to teach him about that religion. Çaybon followed up on the request, meeting with Dorador at his house at a later date.

In the mind of Çaybon, Ayala's interest in Arabic demonstrated that the bishop had some degree of attraction to Islam. Given Dorador's knowledge of Arabic, Çaybon probably thought that the priest also had an interest in Islam. Çaybon might have been an *alfaqui*, a teacher of Muslim law, given his ability to write in Arabic and the fact that he made a point of traveling to Dorador's house to speak with him about Islam. Given the possibility that Çaybon served as an *alfaqui*, his opinion on the relationship between Arabic and Islam probably influenced the views of other Moriscos. Such evidence helps the modern reader to understand why Spanish authorities sought, over the course of the sixteenth century, either to eradicate the use of Arabic among Granada's Islamic community—as did Ávalos and Guerrero—or to use it on a limited basis—as did Talavera, Ayala, and the Jesuits.[71]

CONCLUSION

This chapter has examined how authorities in mid-sixteenth-century Granada advocated a range of language practices in order to catechize Islamic communities, generally using a combination of both Arabic and Castilian. All churchmen, regardless of whether they advocated some use of Arabic, maintained a common goal: the conversion of Spain's Islamic communities and their eventual assimilation into a Castilian-speaking society. As the next chapter will demonstrate, other Romance languages such as Valencian were also acceptable.

Clerics undoubtedly differed in the degree to which they supported or allowed Arabic usage and, more generally, in the ways that they envisioned the development of religious and cultural assimilation. Even though some of the figures examined here advocated particular usages of Arabic, none appear to have viewed Arabic as more than an interim language, a temporary tool of catechesis. Even those clerics who used Arabic or supported such approaches still aimed for it to fall out of use eventually. Within this context, the move to prohibit Arabic in 1567 does not represent a radical departure from previous methods of Christian indoctrination. Rather, the royal decree constituted a next step in a process of catechesis and acculturation that already had begun. That process, if we can describe it as such, certainly was uneven and varied, but it had been in place for decades.[72]

Though they shared common ground, churchmen certainly did not view Arabic in exactly the same ways. Each of the clerics examined here worked in different situations: Hernando de Talavera reached out to recently conquered Muslims, Martín Pérez de Ayala ministered to Moriscos fifty and sixty years removed from Islamic sovereignty, and the Jesuits served Moriscos at a still later date and in a more urbanized, increasingly Castilian, Christian environment. As a whole, they demonstrate pragmatism, using languages in distinct ways, each aiming to foster religious conversions in their unique circumstances.

CHAPTER 3

ARABIC AND *ROMANCE* IN VALENCIA, CA. 1540–1600

In 1561 Francisco de Navarra y Hualde, the archbishop of Valencia (1556–63), received permission from King Philip II to call an assembly of prelates and civil officials, relating to the conversion of Valencia's Moriscos. Navarra wished to renew local efforts in providing religious instruction to the Moriscos, at least in part to facilitate their loyalty to the Spanish Crown, as rumors circulated about a possible attack from North Africa. At the assembly, they decided that Valencia's Moriscos "ought to be stripped of the privilege of reading and writing in Arabic," and that they "should learn the common language of the kingdom." All told, however, they stopped short of prohibiting Moriscos from speaking Arabic.[1]

Together with their restriction of Arabic, the Valencian authorities made a curious addendum. They urged clerics to approach this matter "with as much benevolence as possible," ensuring that the Moriscos "receive doctrine more by love than by fear."[2] Though the Crown did not uphold these linguistic restrictions for Valencia's Moriscos, the discussion reveals an important insight regarding Spanish attitudes toward Arabic. While taking Arabic away from the Moriscos was, in one sense, an oppressive act, marginalizing Spanish Islamic communities, local authorities considered it in a different light. From their perspective, the restriction of Arabic could liberate the Moriscos from their past, facilitating their conversion and integration into the Catholic Church.

Current scholarship on the conversion of the Moriscos tends to say the following about the place of Arabic: First, with regard to language practices, clerics who worked among the Moriscos chose to support either Arabic or a Romance tongue. Second, those few individuals who either knew Arabic or supported its use engaged in a symbolic act of goodwill toward these new Christians of Islamic descent. The vast majority, however, did not learn Arabic and/or lobbied against its use. In doing so, they contributed to a dominant culture of derision directed toward Spain's Islamic communities.[3]

Several leading figures from the sixteenth-century Spanish kingdoms appear to fall into one of the categories just described: favoring the use of Arabic and thus extending goodwill toward the Moriscos or forbidding Arabic and thus marginalizing the Moriscos. An examination of attitudes toward Arabic, however, reveals a more complex history. In what follows, this chapter covers several individuals who appear to have adopted opposing stances regarding the place of Arabic within the conversion of Valencia's Moriscos. But when Spanish churchmen reflected on language use, they thought about particular contexts. Clerics, for instance, might advocate using Arabic for preaching sermons, teaching doctrine, and/or administering confession. Moriscos might use the language for reading the Qur'an, for writing commercial agreements, or for speaking with family members at home. Accordingly, each case in this chapter demonstrates the difficulty of categorizing individuals as either proponents or opponents of Arabic. Some of these tendencies reveal themselves in the documentation of Valencia's Inquisition, which offers insight into how some Moriscos used Arabic.

THE INQUISITION AND ARABIC-LANGUAGE CRIMES

In the second half of the sixteenth century, Valencia's Inquisition authorities prosecuted particular usages of Arabic among Moriscos: the instruction in reading and writing Arabic, as well as the possession of Arabic books. The records of Valencia's tribunal of the Inquisition from 1550 to 1580 reveal the prosecution of Juan de Guzmán Alarave, a native of Fez, accused not only of "being an alfaquí and teaching the sect of Mohammed to many people in his own house" but also of teaching children "prayers of Moors and how to read and write in Arabic." The tribunal confiscated his property and sentenced him to perpetual imprisonment. In two similar cases, the Valencian Inquisition prosecuted men for practicing Islam and teaching Morisco children how to read, presumably in Arabic. One had "taught three Morisco boys how to read, with the intention of instructing them in the sect of the Moors," and another had "taught the children of the new converts how to read, as well as the prayers of Moors."[4]

In one of these *relaciones* (trial summaries), the practice of teaching children to read is linked explicitly to instructing them in Islamic doctrine: "[teaching] three Morisco boys how to read, *with the intention* of instructing them in the sect of the Moors." Another trial summary reveals similar wording: "[teaching] children of the new converts how to read, *as well as* the prayers of Moors." In these cases, reading Arabic did not, on its own, constitute a cause for a trial, but it does appear to have served as an aggravating factor in Inquisition trials.

By the late 1580s and 1590s, several Spanish officials perceived a decline in Arabic and an increase of Romance language proficiency among Valencian Islamic communities (as we will see in the later parts of this chapter). The local branch of the Holy Office, however, continued to prosecute specific usages of Arabic, convinced that they denoted adherence to Islam. A register of the Valencian tribunal from 1587 to 1595 reveals several prosecutions of individuals not only for possessing Islamic texts written in Arabic but also for reading and writing in Arabic.

One case dealt with a father who had taught his children to read and write in *algarabía* (vernacular Arabic), while another dealt with a man who "knew how to read and write in Arabic but did not know Christian prayers." In both cases, the tribunal ordered the men to remain under arrest until they received proper instruction in the Catholic faith. The tribunal also prosecuted several other individuals who admitted not only that they knew how to read and write in Arabic but also that they were ignorant of Christian prayers. Similar to the examples above, many of these cases against Moriscos made references to Arabic in which the language denoted some adherence to Islam. In one case, the Valencian tribunal charged a man with having "some papers written in Arabic, which were taken from the Qu'ran of Mohammed." Similarly, another man found himself accused of having "some papers written in Arabic, which foretold what was to happen between Moors and Christians."[5]

In these cases, Arabic raised eyebrows because it served as an expression of Islam. In each instance, the trial record indicates that the defendant was guilty of at least two charges: first, "[not knowing] either how to cross himself or how to bless himself or how to recite Christian prayers," and second, "[saying] that he knew how to read and write in *algarabía*." Similarly, the defendant in the second case "did not know any Christian prayer *and* said that he knew how to read and write in *algarabía*." In the same vein, other cases described the defendants' use of reading and writing in Arabic adjacent to the charge of instruction in Islamic doctrine or the reading or possession of Islamic texts. Pedro Rochet, for example, faced charges of "teaching people of the Moorish caste how to read and write in *algarabía and* about the sect of Mohammed." For Rochet and others, the tribunal identified reading and writing in Arabic as suspicious traits in themselves, though they do not appear to have been sufficient to constitute charges in their own right. Reading and writing in Arabic, then, served as aggravating factors, adding weight to a charge of secretly practicing Islam.[6]

It is noteworthy that none of the records accuse anyone of *speaking* Arabic. This absence suggests two possible conclusions. First, Valencian Moriscos spoke Arabic less than, say, the Moriscos of Granada at the same time. Second, Inquisition officials may have viewed reading and writing in Arabic as more suspicious than speaking it; as the records show, reading and writing in Arabic often went hand-in-hand with the possession of Muslim religious texts.

AYALA AND HIS PREDECESSORS: COOPERATIVE ATTITUDES TOWARD ARABIC

When Martín Pérez de Ayala left Guadix in 1560, his work among the Moriscos had not ended. After serving as the bishop of Guadix and then Segovia, Ayala became the archbishop of Valencia in 1564, following the death of Francisco de Navarra and an extremely short episcopate by Acisclo Moya de Contreras, who died less than two weeks after his installation as archbishop. As the new archbishop, Ayala faced many challenges. Scholarship has suggested that previous archbishops frequently had neglected the task of instructing the Moriscos in Christianity. Ayala also arrived at a tense time, not long after Philip had forbidden Valencia's Moriscos from bearing arms, hoping to prevent their rumored conspiracy with North African Muslims. Philip's decree, however, did not quell local fears of a Morisco rebellion, which continued through the 1560s, especially after news arrived of the revolt in the Alpujarras.[7]

Having had many years of experience working among the Moriscos, Ayala probably seemed an ideal candidate to lead the archdiocese of Valencia and its large Islamic-Christian community. He died, however, just under two years after his appointment. Still his brief tenure as archbishop reveals significant insight regarding the place of Arabic within efforts to convert the Moriscos.[8]

In 1566, the year that Ayala died, the Valencian publisher Juan Mey released two books that related to the conversion of the Moriscos. Ayala authored one, a small catechism that contained basic prayers and tenets of the Catholic faith in both Castilian and Arabic. The other text was a posthumous publication authored by Jorge de Austria, former archbishop of Valencia (1538–44), and Antonio Ramírez de Haro, former apostolic commissioner for the reform of the Moriscos in Valencia. An examination of both books provides an opportunity to explore how Ayala's ideas regarding Arabic compared to those of earlier religious leaders in Valencia.[9]

"The instructions" authored by Austria and Ramírez de Haro made no indication whether churchmen should use Arabic when preaching to the Moriscos.[10] The book does, however, address how the Moriscos themselves could and could not use Arabic. First, the authors ordered that no one give Islamic names to children: "Under penalty of one ducat, no one shall give a Moorish name to his sons; nor shall he address them by a Morisco name. Rather, he shall use a Christian name, under penalty of six coins."[11] In stating these rules, Austria and Ramírez de Haro gave insight into two problems among the Moriscos, both related to naming practices. Some Morisco parents gave Islamic names to their children; other parents had given Christian names to their children but continued to address them informally by Islamic names. The authors opposed any attempt to retain Islamic names, whether formally or informally.

Besides naming issues, Austria and Ramírez de Haro also dealt with the Moriscos' spoken language, more generally. They noted, "Fathers and mothers shall push their children from a young age to speak the Valencian language so that when they are older, they can leave Arabic behind more easily." Austria and Ramírez de Haro thus encouraged Valencia's Moriscos to speak Valencian. Their position did not amount to a prohibition of Arabic among Islamic communities. Instead, they implicitly tolerated spoken Arabic while aiming for its eventual abandonment.[12]

While Austria and Ramírez de Haro did not encourage clerics to use Arabic, Ayala made it a priority. His Castilian-Arabic catechism provided clerics with a bilingual aid for explaining Christian doctrine to Moriscos. Ayala's text followed the format of contemporary catechisms, including the sign of the cross and basic prayers (the Our Father, the Hail Mary, the Apostles' Creed, the Hail Holy Queen), which "any Christian ought to know." It also contained the confession of sins, the Ten Commandments (each with a brief explanation), the six precepts of the Church, the seven deadly sins, the corporal and spiritual works of mercy, the sacraments, the cardinal and theological virtues, and the prayers and responses for the Mass. After writing the text in Castilian, Ayala "ordered it [to be] translated into the common Arabic language of this kingdom so that those . . . who did not understand the Spanish language would not fail to take advantage of instruction in the Christian faith and religion."[13]

Within the text, Ayala took steps to make the catechism accessible to churchmen who had rudimentary or no knowledge of Arabic. Almost all the content exists in both Castilian and Arabic translation, with one line in Castilian followed by one line in Arabic (fig. 3). The Arabic text, furthermore, appears in Roman characters, thus facilitating use by clerics with limited knowledge of Arabic. The catechism also included instructions explaining how to teach the doctrine and how to pronounce the Arabic words. Though almost the entire text is bilingual, the opening letter and the closing section are written in Castilian only, thus again strongly suggesting an audience that utilized Castilian as a primary language. Ayala's catechism, therefore, does not seem to have been destined for a general readership. The book's structure suggests that he intended clerics to read it and then teach its contents to the Moriscos.

Unlike Austria and Ramírez de Haro, Martín Pérez de Ayala went to significant lengths in encouraging churchmen to use Arabic when instructing the Moriscos. Thus as archbishop of Valencia, he continued in a similar direction to that which he had pursued as the bishop of Guadix, when he pushed churchmen to use Arabic for preaching and for other pastoral duties, such as administering the sacrament of confession. Ayala certainly differed from his predecessors in the degree to which he called for clerics to use

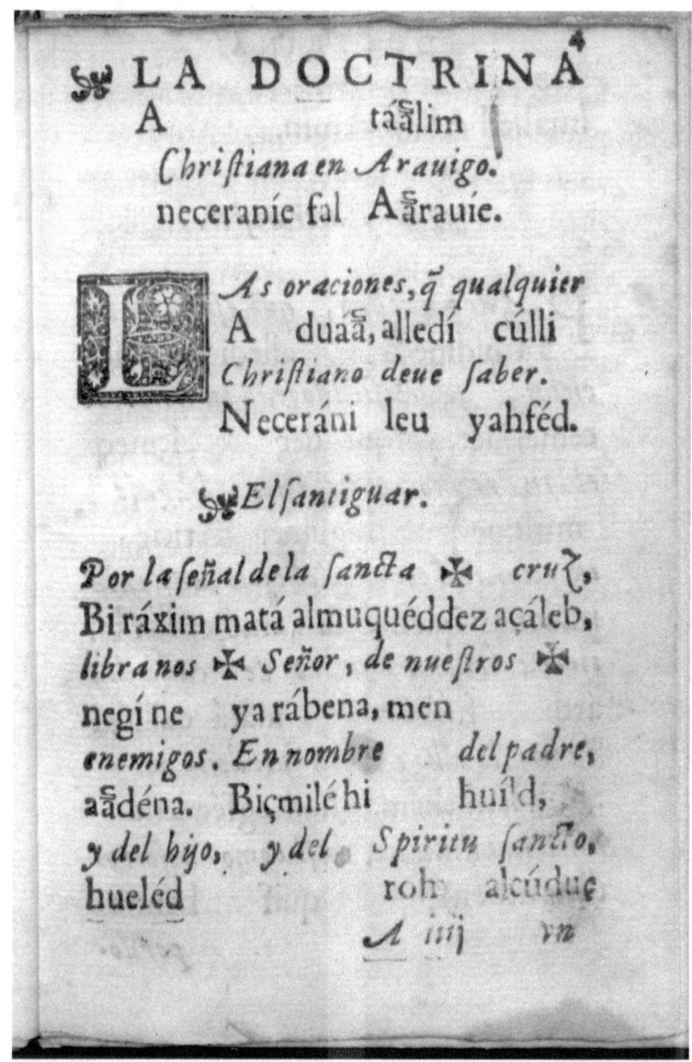

LA DOCTRINA
A táālim
Christiana en Arauigo.
neceranie fal Aārauie.

LAs oraciones, q̄ qualquier
A duáā, alledí cúlli
Christiano deue saber.
Necerání leu yahféd.

El santiguar.

Por la señal de la sancta ✠ cruz,
Bi ráxim matá almuquéddez açáleb,
libranos ✠ Señor, de nuestros ✠
negí ne ya rábena, men
enemigos. En nombre del padre,
aādéna. Biçmiléhi huí'd,
y del hijo, y del Spiritu sancto,
hueléd roh alcúduç
A iiij

FIG. 3 | Martin Pérez de Ayala, *Doctrina christiana*. Biblioteca Valenciana Nicolau Primitiu. Photo: BIVALDI.

Arabic. Still, he did not oppose the methods that Austria and Ramírez de Haro delineated. In fact, he shared significant ground with them.

As archbishop of Valencia, Ayala convened a diocesan synod in 1566. During this meeting, he ordered Valencian clerics to continue adhering to the 1548 synod celebrated by Tomás de Villanueva. Ayala's confirmation of this synod is significant because that earlier assembly had directed Valencia's priests to follow everything already established by Jorge de Austria and Antonio Ramírez de Haro. By extension, Ayala thus confirmed the measures recommended by Austria and Ramírez de Haro.[14]

Ayala made more than a merely formulaic connection with these earlier leaders of the Church in Valencia. As the bishop of Guadix, Ayala had advocated language practices similar to the ones supported by Austria and Ramírez de Haro. He had indicated, for instance, that Moriscos had to take Christian names at baptism. He also required Moriscos to demonstrate knowledge of Castilian prior to receiving the sacrament of marriage in the Church. Similarly, Austria and Ramírez de Haro, writing for the archdiocese of Valencia, had pushed Valencian. All parties thus agreed upon encouraging the Moriscos to use Christian names and to speak a Spanish Romance language rather than Arabic.[15]

There remains further space for compatibility among these Valencian religious leaders. Ayala's desire to see clerics use Arabic could have fit within the recommendations made by Austria and Ramírez de Haro. Though the latter two men discouraged the Moriscos from using Arabic, they did not explicitly forbid clerics from utilizing it. As we have seen already, Ayala saw eye to eye with Austria and Ramírez de Haro in that he did not encourage the general use of Arabic among Moriscos; like his predecessors, he wished that the new converts eventually would learn one of the Spanish Romance languages. He differed, however, in his explicit call for Catholic clerics to use Arabic for the benefit of the Moriscos who did not understand Castilian (or Valencian) well.

Ayala thus demonstrates that one could encourage clerics to use Arabic while simultaneously pushing Moriscos to learn a Spanish Romance language. Ayala and his predecessors differed in their promotion of Arabic *by clerics*. But they concurred in their desire to encourage the local language (Valencian) and to discourage the use of Arabic *by Moriscos*, hoping that the language eventually would fall out of use as a vernacular of these New Christians. Thus regarding language policies and practices, these Spanish churchmen did not stand in opposed camps. They might have called for different methods, but they shared the ultimate goal of Christianizing the Moriscos. They aimed to do so partly through discouraging this Islamic people's use of Arabic and encouraging them to use the language of the local Old Christian populace.[16]

TABLE 1. Language practices advocated by Valencian archbishops

	Valencian among Moriscos (e.g., names, language learning)	**Arabic among clerics (e.g., religious instruction, preaching)**	**Restrict Arabic among Moriscos (e.g., names, reading and writing)**
Austria	X		X
Navarra	X		X
Ayala	X	X	X

AYALA AND PHILIP II: COLLABORATION BY CHURCH AND CROWN

The two books examined above indicate that leading churchmen identified different ways of using languages. In Valencia around the mid-sixteenth century, clerics had permission to speak in Arabic, and sometimes they received enthusiastic encouragement to do so. The Moriscos did not have the same status; authorities pushed them to learn a local Romance language, in hopes that they eventually would abandon their native Arabic. At the same time, King Philip II also made distinctions in the ways that Arabic might (and might not) be used in his kingdoms.

In the same year (1566) that Ayala published his Arabic-Castilian catechism, Philip prohibited Arabic among Granada's Moriscos. Their two actions appear to exist at counter purposes, but in fact, the two men pursued similar goals. Like Ayala, Philip distinguished between the use of Arabic among Moriscos and its use among clerics. His directive against Arabic banned the language specifically among Moriscos. In no way did he prohibit clerics from using Arabic. Thus Philip implicitly permitted a bilingual catechism like Ayala's because it was intended for churchmen. Like Austria and Ramírez de Haro, Philip did not explicitly encourage clerics to use Arabic; at the same time, he did not forbid it. While Ayala and Philip differed in their views on the clergy's use of Arabic, they saw eye to eye in their wish for the Moriscos to leave Arabic behind. It is also worth noting that even if Philip had intended to prohibit clerics from using Arabic, Ayala may not have faced trouble because the royal decree applied to Granada, not Valencia.

Ayala and Philip had a history of close collaboration. Throughout his short autobiography, Ayala depicted himself as Philip's loyal servant. As a delegate to all three terms of the Council of Trent, Ayala regularly aimed to comply with Philip's ideas regarding religious reform. Philip sought to ensure that Catholic reform in Spain would take place on his terms and by his authority, not that of the papacy. Therefore, Ayala and other Spanish delegates favored affirming not papal power but that of local prelates and provincial councils, over which the Spanish Crown presumably would exercise more direct influence than it could over Roman authorities.[17]

Ayala and Philip also shared much in common regarding how to approach the conversion of the Moriscos. After accepting his appointment as the archbishop of Valencia, Ayala met with Philip in 1564 to discuss the king's wishes for this important diocese. Among other topics, they discussed how to instruct Valencia's Moriscos in Christian doctrine. For the following year (1565), Philip aimed to amplify efforts to encourage the Moriscos' conversion. His plan included each Spanish bishop ensuring the instruction of the Moriscos through "good catechisms." Ayala accepted Philip's idea enthusiastically, offering "to do it at his own expense." Philip added that the Inquisition would have nothing to do with the Moriscos, except those who shamelessly sinned in public. He wished for inquisitors to forgive the Moriscos of everything they had done in the past. Therefore, prior to Ayala's tenure as archbishop of Valencia, Philip aimed to incorporate the Moriscos more fully into the Church, and he wanted Ayala to play an important role in that effort. The archbishop's death in 1566, however, meant that Philip would have to find others to help foster the conversion of the Moriscos.[18]

At approximately the same time that Philip looked to augment the religious instruction of Valencia's Moriscos, he also considered prohibiting the Granadan Moriscos' native Arabic. These two impulses may seem at odds with one another, but in Philip's mind, they pointed in the same direction. For him, the prohibition of Arabic did not suggest a concession of failure to incorporate the Moriscos among other Christians. Instead, by prohibiting the Moriscos' language, he removed an obstacle toward their conversion. Thus rather than working in two contrary directions in Granada and Valencia, Philip hoped in both cases to take steps toward fostering the Moriscos' religious conversion and assimilation.

Although he supported the religious instruction of the Moriscos in both Granada and Valencia, he took different approaches in each place with regard to the Moriscos' use of Arabic. Early in 1568, Philip followed the advice of local Church leaders and restricted the use of Arabic for Valencia's Islamic communities. But he did not go to the same extent as he had in Granada: "Among other things, the prelates convened in that city for the instruction and reformation of the new converts of that kingdom have recommended that it would be very appropriate—and for the good of the matter mentioned above—to order that any contract, will, donation, or other public act written in the Arabic language have no force or obligation at all. For by taking this measure, the Moriscos would push themselves harder to learn the vulgar language of the Old Christians of the aforementioned kingdom." Philip focused on prohibiting Valencia's Moriscos from using *written* Arabic for any public transaction, stopping short of a more general ban of Arabic as he had done for Granada. Though the recommended action focused on certain written acts, Philip hoped its influence would prove more wide-ranging. For Philip and for the prelates who advised him, the prohibition of Arabic contracts and wills could pressure the Moriscos to learn Castilian and/or Valencian, which in turn would prove beneficial for the "instruction and reformation of the new converts."[19]

In the same letter, Philip also addressed the possibility of a more general prohibition of Arabic: "The aforementioned prelates have also advised us that it would be good to take the Moriscos' spoken language away from them, Morisco dress from the women, and other customs. Because it seems that taking away so many things at once would be inappropriate, we respond [to the prelates] that during visitations, they observe and determine when would be a good time to take away all or part of the above." Though Church authorities recommended a universal ban on spoken Arabic among Valencia's Moriscos, Philip II stopped short of pushing the matter forward.[20]

Philip's letter, written in early 1568, came at an interesting moment. About one year earlier, as seen in chapter 2, he had enacted the general prohibition of Arabic among Granada's Moriscos, in addition to banning several other Arab-Islamic customs. Some of his advisers at court, notably the Count of Tendilla, discouraged him from enforcing the 1566–67 Granada decree in order to avoid a violent response by the Moriscos. Philip resisted this counsel and proceeded to implement the law; within two years, in December 1568, the Moriscos' second Alpujarras revolt began.[21] The revolt, however, started too late to have influenced Philip's more limited restriction of Arabic in Valencia. But what happened in Granada still may have led him to take a more restrained approach in Valencia. Given Granada's recent Islamic history, Philip perhaps believed that he needed a wide-ranging prohibition of Arabic there. Valencia, however, had existed under Christian rule since the mid-thirteenth century; if Philip considered Valencia's Moriscos as more assimilated, it is plausible that he considered the same kind of restriction on Arabic as unnecessary and imprudent for that population.

Still other factors may explain why Philip prohibited written *and* spoken Arabic among Granada's Moriscos in 1566–67 but only written Arabic among Valencia's Moriscos in 1568. He may have believed that he made a mistake in Granada, or perhaps local politics influenced the different approaches. Regardless of the answer, the evidence demonstrates that Philip made distinct linguistic decisions in Granada and in Valencia. He understood that he could restrict Arabic in different ways. He recognized the diverse histories and needs of the regions under his rule; he considered and implemented distinct measures in his hope of converting and assimilating the Moriscos.

In determining how to proceed, Philip carefully considered the recommendations made by leading churchmen. At times, he differed with them. For instance, he seems to have had little desire to encourage clerics to use Arabic, yet he did not prevent them from using the language or calling for its use (as in Ayala's case). He also did not follow the counsel of the Valencian prelates to ban both written and spoken Arabic, seeing the suggestion as inappropriate for the moment. Despite some differences in approach, Philip and his leading churchmen could all agree that as long as the Moriscos continued to use Arabic, they remained in danger of perpetuating the religious and political threat of Islam. Though Philip, Ayala, and other prelates differed in degree with regard to Arabic, they did not take oppositional stances. They all agreed that in order to become Spanish Christians, the Moriscos eventually needed to abandon their native Arabic. In restricting their use of Arabic, these religious leaders attempted not to ostracize the Moriscos but to facilitate their incorporation within the Catholic Church.

Despite the fact that Ayala supported particular usages of Arabic in both Guadix and Valencia, Arabic-speaking clerics remained few and far between. In 1564, the year that Ayala became archbishop of Valencia, the Jesuit Jerónimo Doménech provided some insight on the availability of clerics proficient in Arabic. Doménech served the Catholic Church in Valencia before joining the Society of Jesus. After becoming the provincial of the Jesuits in Sicily, he wrote, "Many times we have tried in Sicily to find someone who could read the Arabic language. [. . . E]veryone had a strong desire that some of our men would learn this language, and we have not been able to find a person to do it."[22] Doménech, a native of Valencia, who had spent time not only in Sicily and Rome but also in Paris, could think of only one Jesuit who knew Arabic well enough to teach it: "I understand that in Majorca there is a Jesuit priest who knows this language very well and used to teach it here. I also have found a printed grammar and vocabulary, and I understand that this priest, who is a native of Gandia, is an enthusiast of the language."[23] Doménech requested that this Jesuit, Jerónimo Mur, leave Majorca and go to Sicily "for a few months to teach this language." Doménech, however, did not succeed in his effort to support the clergy's use of Arabic. He eventually returned to Valencia and played a leading role in the local Jesuit college. After his return, he continued to call for churchmen to study Arabic, but it never became a major or even a significant part of instructing the Moriscos in Christian doctrine.[24]

JUAN DE RIBERA AND THE 1587 ASSEMBLIES: OLD QUESTIONS, DIFFERENT APPROACHES

When Ayala died in 1566, just under two years after his appointment, Philip named the senior Dominican friar Fernando de Loaces as archbishop of Valencia. Loaces came with over twenty years of experience as a bishop, beginning in Elne (France) and then taking appointments in Lérida, Tortosa, and Tarragona. The elderly Loaces spent even less time than Ayala as archbishop of Valencia, dying after less than one year in office. The king might have decided that enough was enough and that the archdiocese of Valencia needed some young blood, as it were. He chose Juan de Ribera, the bishop of Badajoz. At thirty-six years of age, Ribera had a significant advantage on his two predecessors, who had received their appointments at the ages of fifty-nine and eighty-three. If Philip wanted an archbishop who would stay around a long time, he got just that. When Ribera died in 1611, he had served as archbishop of Valencia for forty-two years (1569–1611).

Just as Ayala had inherited a challenging position, so did Ribera. Ribera's appointment in December 1568 coincided with the start of the Alpujarras revolt in the kingdom of Granada. When news of the uprising arrived in Valencia, it fed ongoing fears that local Moriscos were engaged in a conspiracy with North African Muslims, planning a rebellion of their own. The fears were not unfounded, given that sixteenth-century Inquisition sources reveal the practice of Islam as common among Valencia's Moriscos.[25]

The most recent and detailed work on Ribera demonstrates that in his first ten years as archbishop, he made a colossal effort to reach out to local Moriscos. Together with Inquisitor General Gaspar de Quiroga, the king, and local nobles, Ribera helped coordinate a 1571 concordia, which offered immunity to those Moriscos who had been convicted of heresy. The accord meant a second chance for Valencia's Moriscos, including relapsed heretics and anyone currently in Inquisition prisons. Ribera also embarked on several additional initiatives, creating new parish churches for Moriscos and increasing salaries for diocesan priests in the hope of attracting more interest in ministering to the local Islamic community. He also brought Jesuits to enhance his apostolate to the Moriscos, and he took on a new enthusiasm for preaching, inspired in no small part by the work of his close friend, Louis of Granada.[26]

These many initiatives, however, appear to have failed. His effort to raise priestly salaries resulted in many absentee priests, and Moriscos complained that they had received little or no instruction in Christian doctrine. Even when priests did fulfill their duties, they battled against hostility from both Moriscos and the nobles for whom they worked. Even the Jesuits, who had seen some success in Granada as well as countless other locales in Europe and abroad, began to consider the situation a failure. The Inquisition concordia of 1571, furthermore, had not improved relations with the Moriscos. While Ribera embarked on his new position with optimism that he could evangelize the Moriscos, he eventually grew disillusioned, going so far as to request a transfer in 1577. In the end, he stayed in Valencia, but his sermons demonstrated growing dissatisfaction with the Moriscos whom he viewed as actively hostile and skilled impostors. To boot, rumors continued of a possible uprising among Valencia's Moriscos. By 1582 the once-optimistic Ribera wrote to Inquisitor Quiroga, asking him to push Philip to expel the Moriscos.[27]

Soon after Ribera's letter to Inquisitor Quiroga, the Council of State recommended that King Philip expel the Moriscos. The monarch, however, postponed the decision, instead ordering new efforts aiming at religious instruction for the Moriscos. While Philip thought that the Moriscos still could, over time, become Christians, it appears that Ribera considered their case as hopeless. Nonetheless, he obeyed the king's orders, designing a new set of initiatives, perhaps the most ambitious ever attempted for reaching out to the Moriscos. He continued to fund Morisco parishes, he oversaw several assemblies dedicated to discussing the conversion of the Moriscos, he continued to employ the Jesuits, and he republished or reedited earlier manuals and orders related to the instruction of the Moriscos.[28]

In 1587 Philip II called a meeting in Madrid to discuss the religious instruction of Valencia's Moriscos, among other topics. At the Madrid meeting, the Church and Crown officials present, including Inquisitor Quiroga, discussed several topics before addressing the use of Arabic. They addressed the question of who had the responsibility of instructing Valencia's Moriscos, and they also considered removing the Granadan Moriscos from Valencia so as to avoid potential relapses into Islam. Given the order of the subjects addressed, the authorities present seem to have viewed Arabic as a topic of secondary importance in the conversion of the Moriscos. That they even raised the question of who should attend to the Moriscos suggests that their religious instruction had been neglected. Thus some fundamental problems required discussion and only afterward could the members of the assembly proceed to language practices.[29]

Although language appears only as a secondary concern at the meeting, the issue still sparked some debate when eventually proposed:

> There were many opinions, one of which favored [instruction] in Arabic, holding it as necessary that those who have to instruct and preach doctrine learn the language that the new converts understand and know, presupposing that they do not know any other language but Arabic. But all the men present concluded that presenting and teaching Christian doctrine and relevant issues be done in Castilian and Valencian because, in general, all the aforementioned new converts know or at least understand them, and the men or women who do not know or understand [these languages] are few. These individuals shall be obligated to know and understand through instruction in [these languages].

Although one party raised the possibility of using Arabic, it appears that the rest of the assembly members convinced him against it. They believed that Valencia had very few monolingual Arabic speakers, emphasizing instead that the great majority of Valencia's Moriscos knew either Castilian or Valencian. As a result, the assembly deemed instruction in Arabic unnecessary. They also called for the publication of catechisms in Castilian and Valencian but not in Arabic.[30]

Whether the men at the assembly were correct in their assessment of the Valencian Moriscos' linguistic abilities would have been a controversial question for some. A contemporary authority on language, Bernardo de Aldrete, confirmed the opinion expressed in the record above—namely, that by the late sixteenth and early seventeenth centuries, the use of Arabic among Valencia's Moriscos was actually not widespread. The Jesuit Ignacio de las Casas, however, considered the number of Arabic speakers as sufficiently large to call for local clerics to study their language. Still, despite favoring the use of Arabic as a tool for preaching, Las Casas did not deny that the vast majority of Valencia's Moriscos did, in fact, know at least some Valencian.[31]

In the same year that Philip called the Madrid assembly, he also requested that Ribera preside over another such meeting to examine and respond to the Madrid group. Ribera and the others in attendance developed a complex set of opinions regarding the Moriscos. He and his men generally agreed with the conclusions from the Madrid assembly and called for their promulgation throughout all Spanish bishoprics.[32]

Ribera followed royal orders and called his own assembly to discuss the matters raised in Madrid. Among those present was the Jesuit Jerónimo Doménech. With regard to linguistic issues, all the assembly members agreed to commission two catechisms, "for instructing the new converts, one printed in the Castilian tongue and the same one in Valencian. This seemed very good to everyone." While each individual agreed on the language(s) for the catechisms, all except one consented to the exclusion of Arabic as a language of instruction. Ribera and most of the others aligned themselves with the Madrid group, deciding in favor of Castilian and Valencian over Arabic: "All those from the assembly were of the opinion that everything contained and declared in the aforementioned resolution from Madrid was very well considered. They agreed that catechesis and instruction should be conducted in Castilian and Valencian and that the catechism should be published in these two languages. One from the assembly, however, was of the opinion that doctrine should be imparted in the Arabic language." Given his history of advocating the study of Arabic, Doménech probably was the sole objector at the assembly, trying yet again to rally support for using the

Moriscos' traditional language. He did not succeed. In the rest of the meeting, Doménech reveals that he envisioned a limited use of Arabic, mirroring the position taken by Martín Pérez de Ayala. Like Ayala, Doménech considered the use of Arabic for religious instruction as beneficial. In other contexts, however, he seems to have viewed Arabic as a hindrance to the Moriscos' conversion.[33]

Both assemblies discussed whether to establish a university chair in Valencia for the study of Arabic. The individuals who raised the issue pointed to the recent royal order to create professorships of indigenous languages in America. In spite of what the Crown desired for the other side of the ocean, the Madrid and Valencia assemblies decided against the establishment of a parallel position for Arabic. In fact, at both meetings, the individuals present dismissed the idea immediately, for all agreed that a chair of Arabic "was in no way appropriate." In a similar vein, both groups agreed "that the children of the new converts should not learn to read Arabic and that prelates and local judges should prevent it. All agreed with this resolution and indicated that His Majesty ought to release a pragmatic on the issue."[34]

All the men assembled with Ribera opposed both the establishment of a professorship of Arabic and the instruction of children in reading Arabic. Yet among this group, one (probably Jerónimo Doménech) believed in using Arabic for instruction in Christian doctrine. In Madrid, the question of preaching in Arabic had elicited "many opinions," while the subject of whether to establish a professorship of Arabic apparently found no supporters, even among the individual who advocated preaching in Arabic. At both assemblies, therefore, support for religious instruction in Arabic did not amount to backing other uses of Arabic.

As we have seen, a similar mode of thought manifested itself in other churchmen, such as Martín Pérez de Ayala. Ayala called for using Arabic in religious instruction and in the sacrament of confession. Yet he also encouraged Moriscos to use Christian names and to learn Castilian. Ayala's actions can help explain the stance probably taken by Doménech and some others. Religious instruction in Arabic could serve an ad hoc purpose: namely, facilitating the conversion of those Moriscos who did not yet understand Castilian or Valencian. This limited use of Arabic, by clerics, would remain in place only as long as necessary (i.e., until all Moriscos spoke one of the Iberian Romance languages). In this context, then, Arabic was valuable only insofar as it facilitated conversion to Christianity. A professorship in Arabic and instruction of children in reading Arabic, however, might have imputed value of the study of Arabic in itself and contributed to its long-term survival. Thus for the churchmen under examination here, preaching in Arabic represented a very different goal than establishing a professorship of Arabic or allowing Morisco children to learn how to read in Arabic. The Spanish kingdoms had some precedent of churchmen advocating *limited* uses of Arabic for the religious instruction of the Moriscos.

As a whole, the 1587 assemblies opposed the use of Arabic for religious instruction and for academic study. Still, they did not recommend a general prohibition against Arabic and other Morisco customs. Probably bearing in mind the violent repercussions of the 1568 Alpujarras revolt, the assembly members chose different tactics: "[The disuse] of their dress could be effected little by little and with gentleness, and the same appears true in the case of their language, that it be taken away from them little by little through the most delicate means possible. Because if they are inclined to accept [Christian] doctrine, we have reason to believe that they will be idle in leaving behind anything serving as an obstacle or impediment to it."[35] Recognizing the practical difficulty of forcing people to leave behind their customs, the assemblies recommended a more gradual approach to eliminating the Moriscos' traditional language and dress. The officials at these meetings commented, furthermore, that "many [new converts] spoke the Valencian tongue and wore clothes that differed little from what others of that kingdom wore."[36] They discerned, therefore, a significant degree of acculturation among Valencia's Moriscos; thus their understanding of local conditions in Valencia led them to recommend tactics that departed from those adopted in Granada.

Rather than seek a rapid resolution to the challenges regarding Valencia's Moriscos, the 1587 assemblies looked for a long-term approach. Instead of prohibiting Arabic dress, they recommended ordering tailors to stop making clothes in that style. Thus the Moriscos who had such clothes could continue to wear them, but they eventually would fall out of use altogether. Similarly, the assemblies avoided a general prohibition of Arabic in Valencia, but they still recommended that Morisco children not learn to read or write in that language. If children could not do so, then Arabic presumably would fall out of use over time, as a language used predominantly among older generations. Authorities thus found instruction in reading and writing, in particular, more undesirable than speaking. They believed that reading and writing would preserve Arabic in a way that only speaking would not have achieved. Accordingly, the Valencian Inquisition prosecuted not only the possession of Arabic-language books but also the instruction of children in the reading and writing of Arabic.[37]

Ribera's 1587 assembly differed from Philip's 1566–67 decree for Granada in another way. Ribera's assembly indicated that "it was worth enforcing through penalties or censures that no Old Christian speak with the new converts in the Morisco tongue." The Granada decree prohibited Moriscos from using Arabic and said nothing about Old Christians; the 1587 Valencia assembly, however, took a different course. Old Christians in Granada technically could continue to use Arabic, but in Valencia, the language remained licit only when spoken among Moriscos. Again, the authorities trusted that if they confined Arabic to the spoken realm, it might decline until falling into disuse.[38]

Altogether, the 1587 assemblies on Valencia's Moriscos demonstrate that officials of the Church and Crown identified different ways of using Arabic. Though someone might support clerics using Arabic for religious instruction (like Doménech), he might not have backed the use of Arabic by Moriscos. It seemed that some uses of Arabic would facilitate the Moriscos' conversion, while others might hinder it. Similarly, while some people would not advocate Arabic as a tool for religious instruction, they did not necessarily oppose all uses of the language. Although authorities posited a variety of ways to incorporate the Moriscos within the Catholic Church, they did not divide into two oppositional parties. Instead, the discussion about Arabic included multiple approaches. Each one, however different, aimed at the *eventual* elimination of Arabic and the concurrent acculturation of the Moriscos.

THE 1595 ASSEMBLY ON THE MORISCOS: MOVING BEYOND LANGUAGE

Although the officials at these assemblies continued renewing efforts to convert the Moriscos, they met with limited success. When Philip II convened yet another meeting in 1595, the officials present still sought to implement some measures that had been recommended over twenty years earlier, in

1573. They also recognized that the Moriscos had received poor instruction. Still, they continued to push for renewed efforts. Consequently, they concluded that ministers who used "lenience and gentleness" should approach the Moriscos once again as "new plants."[39]

Despite acknowledging similar problems as noted in earlier assemblies, the discussion in 1595 reveals changes in opinion. If the delegates to the 1587 assembly considered Arabic as a topic of secondary importance, the officials at the 1595 meeting deemed it even less significant in explaining why previous religious instruction had failed. Accordingly, the desire to employ "lenience and gentleness" did not by any means suggest an intention to use the Moriscos' traditional language. Rather, they decided to retain the previous assemblies' decisions against establishing a professorship of Arabic; they also desired to ensure at all costs that Morisco parents not teach their children to read and to write in Arabic, favoring Castilian or Valencian instead. Similarly, they called for preaching only in Castilian and Valencian, and they encouraged Archbishop Ribera to undertake the task of revising the Latin catechism drafted by the late Martín Pérez de Ayala. Still, like the 1587 assembly, they avoided a prohibition of Arabic and traditional dress among Moriscos. Altogether, the authorities made no effort at the 1595 meeting to call for the clergy to use Arabic. They believed that the fundamental problems with converting the Moriscos lay elsewhere.[40]

One of their primary concerns related to hiring more pastors so that "the elderly, women, and children could hear Mass and receive instruction more effectively and comfortably." This observation was by no means a novel one. In 1573, only a few years into Juan de Ribera's long tenure as archbishop of Valencia, authorities had arrived at similar conclusions. Ribera had long faced the challenge of having an insufficient number of priests. The 1595 assembly, then, recommended a temporary papal dispensation on the ban of foreign clerics and religious as pastors, hoping that some foreign churchmen might help make up for the lack of priests in Valencia. Besides staffing problems, some assembly members feared that the presence of the Inquisition obstructed the instruction of the Moriscos. In their view, that institution's threat of punishment already had proven itself as an ineffective tool for the conversion of the Moriscos. The majority at the assembly thus advocated suspending the Inquisition's jurisdiction over the Moriscos for two years, during which time they would receive instruction in Christian doctrine.[41]

In reflecting on how to proceed, the officials at the 1595 assembly also considered a petition from some of Valencia's Moriscos. In it, they expressed a desire to receive instruction in Catholic doctrine, underlining that previous attempts left much to be desired. The Moriscos complained, in general, that past efforts had not fulfilled Philip II's wishes: "The ministers in charge of the catechesis and instruction [of the Moriscos] entrusted these duties to unlearned persons with little experience, lacking any zeal for the salvation of souls. They have gone only to celebrate Mass for them and to recite the prayers with the speed of blind people. They attempt, rather, only to complete their duties according to the letter of the law and find opportunities to charge monetary fees rather than provide instruction." To some degree, the majority at the 1595 assembly appears to have agreed with the Moriscos, emphasizing once again that factors beyond language, such as the improper disposition of clergy, comprised the main problems in the instruction of the Moriscos.[42]

Some officials at the assembly did not agree with the Moriscos. Instead, they located the problem not in the lack of ministers, in a lack of good instruction, or in the presence of the Inquisition but in the refusal by some Moriscos to accept Christian doctrine. They did underline, albeit very briefly, some Moriscos' refusal to learn *Aljamía* (Castilian) as a reason they had not received doctrinal instruction: "Those who are not instructed in Christian doctrine have only themselves to blame, for there has been no lack of instruction, provided by their pastors and other religious. [The Moriscos] flee from them, thus inviting obstacles [to instruction], such as not wanting to know Castilian and other reasons, so that they would not be taught." The individuals who articulated this position, however, identified the main problem not in language but in the Moriscos themselves. In this view, the Moriscos had received sufficient instruction and also had received the benefit of several years in which they theoretically had not been subject to the Inquisition's jurisdiction. In the words of one observer, however, the Moriscos used this instruction and privilege for perverse ends: "only to flee and reject the Gospel law." At this point, therefore, some individuals explained the failure of conversion efforts by describing a deep-rooted revulsion of the Moriscos to Christianity.[43]

While they disagreed on the particulars of the problem, all concurred that Arabic preaching was not an essential element. Instead, they contended that most Moriscos knew Castilian and/or Valencian sufficiently well; thus factors other than language and comprehension constituted the important obstacles to the Moriscos' conversion. Although some religious leaders continued to have hope, the available evidence also suggests a fear, at least among some, that they could not fix the problem. Nonetheless, as the following section illustrates, even a disillusioned churchman still might push for new initiatives, including the use of Arabic.

THE AYALA-RIBERA CATECHISM OF 1599

After more than thirteen years of attempting to foster the Moriscos' conversion, Ribera endorsed their expulsion in 1582. He made his convictions known in written arguments submitted to the "Lisbon assemblies" of 1581–82. Philip, however, stalled the decision.[44]

Given Ribera's stance, it may come as little surprise that with regard to using Arabic for evangelization, he expressed skepticism: "To look for preachers who know Arabic would be impossible and when they are present, it would not be appropriate to teach the Moriscos in that language because of its lack of the terms necessary to teach the principal mysteries of our faith." While Martín Pérez de Ayala advocated the use of Arabic in a Christian context, Ribera seems to have opposed it. Though Ayala and Ribera appear to have espoused contrary stances, a further examination of Ribera's writings calls this assessment into question.[45]

When the Crown did not accept Ribera's recommendation of expelling the Moriscos, the Valencian archbishop had to accept King Philip's view that the Moriscos still might be helped. Ribera thus continued to make efforts to offer them religious instruction. In 1595 Philip requested that Ribera take up the task of preparing for publication the Latin catechism that had been drafted by Ayala several years earlier, a different text than the 1566 bilingual Arabic-Castilian catechism authored by Ayala. The bilingual catechism is a short text, which contains Castilian and Arabic (with Roman letters) versions of prayers, Mass parts, and Catholic doctrine. The text discussed now is a much longer text, in Castilian, based on a dialogue between a Christian teacher and a Muslim disciple. Finally released in 1599, the Castilian catechism formed one part of Ribera's ongoing initiatives toward Moriscos.

Given Ribera's reluctance toward using Arabic, it will come as no surprise that the catechism neither contained Arabic nor encouraged clerics to learn the language. Nonetheless, Ribera still made some room for the Moriscos' traditional tongue. Of particular interest is the first dialogue: "On the occasion for the catechism, which was the reasoning of a Christian cleric, adept in the Arabic language, with a Moor from Barbary." The cleric serves as the teacher in the dialogue and indicates here that he will serve as an interpreter for the Muslim disciple:

> I am your interpreter, because many of these new converts do not understand well the vernacular Castilian language, and I state and translate into Arabic what [the priest] has preached in the vernacular, in the same order, and almost without losing a point. It is all done with such brevity that in just over one hour, the prelate has preached, and I have put it into Arabic. Therefore, through the favor of God and by his love, and for the benefit of your good wishes, I will instruct you in what I have heard from the prelate because I understand your language well.

Although Ribera elsewhere expressed disapproval of using the Arabic language for religious instruction, here he seems to have approved of its use by interpreters.[46]

Just a few lines after indicating his ability to serve as an Arabic interpreter, the teacher elaborates on the origins of his linguistic skills and states that he will have to obtain a license from the bishop in order to instruct the disciple in Catholic doctrine:

> It is true that I know well the common language of Africa and even the Ceneti [language], which (as you know well) is more barbaric and obscure. And this is no wonder because I have lived in Africa more than five years, and I learned it with eagerness; and thus, I speak it as well if not better than Castilian. Thus, I will speak to the bishop, and I will tell him of your good disposition. And I know for certain that he will give [me] his license and blessing so that I will have authority in instructing you. Then, I will teach you in the same way that he has done for his subjects, for

> everything he has preached, I have written down, at least the substance of it.

The cleric proficient in Arabic thus was not simply a passing reference in the catechism. His linguistic ability is featured prominently, in the title of the first dialogue. In the body of that section, the cleric elaborates on his skills, their origins, and the permission that he is confident he can obtain in order to guide his disciple.[47]

How can one make sense of Ribera's attitude toward Arabic? On the one hand, he stated clearly that the Arabic language could not convey Catholic doctrine appropriately, and he also noted his reservations regarding the study of the Arabic language. On the other hand, he approved a catechism in which the teacher of doctrine is a cleric fluent in Arabic. Did Ribera contradict himself?

Perhaps Ribera opposed the use of Arabic and simply published the catechism because he wished to obey Philip II's orders. If one considers his previous recommendation of expulsion as well as his comments regarding Arabic, such a reading makes sense. Perhaps Ribera had had enough after learning that Philip postponed the recommendation of expulsion. It seems reasonable that—convinced of the need for expulsion—Ribera wished to show the king that any attempt to instruct the Moriscos would be futile. Accordingly, it has been argued that Ribera "mounted an aggressive campaign of evangelization—not to achieve the true conversion of the Moriscos so much as to prove their apostasy to the king."[48]

The fundamental structure of the catechism also might support this reading. The text presents a dialogue between a master—a Christian priest fluent in Arabic—and a disciple, a Muslim from the Barbary Coast. The catechism thus avoided the actual situation that priests encountered in Valencia, where very few priests knew Arabic, and the local population included Moriscos, but generally speaking, not Muslims. Given this difference between the text and the reality of late sixteenth-century Valencia, it has been suggested that Ribera effectively side-stepped the actual substance of the problem that he and other local churchmen faced. Ribera's actions may imply that he considered the situation as having no real hope of success. He thus "pursued projects designed to fail," and merely sought to carry out his duties obediently. According to this line of thought, Ribera had no real interest in the catechism and its Arabic priest-interpreter. He published the text only to show that it would make no difference.[49]

While a plausible reading, Ribera's writing reveals another possible interpretation. Sources from the final decade of the sixteenth century suggest that he might still have harbored hope for the conversion of the Moriscos. The following paragraphs offer a further examination of the catechism and one of Ribera's letters.

In the preface to the 1599 catechism, addressing himself to his fellow clerics, Ribera wrote that Ayala's catechism should provide a model of how to teach doctrine to all Christians. He recommended the text to them in multiple ways, calling it "a most important means for the exercise of your position" and a "benefit of your parishioners." He called on them to "take advantage of this Catechism," to read it "many times," and to make it "very familiar, and even committing it (if possible) to memory. This I urge of you." Ribera thus expressed his approval of a catechism originally drafted by Ayala, a point worthy of note since the two men have been considered as espousing opposing techniques for the evangelization of the Moriscos. It is possible, though, that Ribera only wrote these words in order to show his good faith as a servant who complied with orders. Nonetheless, given the numerous endorsements and exhortations that he offered, it also seems plausible that he meant what he said.[50]

Ribera's preface to the catechism also seems to suggest that he actually had hope for the text. While Philip II did ask Ribera to publish Ayala's catechism, Philip also gave Ribera license to add or detract from the text according to what Ribera thought appropriate: "His Majesty resolved that [. . .] the Patriarch [Ribera] be sent a letter so that he might examine the catechism written by the archbishop Martín de Ayala and send it to His Majesty [after] adding and taking away that which is appropriate." In his preface to the Ayala catechism, Ribera noted, furthermore, that he and a team of other learned men examined the book before approving it for publication: "It was necessary to spend a few months organizing the materials and chapters and in adding and moving words and clauses for greater clarity of the doctrine. I did this together with some learned persons, both those whom I have in my company and others from outside, alike." If Ribera or any of his team of scholars objected to the prominent role of an Arabic interpreter in Ayala's manuscript, or to anything else, it seems that they had the opportunity to adjust the text accordingly. Furthermore, the apparently detailed work that Ribera and his men put into the text suggests an actual interest in seeing it make a positive impact on the Moriscos.[51]

Ribera also demonstrated investment in the book when he commented on Ayala, the original author. In this passage, he seems to have gone well beyond merely complying with Philip's order to publish the catechism. Ribera lavished praise on Ayala:

> In addition to his abundant academic preparation, to which his many other works testify, he was always very much esteemed as a person, both by His Majesty the King our Lord Philip II (all glory to him) and by all the others who knew him. Particularly during the Council of Trent, his opinion held much weight among all the other delegates present. And (importantly) he was particularly aware of the situation of the newly converted Moors, since he was Bishop of Guadix, where there were many [Moriscos] during his time: and it was during this time there that he began to compose the Catechism. Afterward, he was moved to Segovia, and since there are none [Moriscos] there, he stopped writing: but, at the end of his life, being promoted to this Archbishopric, which produced the same situation and needs as in Guadix, he returned to composing this work. All this is to say that the lord Archbishop was not only educated and prudent but also experienced and completely aware of the needs of these people; therefore it is manifest in the truths I have said that it is enough to know the author to esteem the work.

Ribera lauded not only Ayala's learning and character but, more importantly, his "complete awareness" of the Moriscos' needs. He extolled his predecessor, going beyond the often formulaic approbations that one often finds in early modern printed works. Given his admiration of Ayala, at least two conclusions seem possible: First, perhaps Ribera actually did think that the catechism could help local priests. Second, he may have been willing to concede that an Arabic priest-interpreter was an asset to the conversion of the Moriscos, even if they received instruction otherwise in Castilian or Valencian. One scholar has suggested that the Arabic-speaking cleric in the Ayala-Ribera catechism may have been inspired by Bartolomé Dorador, Ayala's Arabic-speaking priest-interpreter in Guadix. Like the priest in the catechism, Dorador himself had learned Arabic by living in North Africa. The possibility that a real priest—who had himself worked among Moriscos in Guadix—served as the model for the cleric in the dialogue further suggests that Ribera may have had real hope for the catechism.[52]

Perhaps the most convincing explanation for why Ribera published a text that included an Arabic interpreter comes from a letter that he authored late in his life, approaching the time of the Moriscos' expulsion in 1609–14. Discussing the possibility of allowing Morisco children under a certain age to stay in Spain, Ribera suggested using the rents from two schools in Valencia to pay for the upkeep of the children who would have been left without their parents. The schools, Ribera argued, should be closed, for the students who attended them were worse off than those who did not. For Ribera, "the program of studies in those schools was not appropriate but rather detrimental, and if some benefit might have arisen, it would have come from identifying someone who could preach in Arabic to the Moors." Ribera, then, thought that in an ideal situation, the Church would have provided Arabic sermons to Islamic communities. Nonetheless, in his experience, finding preachers with the appropriate linguistic capacity had proved nearly impossible, and even when available, preaching to the Moriscos in their native tongue still posed problems for the translation of Christian concepts from Romance languages into Arabic.[53]

Still, much evidence suggests that even after calling for the Moriscos' expulsion, Ribera did have an interest—albeit limited—in Arabic as a language of religious instruction and in publishing Ayala's catechism, more generally. It remains true that Ribera expressed frustration at the Moriscos' situation, and it is likely that after having his 1582 call for expulsion postponed, he wished to convince the king and everyone else of the good foundation for his conclusion. Nonetheless, those conclusions do not exclude the possibility that Ribera, even in his vexation, continued to harbor some hope that his priests still could serve the Moriscos.

CONCLUSION

In 1605 the Jesuit Ignacio de las Casas wrote to Pope Clement VIII, explaining the "most pitiful and wretched" situation of the Moriscos. By that time, Church and Crown authorities had spent decades considering how to deal with the Moriscos. Las Casas, himself a Morisco, had an answer for why these new Christians had yet to leave their Islamic past behind. He faulted Old Christians for rejecting the Moriscos; specifically, he blamed his fellow churchmen for failing to instruct the Moriscos properly in Christian doctrine. He noted a linguistic obstacle: "no one knew how to preach to them in their native Arabic language," and the Moriscos "did not understand the Spanish language sufficiently well." Overall, Las Casas linked the clergy's ignorance of Arabic with a general disdain toward the Moriscos. Las Casas's framework—with Arabic use denoting goodwill and ignorance of Arabic representing hostility—has endured in recent scholarship. Undoubtedly, Las Casas represented the opinions of some clerics. As the preceding sections have shown, however, his dichotomy does not reflect the views of many high-ranking churchmen in Valencia.[54]

While Las Casas viewed the clergy's lack of Arabic as a crucial obstacle, many others believed the problem was deeper than language. Around the time of the expulsion, one observer described the Moriscos of Castile—dispersed in regions such as Ávila and Olmedo—as individuals who "lived among Christians and, for the most part, spoke our vernacular very well and dress like us, [even though] they are as Moorish in their faith as the Moriscos of Valencia." Thus according to some, the fact that some Moriscos blended in with the Old Christian populace posed a threat. We find similar observations in the papers of Archbishop Ribera. Written in response to Philip III, one letter reads as follows: "Because they understand and speak our vernacular, dress like us, and frequently use the same arms—both defensive and offensive—our enemies have a great multitude of soldiers, armed and ready for their service and our harm. Thus, it is certain that on any occasion—whether an attack or defense—they will blend in among our armies, serving as spies for our enemies so that they can turn against us in any threat of war." According to this view, assimilated Moriscos who knew Castilian or Valencian still posed a major threat, especially because they seemed to blend with their neighbors.[55]

Like others, Archbishop Ribera also had begun to identify the conversion of the Moriscos as virtually hopeless. In a 1602 letter to King Philip III, Ribera wrote:

> Their purpose and tenacity against the Catholic faith is one in all of them, as is their hatred and loathing of their natural King and their desire to see themselves under the sovereignty of the Turk or any other tyrant who will let them live freely in their sect. All this

> is to say that at the heart of the matter, their outward characteristics make no difference: some go about dressed like Christians and others in the Moorish way; some know and regularly speak *aljamia* (Romance), and others do not; some live in separate places that have no Moriscos, and others live mixed among Old Christians. But we all know with certainty that they are Moors and that they live in the sect of Mohammed, keeping and observing the rites of the Quran as much as possible while despising the holy teachings of the Catholic Church. Speaking properly, we should not call them Moriscos but rather, Moors.

By this point, Ribera thought that the linguistic abilities of the Moriscos (or Moors, as he would say) had little or no bearing on their religious inclinations. Knowledge of Castilian or Valencian and the attendant ability to understand Catholic priests more fully had not inclined them closer to Christianity. Rather, they continued to practice Islam in secret. In his estimation, then, the primary obstacle to the conversion of Spain's Islamic communities lay not in a linguistic barrier but rather in the Moriscos' deep-rooted revulsion toward Catholicism.[56]

In exploring attitudes toward Arabic in sixteenth-century Spain, Church leaders appear to have had two options: using the language and making connections with the Moriscos or opposing its use and thus disdaining and marginalizing the Islamic peoples. This chapter has shown, however, that Spanish authorities adopted more complex positions. Calling for some use of Arabic did not amount to an all-encompassing support of the language. Similarly, those who decided against using Arabic in religious instruction by no means gave up on the Moriscos. Rather, they remained invested for many years in finding ways to facilitate the Moriscos' conversion. Thus efforts to restrict the use of Arabic did not directly imply or lead to the eventual expulsion. Most Church leaders, regardless of whether they supported some use of Arabic, wished for the language to fall out of use eventually. As time passed, many leading figures dismissed the notion that some kind of linguistic or cultural issue explained the Morisco problem. As they saw it, converting the Moriscos would require far more than having churchmen learn Arabic. But at that late stage, even a proponent of expulsion still might have shown hope and participated in a renewed effort to teach doctrine, sometimes through an Arabic interpreter.

CHAPTER 4

NATIVE TONGUES AND SPANISH IN NEW SPAIN, CA. 1520–85

As the last two chapters have shown, Philip II sought various ways of restricting the Arabic language and propagating Castilian or Valencian in its place. Still, he permitted churchmen to use Arabic, and in some cases, he tolerated the temporary use of the language by Moriscos. The pages that follow will show that the Crown's position regarding Amerindian languages mirrors its stance toward Arabic but also departs from it in important ways.

In the Spanish Crown's Laws of the Indies, all missionaries were ordered to "know the language of the Indians." The next law, however, orders churchmen to ensure that the native peoples learn Castilian Spanish. Taken together, these two laws seem rather curious.[1] This chapter explores the logic behind the Crown's apparently contradictory legislation related to language.

The general subject of language and communication between native Mesoamericans and Europeans has proven a fruitful field of study for years among students of Latin American history. Among the first modern scholars to devote attention to this broad topic was Robert Ricard, in his seminal work, *La conquête spirituelle du Mexique*. Approximately fifty years after the publication of Ricard's work, the discussion intensified, with multiple monographs addressing the related topics of language, evangelization, and conquest. In recent decades, a growing cadre of scholars has enhanced the field by examining indigenous-language sources with great energy. Some of the latest fruits of their efforts have resulted in a sophisticated discussion examining language use in different contexts within colonial Mexico.[2]

Despite the extensive literature devoted to language and communication in colonial Mexico, scholars have been bewildered by the Spanish Crown's official legislation related to language. In a landmark study on language policy in Mexico, published in 1972, Shirley Brice Heath noted, "The Conquistadors walked into a solution and made it a problem. . . . Despite recognition by Isabella and later Spanish monarchs of the use of language as an instrument of empire, the Conquistadors failed to perpetuate Nahuatl as the standard tongue or to introduce Castilian in its place." In Heath's view, therefore, the Crown had two options and did not execute either one effectively. Following the publication of her work, there has been no systematic attempt to revisit the subject.[3]

Recent work on colonial Mexico has echoed Heath's general assessment, indicating that the Spanish Crown had two options: using indigenous languages or propagating Castilian. Given these choices, Spanish monarchs and their officials adopted conflicting positions, vacillating between Castilian, on the one hand, and Nahuatl and other indigenous languages, on the other.[4] Unlike the Crown, churchmen were more uniform in calling for the use of indigenous languages.[5] Clerics also had their share of tension over linguistic politics, as the last half of the sixteenth century witnessed significant hostility toward native tongues.[6] Nonetheless, both the Church and the Crown pushed the use of indigenous languages during the seventeenth century.[7] At the same time, the Crown attempted to propagate the use of Castilian among indigenous peoples.[8] Altogether, it is commonly thought that the Spanish Crown swung from one side of a language debate to another.[9]

This chapter suggests a different vantage point for considering the Crown's legislation related to Amerindian languages. It posits that the so-called debate over whether to implement Castilian or to use indigenous languages is a red herring. To be sure, sixteenth-century sources do demonstrate different opinions regarding exactly how Europeans should communicate with natives. However, those references are scattered throughout different documents, and they do not reveal a coherent debate between two opposed sides (e.g., advocates of Castilian vs. backers of indigenous languages). Calling these sporadic recommendations a debate leads to viewing Spanish authorities in an overly ideological light, engaged in a battle between open-minded advocates of indigenous cultures and inflexible defenders of Castilian expansionism.

To understand the Crown's legislation related to language, it is helpful to examine the recommendations made by New Spain's leading churchmen. In Iberia, when King Philip II considered the future of Arabic for the Islamic community of Granada, he paid attention to the advice of Church authorities.[10] Similarly, for New Spain, the recommendations of leading churchmen appear to have inspired the royal orders to support the use of both Castilian and indigenous languages.

The following pages emphasize that the Spanish monarchs permitted a kind of linguistic coexistence between Castilian and indigenous languages. In doing so, they did not aim to defend anything like the contemporary conviction that governments should protect multiple languages. Instead, the Crown's approach reflected the practical mindset of Mexico's churchmen. Officials of the Church dealt with language questions on an ad hoc basis, making numerous pragmatic decisions that served specific problems. In some contexts, Castilian or even Latin seemed a suitable choice to Mexican clerics. The same men simultaneously deemed indigenous languages more appropriate for other situations.

This chapter highlights that, for Mexico's churchmen, calling for the use of Castilian was not necessarily a vote against indigenous languages; by the same token, emphasizing the study of native tongues did not exclude acknowledging Castilian as a useful language for Amerindians to learn. Churchmen generally did not view language practices in terms of two exclusive options: Castilian or indigenous languages. Instead, the choices to be made were far more complex and reflected the realities of dealing with a diverse population.[11]

CONVERSION, LANGUAGE, AND CONQUEST IN MEXICO: THE CURRENT CONSENSUS

Since at least the 1980s, scholars have demonstrated an increasing interest in studying colonial Latin America from the vantage point of indigenous peoples. Consequently, research from a variety of disciplines has convincingly challenged the notion that Spaniards occupied a clearly dominant place in the history of the conquest and the ensuing colonial society. In its place, this scholarship has highlighted the ways in which Amerindians weaved many of their own traditions into the fabric of what became Latin American societies. As a whole, the field now emphasizes that the *mestizo* ("mixed") cultures of colonial Latin America developed through the confluence of several different actors: Amerindian, African, and European.[12]

In addition to the field's increased attention to indigenous perspectives, students of colonial Latin America also have made advances in examining the Catholic clerics who spent most of their time "on the ground" with native peoples. Some of the best work has explored how missionaries and native peoples collaborated, with both showing flexibility in accommodating new ideas. Existing scholarship has described the friars as men ahead of their time, so to speak, given the interest and effort that so many invested in studying indigenous languages and cultures.[13]

While acknowledging the remarkable abilities of many friars, the same scholarship also has described them as limited by their zeal for the conversion of souls. While their Christian beliefs often motivated them to study local languages and customs with ardor, some scholars have faulted the friars for that same religious fervor, which generally kept them from the more modern appreciation of diverse cultures for their own sake. The friars' idealism led them to passionate defenses of indigenous people's rights. It also gave them a degree of tunnel vision, as it were: they so eagerly desired the conversion of the native peoples that they blinded themselves to their flock's ongoing participation in indigenous religious devotions. Altogether, despite the inroads that friars made among native peoples, their conversion efforts fell far short of what they had envisioned.[14]

Since the 1980s, scholars have challenged earlier historical narratives, which viewed the sixteenth century as the beginning of a "spiritual conquest" or of a more-or-less steady "Christianization."[15] Despite the undeniably tremendous Catholic presence in these former territories of the Spanish Crown, scholars in recent decades have shown increasing interest in the challenges of translating Christianity into new languages. Scholars have emphasized misunderstandings, unforeseen outcomes, and in some cases, irreconcilable worldviews. For instance, a classic study of the Nahua-missionary encounter argues that missionary friars faced insurmountable obstacles, given the fundamental differences between Nahua and European worldviews. As a result, the Nahuas became sufficiently Christian for the new colonial society but retained their fundamental ideological and moral orientation. For the Maya, recent scholarship contends that missionary friars lost control of the Christian concepts that they introduced. The words intended to convert the Maya were themselves converted to new uses, fundamentally different from their original meanings. In the Spanish Philippines, similarly, converts to Christianity understood the new religion in ways that bore no relation to the intentions of the priests.

In general, important scholarship has described churchmen as somewhat obtuse, either unaware of or unwilling to accept their congregations' continued interest in their native religious customs, failing to appreciate the complexity of the cross-cultural situations in which they lived and worked.[16] The pages that follow suggest that, although it is evident that the friars were not modern linguists, sixteenth-century Spaniards actually were sensitive to the relationship between language and thought and responded in practical ways.

Though scholars have devoted much attention to mendicant friars, the highest-ranking clerics of Mexico—its archbishops—have received surprisingly little attention, given their position of influence.[17] This chapter focuses on the records of the provincial councils called by Mexico's archbishops in the sixteenth century, in addition to other early assemblies. Other sources exist for the study of language use and religious instruction, but the records from these assemblies have the benefit of providing an overview regarding the perspectives of leading clerics.[18] These documents rarely form a subject of study in themselves perhaps because one might argue that they explain only the clerics' ideals and not the reality of their actions. It is true, of course, that the bishops issued directives and did not know what would result. Nonetheless, these churchmen also made a habit of candidly explaining the real challenges that they faced, thus offering useful insight into the ideals and shortcomings of their fellow clerics.

This chapter and the next may be criticized for a perhaps "top-heavy" or Eurocentric focus on influential churchmen of Mexico. With regard to this potential critique, two points seem worth noting. First, as scholars of colonial Mexico know well, its history is difficult—if not impossible—to comprehend independently of European history.[19] Second, these chapters do not in any way aim to suggest that Mexico's churchmen occupied a more important place than others in the history of New Spain. They remain, nonetheless, significant individuals whose complex perspectives have been underappreciated.

Reading these sources reminds us that leading churchmen made significant contributions to the dynamic, multifaceted cultures of colonial Mexico. The *mestizo* societies of Spanish America emerged not only from the resilience and adaptability of people "on the ground." Rather, the process was a shared one, as this flexibility also manifested itself in high-ranking Church authorities.

MANY PEOPLES, MANY LANGUAGES

In the words of the chronicler and conquistador Bernal Díaz, Cortés and his men stood in awe when they first glimpsed the city of Tenochtitlan, or Mexico: "With such wonderful sights to gaze on, we did not know what to say, or if this was real that we saw before our eyes. On the land side there were great cities, and on the lake many more. The lake was crowded with canoes. At intervals along the causeway, there were many bridges, and before us was the great city of Mexico." Now known for its achievements in agriculture, architecture, astronomy, mathematics, writing, and—infamously—for its practice of human sacrifice, the so-called Aztec Empire boasted a sophisticated civilization. And the Spaniards knew it.[20]

For the purpose of this chapter, it is worth emphasizing that this advanced society consisted of a relatively loose confederation of *altepetl*, or *pueblos*, as the Spaniards called them.[21] Each altepetl would have had a territory, a set of smaller communities or units (*calpolli*), and a ruler (*tlatoani*). In general, the people of an *altepetl* also shared an origin story, a special god, a temple, and a central market. An alliance of three leading *altepetl*—Tenochtitlan, Tetzcoco, and Tlacopan—commanded tribute from subordinate *altepetl*. Besides this obligation, this association of cities shared little else other than a common language: Nahuatl (for this reason, it may be most appropriate to speak of Nahuas instead of Aztecs). The traditional image of a unified Aztec Empire led by Montezuma (*Moteuczoma*) appears to stem at least in part from the Mexica people (the inhabitants of Tenochtitlan), who rewrote their history in order to emphasize the power of their ruler. Though Tenochtitlan did become the most powerful among the three cities of the triple alliance, it often had limited influence over other *altepetl*. The semi-independent cities of the "Aztec Empire" each had their own sense of ethnic identity and often went to war with one another. Each person would have identified not as an Aztec but rather with an *altepetl*. After Spaniards arrived, they built their own settlements, but they organized virtually all of their other activities around the already existing *altepetl*.[22]

This highly local culture of the Nahuas seems one of the principal factors that influenced the ways in which churchmen proceeded to evangelize. They could not approach each new community as though it formed part of a unified "Aztec" people. Instead, each city or town potentially required different plans. Despite this immense cultural diversity, a substantial subsection of Mesoamerica's indigenous population at the time of the European arrival spoke Nahuatl either as a native tongue or as an acquired language. For this reason, large numbers of Spaniards would learn Nahuatl during the sixteenth century, perhaps contributing to the further expansion of the language. In fact, at one point, Philip II hoped that Nahuatl could become a primary language for all indigenous peoples in the region. Despite its widespread utility, Nahuatl had limited applicability, and Philip eventually emphasized the study of all native languages. Europeans would venture well beyond the borders of the former Aztec Empire, interacting with people who spoke languages very different from Nahuatl.[23]

The immense linguistic diversity of Mesoamerica was apparent to Europeans—at least to some degree—from as early as 1519. In his chronicle, Bernal Díaz recorded that he and his men worked with an interpreter named Jerónimo whom they met near the coast of Cozumel and who helped them while in the Yucatan. They would need another interpreter, Malintzin, once they began to interact with Nahuas. Although Nahuas and Mayas both lived in Mesoamerica, their languages came from entirely distinct linguistic families, with Nahuatl now classified as part of the Uto-Aztecan family and the Maya language family comprising several distinct languages. Altogether, it is hard to overestimate the range of languages that coexisted in sixteenth-century New Spain.[24]

Altogether, it seems clear that Catholic churchmen had their work cut out for them, so to speak. They would have to adapt their message not only to the peoples of a "New World." They also would have to readapt that message several times over in order to evangelize people from a wide range of cultures. It is true that they had a highly useful tool in one already widespread indigenous language (Nahuatl). As the Spanish presence in Mesoamerica expanded, the Crown's territory encompassed lands far beyond the former Aztec Empire. Given the array of peoples and languages, the situation offered no clear solutions regarding how to convey Christianity.

FRIARS: SELF-GOVERNING AND IN SHORT SUPPLY

Responding to the diversity of native peoples and tongues, the mendicant ("begging") friars led the Church's efforts in Mexico for much of the sixteenth century. The friars possessed several characteristics that made them ideal people for the challenge. Hernán Cortés himself asked King Charles to send Franciscan friars, thinking that their apostolic poverty would provide a better model of Christianity than would secular (diocesan) priests and bishops.[25] Originally inspired to live according to the poverty of Jesus Christ and his apostles, the Franciscans, Dominicans, and Augustinians each took vows of poverty, as well as chastity and obedience. They served as the first major teams of preachers, all arriving within a decade following the defeat of the Aztec Empire in 1521.

Each order had distinctive qualities. Among the three, the Augustinians had the longest tradition, inspired by their founder, St. Augustine of Hippo (354–430). St. Dominic Guzmán (1170–1221) had founded the Dominicans to combat heresy through preaching. While all the mendicants took vows of poverty, this trait stands out most clearly in the story of St. Francis of Assisi (ca. 1181/82–1226), who abandoned a wealthy family inheritance to preach the Gospel through service. Though each order had unique qualities, they all took the study of indigenous languages seriously, with each group able to boast dozens of men who studied native tongues.

In New Spain, the friars exercised an unusual degree of authority. Mexico had no bishop for nearly five years after the arrival of the famous band of twelve Franciscans in May 1524. When Charles I recommended Mexico's first bishop in 1527, he chose a man who came from the Franciscans, Juan de Zumárraga (1468–1546). Zumárraga, however, would not arrive until December 1528 and only received his formal ordination as bishop in 1533. Zumárraga would die just one month before the papal bull that named him as archbishop arrived in Mexico. Mexico's second archbishop, the Dominican Alonso de Montúfar (1489–1572) likewise came from the mendicant orders and occupied the highest position in the archdiocese for over twenty years (1551–72). Altogether, there is much to support the claim that the mendicant friars dominated the first fifty years of the Catholic Church in Mexico. After that point, the numbers of secular clerics would grow.[26]

The relative independence and influence of the friars led many of them to form very close relationships with their native charges. Friars and natives interacted for many reasons: religious instruction, of course, but also for other purposes, ranging from settling legal disputes to obtaining health care. Given the friars' bonds with many native peoples, they often sought to protect them from the Spaniards who attempted to take unfair advantage of indigenous labor and resources. Altogether, the independence of each community of friars allowed them to adapt to the needs of specific indigenous communities. While officials of both the Church and the Crown would seek to intervene in the friars' local affairs, these missionaries also resisted some of those initiatives, claiming a better understanding of the needs of the native peoples in their particular area.[27]

These often intimate relationships between friars and natives, however, did not always serve to propagate Catholic evangelization. For instance, the friars' urge to protect indigenous peoples also led to segregating the natives into distinct communities, apart from Spaniards. Living on their own probably facilitated the preservation of indigenous religious devotions, though many sixteenth-century writers attributed this phenomenon to Satanic influence. Separating indigenous communities from Spaniards also may have cultivated a greater sense of paternalism among the friars, who felt an increasing duty to protect their "child-like" native charges. That paternalistic authority led, in many cases, to tensions among Amerindians, churchmen, and Spanish laymen. It was not uncommon to find complaints issued against friars or secular priests. On some occasions, churchmen's concerns regarding indigenous religious devotions led to violent outcomes. In the early decades of New Spain's history, Church leadership oversaw controversial episcopal inquisitions and extirpation trials, both of which aimed to eradicate indigenous devotions. It is worth noting, however, that after 1570, Amerindians were, generally speaking, not subject to the Inquisition.[28]

This general description should not imply that in every situation, churchmen and Mesoamerican natives enjoyed close relationships. Rather, sixteenth-century sources regularly bemoan a lack of sufficient churchmen. A report from the central Mexican diocese of Tlaxcala in 1571–72 indicates that it was common for one priest to be assigned to upward of one thousand and even two thousand parishioners, often in different villages several miles apart. Other archival materials, furthermore, regularly indicate that authorities in New Spain made multiple requests for more friars and churchmen. Given their limited numbers, clerics relied on indigenous assistants. With churchmen often absent, many Amerindians stepped into positions of leadership. While this book focuses on churchmen themselves, it is important to note that several other studies already have begun to explore the roles that native peoples had in Catholicism.[29]

Altogether, the friars took advantage of their relative independence from central authorities in order to forge intimate relationships with indigenous peoples. While that independence may have assisted their evangelization efforts, it also seems to have worked against them in some ways. Eventually, while both the regular and secular clergy made inroads among Mesoamerica's native communities, they also found themselves limited both by numbers and by social tensions. Though they reviled many indigenous devotions as idolatrous, they also found native languages and customs that they put to use in support of their evangelization efforts. Just how they would strike a balance between indigenous and Christian elements remained to be seen. The balance would be a highly pragmatic one, aiming to resolve the unique challenges posed by a wide range of peoples and situations.

PRAGMATIC COMMUNICATION AFTER THE FIRST ENCOUNTER

In 1519 Hernando Cortés arrived in present-day Mexico with four clerics. Secondhand sources claim that his chaplain, Juan Díaz, learned a number of Amerindian languages. During the first years of contact, only a few priests were available to carry out the duty of teaching the natives. Given a shortage of priests, the duty of both evangelizing and "civilizing" the natives theoretically fell to the *encomenderos*, the men who took advantage of indigenous labor with the backing of the Spanish Crown. The Crown charged them with teaching European customs, the Castilian language, and Catholic doctrine to the natives. For the final task, they were to rely on the assistance of indigenous interpreters who would instruct other natives in doctrine via the local language. These initiatives, however, produced little success and underscored the need for sending more churchmen to Mesoamerica.[30]

In 1524 twelve Franciscans arrived in Mexico, ready to propagate Christianity. Prior to learning the local languages, how did they manage to communicate their faith to the Amerindians? Some natives managed to learn Spanish quickly and thus made themselves essential collaborators of European missionaries and conquistadors. Throughout the colonial period, native interpreters would remain key figures in the evangelization of indigenous communities.[31]

In addition to working with interpreters, natives and missionaries utilized other methods besides spoken language in order to communicate. An early Franciscan source indicates that some natives used painted images of their sins in order to receive the sacrament of confession. The friars understood that Mesoamerican peoples had image-based writing systems (the Franciscan author here called them forms of writing), and they also managed to utilize them: "Some confessed by taking painted images with certain characters, with which they were able to be understood, and they proceeded to declare [their sins], as this was the method of writing that they used, as Gentiles. Others, who had learned how to write, brought their sins written down."[32] The passage here suggests that while natives and their missionary priests communicated verbally with each other, they also used writing systems—both image based and alphabetic. We do not know whether these particular natives used the alphabet to write in Castilian or in an indigenous language, such as Nahuatl or Otomi. Still, this limited information could suggest at least two conclusions about natives' and missionaries' linguistic abilities in this early context: first, some confessors had acquired sufficient knowledge of local languages to make sense of something written in the Roman alphabet; second, some natives had learned enough Castilian in order to make themselves understood through a combination of speaking, writing, and/or painting.

Just as natives conveyed their sins through their image-based writing, Catholic priests may have used images to communicate basic Christian teachings to natives. Several pictographic catechisms survive to this day, such as one attributed to the Franciscan friar Pedro de Gante.[33] Altogether, natives and Christian missionaries utilized some combination of interpreters, images, and other forms of writing in order to communicate during the early period of contact. While the missionaries had instructed the natives in the Roman alphabet and, presumably, in the Castilian language, they did not seem concerned primarily with imposing their own language to the exclusion of native tongues. Rather, they sought any means possible in order to communicate with natives and thus further their desire to build a Christian new world.

"A LAND OF ONE LANGUAGE"? MARTÍN DE VALENCIA AND THE FIRST FRANCISCANS

Shortly after the arrival of Cortés in Mesoamerica, King Charles I and Pope Leo X commissioned the Order of Friars Minor (the Franciscans) to send men to preach in the new territories. Francisco de los Ángeles, the Franciscans' minister general, chose Martín de Valencia to lead the group. A seasoned servant of the order, known for his *gravitas*, tranquility, self-effacement, and moderation in words, Valencia had worked as the superior of the province of St. Gabriel in Extremadura. Fashioning themselves in the line of Jesus Christ and his twelve apostles, the Franciscans sent Valencia and twelve of his confreres to the New World.[34]

Before their departure, Valencia and the twelve friars received directions from their minister general. Since he knew little about the situation abroad, Francisco de los Ángeles recognized that the friars themselves would know best how to proceed in preaching to the native peoples. Thus his directions contain few specifics regarding how to foster the conversion of indigenous communities. Nevertheless, he did underline what he considered as their fundamental duty: to teach the Gospel. The Franciscans' minister general showed confidence that Valencia and the twelve friars would succeed as long as they "studiously safeguarded the rule [of St. Francis], which is based in the Gospel, observing it purely and simply." In exhorting his men to conduct themselves according to the established Franciscan rule, Francisco de los Ángeles highlighted the friars' behavior as the key to the success of their mission. In a similar vein, he added that "the order and good example that [the natives] will see in your life and conversation will help their conversion as much as words and preaching."[35] Altogether, Fray de los Ángeles made no suggestions regarding language study; instead, he essentially exhorted the friars to preach through their actions.

Valencia seems to have done precisely that. According to his fellow Franciscan, Gerónimo de Mendieta, Valencia was "already old, about fifty when he came to New Spain," and for this reason, "he could not study the natives' language very much." Because he focused on the "essential" tasks that God had given to him—"prayer, contemplation, and spiritual exercises"—he "knew little" of the local language. Despite this limited knowledge, "he did more than the others, by the example he gave of a holy life." In addition to preaching by his actions, as Fray Francisco de los Ángeles had suggested, Valencia also taught native children in the traditional sense: "His standard exercise among the indians was to teach the children to read, beginning with *a*, *b*, *c*, until they could read Spanish, Latin, and Christian doctrine." He taught them "through interpreters." In doing so, he gave them "many good lessons, in keeping with their age and abilities."[36] The fact that he learned little of the native languages and taught children to read Castilian and Latin is reflected in other records of his activity in New Spain.

Shortly after arriving in the new Spanish kingdoms, Valencia convened an assembly to determine how the friars would approach the task of Christianizing the natives. At the Primera Junta Apostólica de México (First Apostolic Assembly of Mexico), Valencia advocated teaching Castilian to the natives. He argued that all clerics ought to take care to "advance and propagate the Castilian language and ensure that the Indians know how to read and write in it." Valencia added that any ministers who failed to teach Castilian to the natives "allowed them to stay closed in their own native language. They are, in my opinion, declared enemies of the well-being of the Natives, of their good order and ability to reason. They intend to disturb the best ecclesiastical government, which is impeded by so many languages that are so different, and they provoke idolatry, which is more apparent in the Indians that do not know Castilian." At this early meeting, Martín de Valencia thus clearly upheld the Castilian language as advantageous to the natives.[37]

Valencia offered several reasons for teaching Castilian to the natives. He argued, for instance, that using Castilian could protect the good order and rationality of the Amerindians. In making this claim, Valencia probably had in mind the linguistic competency of his fellow Spaniards in Mexico. While recent research has suggested that many Spaniards learned Nahuatl during the sixteenth century, it also seems that a large portion of Spaniards either did not learn it or had very limited knowledge of it.[38] Many, therefore, had to rely on interpreters. But an indigenous person who knew Castilian could interact with Spaniards without a mediator. As a result, Amerindians who learned Castilian could have acted upon on their own understanding of a conversation, not relying upon what a third party might tell them. It seems plausible that Valencia was thinking along these lines when he argued that Castilian protected the rationality and good order of indigenous people. When he called for natives to study Castilian, it seems plausible that he did so not out of a sense of cultural superiority. Rather, he might have viewed Castilian as offering Amerindians a practical advantage.

Valencia also saw Castilian as having another pragmatic, administrative benefit over indigenous languages: in his view, "so many languages that are so different" would impede the growth of "the best ecclesiastical government" in Mexico. Instead of a multiplicity of languages, the natives needed to have one language. Why, then, did he not advocate the use of Nahuatl, the already established common language of the Aztec Empire? Valencia had concluded that the natives who did not know Castilian remained "closed in their native language," and thus seemed most likely to practice indigenous devotions.[39] Castilian thus seemed ideal for three practical reasons: first, it would protect the natives' ability to reason; second, it would serve as a common language for people of different backgrounds and thus facilitate "the best ecclesiastical government"; and finally, it would distance the natives from their religious past.

Putting Valencia's support of Castilian into a broader context can help illuminate his views further. At least one scholar has suggested that the records of sixteenth-century Mexico's early ecclesiastical assemblies demonstrate optimism, hopeful of Amerindians' potential to convert to Christianity.[40] If Valencia shared in this early enthusiasm, then his support of Castilian also might denote optimism about the capacity of Amerindians to become devout Christians. It seems plausible that Valencia did not view indigenous languages as problematic in themselves. Instead, his thoughts seem to have followed something like the following logic: if natives would speak a language like Castilian, which did not evoke memories of indigenous devotions, then they might find themselves more free to pursue Christianity. Furthermore, when Valencia suggested that Castilian could protect the Amerindians' ability to reason, he seems to have meant not that indigenous languages were somehow less rational than Castilian or Latin. Rather, the native tongues served as a link to indigenous devotions and thus limited Amerindians' potential to convert to Christianity.

Despite Valencia's support for propagating Castilian, the records from the same meeting indicate that some missionaries had acquired a level of skill in using indigenous languages. Among the twelve friars that accompanied Valencia, at least five—Luis de Fuensalida, Francisco Jiménez, Toribio Motolinía, Juan de Ribas, and García de Cisneros—had learned Nahuatl well enough to author indigenous-language texts, such as catechisms, sermons, dictionaries, and grammars.[41] In fact, individuals with knowledge of native languages had received some preference for appointments as pastors.

Valencia, however, did not consider proficiency in an indigenous language as the most important quality for a good minister to the natives. In fact, he discouraged fellow clerics from placing an excessive emphasis on knowledge of local tongues: "Because they lack the language of the Indians, prelates see themselves almost forced to appoint to the position of curate a less-learned, less-prudent individual of low birth only because he knows the language of that village. I think that if pastors insisted for fifty years that their faithful learn Castilian, it would be accomplished, and all New Spain would be *Terra labii unius* [a land of one language]." For Valencia, proficiency in an indigenous language did not seem crucial to the success of a Christian pastor. He and other members of the clergy felt strongly that formal education and desirable personal qualities ought to determine the selection of pastors.[42] His statement that New Spain could become "a land of one language," seems especially noteworthy. Given the degree to which indigenous peoples outnumbered Spaniards, it is remarkable that he thought it possible to make Castilian the primary—and perhaps only—language of New Spain within just fifty years. The statement seems to underscore the optimism with which Valencia and other early Franciscans viewed their native charges.[43]

Several years later, in 1537, the first bishops of Mexico offered a description of the primary characteristics necessary for clerics in the New World. Like Valencia, they did not consider knowledge of an indigenous language as essential.

> It seems to us that your majesty ought to exercise great care in recommending clerics for these new churches, ensuring that they be men of doctrine and good habits, who lead by positive example, such that these natives will be edified by their ways and their honesty. Along these lines, we inform your majesty that it would be

> appropriate to award the two principal positions of each church to a theologian and a canonist, who can be found in Salamanca and other universities. It would not be inappropriate to increase for them the benefits of the positions because in these lands, little has been shown to them by the establishment, and here, we have more need of letters than in Castile.

For several influential churchmen, therefore, personal qualities and education (not necessarily including training in indigenous languages) constituted the primary needs for the establishment of the new Church in the Americas. Indeed, the letter above identifies the most destructive problem faced by the Church in the New World not in communication obstacles but in "religious and laypersons having no desire to remain here, and having no other goal but making themselves rich and returning to Castile." While Mexico's bishops may have desired at this time that their clerics know an indigenous language, they highlighted personal qualities and theological education of the cleric as fundamental.[44]

In spite of downplaying the centrality of indigenous languages, Valencia still considered them as useful instruments in the conversion of native peoples. In a 1532 letter, he explicitly indicated that the study of native languages by the earliest Franciscans played a crucial part in the conversion of "one hundred thousand" natives:

> We dare to say that each one of us brothers, principally the first twelve companions, have until today baptized more than one hundred thousand, the majority of them being children. And because divine providence wished it so, these brothers of mine were so learned in the languages of the natives that in a very brief time—after much work and care—they [the friars] were able to guide them and teach them to understand the blindness and error of their customs and ceremonies, offering them many sermons in the plazas and markets and wherever else they converged and could produce [sermons] in their own language.[45]

For Valencia at this point, indigenous languages served a highly valuable purpose. In the hands of the friars, they could help facilitate the conversion process.

How do we explain Valencia's strong support for Castilian at the 1524 meeting and his appreciation for indigenous languages in 1532? Perhaps, over time, he grew to appreciate the difficulty of making New Spain a "land of one language" and thus increasingly saw the value of having clerics who knew indigenous languages. It also may help to place Valencia in the context of attitudes toward Arabic in Spain. As shown in chapter 2, several churchmen—including Hernando de Talavera, Martín Pérez de Ayala, and the Jesuits—supported the use of Arabic while also attempting to propagate Castilian among Spanish Islamic communities. Thus it seems plausible that Valencia viewed missionaries' use of indigenous languages as a temporary measure, which eventually would give way to Castilian.[46]

Regardless of how he made sense of them, his thoughts on language represented what many—if not most—influential churchmen in the Americas eventually would uphold. Churchmen did not divide clearly along pro-Castilian or proindigenous lines; clerics who favored Castilian-language instruction among Amerindians did not necessarily oppose the use of native tongues. Valencia, for instance, upheld the value of teaching Castilian to the natives, but he did not do so because he considered Castilian as intrinsically significant. Rather, he viewed Castilian as a useful tool for fostering the religious conversion of indigenous peoples; in doing so, he did not exclude the use of indigenous languages. Valencia seems less invested in the particular language itself and more concerned with adopting any approach that might increase conversions to Christianity.[47]

"IN LATIN, IN CASTILIAN, AND FOR THE INDIANS, IN THEIR OWN LANGUAGE": LINGUISTIC POLITICS AT THE FIRST PROVINCIAL COUNCIL (1555)

When Martín de Valencia held his 1524 assembly, Mexico had very little ecclesiastical hierarchy. Not until 1527 would Charles I recommend the Franciscan friar, Juan de Zumárraga, as the first bishop of Mexico. During most of Zumárraga's tenure, Mexico remained officially part of the archdiocese of Seville in Spain. Only in 1546, shortly before Zumárraga's death, did Pope Paul III name Mexico as an independent archdiocese.[48]

More than thirty years after Valencia's 1524 meeting, the bishops of Mexico held their first provincial council, led by the Dominican friar Alonso de

Montúfar, the second archbishop of Mexico. Montúfar held the council together with Bishop Vasco de Quiroga of Michoacán, Bishop Fray Martín de Hojacastro of Tlaxcala, Bishop Fray Tomás de Casillas of Chiapas, and various other local colonial and Church officials. The ninety-three chapters (*capítulos*) of this first provincial council include discussions of subjects ranging from the teaching of Christian doctrine and the administration of the sacraments to regulations concerning the construction of buildings and the roles of doctors, judges, and notaries in ensuring adherence to Church-related feasts and rites. In keeping with the contemporary European discussion of Church reform at the Council of Trent, Montúfar's council contains a substantial number of sections that clarify duties and appropriate behavior for clerics. Altogether, the council's official record includes an extensive list of topics.[49]

As we have seen, the twelve Franciscans that arrived with Martín de Valencia viewed themselves as resuming the mission of Jesus Christ and his original twelve apostles. The bishops, similarly, considered their work as an extension of the first apostles' efforts. Accordingly, they stated their goal as "desiring to imitate their predecessors [the apostles] . . . in these Western Lands that have gone for so many years without knowledge of the Holy Gospel, an innumerable, barbaric, and idolatrous people now called in recent years to knowledge of our Holy Catholic Faith."[50] The bishops here highlighted their fundamental role as bringing the Gospel to the natives. Although they described the Amerindians as "innumerable, barbaric, and idolatrous," they did not hesitate to call for using indigenous languages (as well as other native customs) as tools for promoting conversion to Christianity. Thus when they described the natives as innumerable and barbaric, they seem less intent on making a cultural judgment; they also may have wished to emphasize the difficulty of their task. In using native tongues, they did not cast Latin and Castilian aside. Like other churchmen before them, the bishops do not seem bound to a particular language as valuable in itself. Rather, they used whatever approaches they could in order to further the evangelization of the Americas.

Throughout the records from the first council, the Mexican bishops repeatedly encourage the use of indigenous languages among clerics who wished to minister to the *Indios*. They ordered them "to learn the language of the *Indios* within a certain time, and he who does not wish to learn shall not receive the duty [of ministering to] the *Indios*."[51] The bishops' desire that priests use indigenous languages seems to mark a departure from Martín de Valencia, who strongly advocated the instruction of the natives in Castilian. But just as Valencia acknowledged the value of both indigenous languages and Castilian, the Mexican bishops also adopted a kind of linguistic coexistence.

In the very first chapter of the council record, the bishops addressed how clerics should communicate Christian doctrine to the natives. Specifically, they explained how to teach the sign of the cross to the Amerindians. The bishops concluded that ministers "were to be diligent in teaching their parishioners and that, in particular, they were to teach them how to bless and sign themselves with the cross, saying it to them in Latin and in Romance [Castilian], so that they might better understand and learn it."[52] Therefore, in describing how ministers should teach key aspects of Christian doctrine, the Mexican bishops advocated using not only indigenous languages but also Latin and Castilian. Their words above also indicate that they did not make sweeping recommendations only in favor of one language over another. Instead, they made more specific proposals, taking particular cases into account when determining the most appropriate language to use.

The bishops also called for churchmen to use Latin and Castilian in conveying several other aspects of Christian doctrine. They directed ministers to use these languages to instruct the faithful in the commandments of the Church,[53] the saints, and the sacraments of the Church, the Ten Commandments, the seven mortal sins, the corporal and spiritual works of mercy, the theological and cardinal virtues, the gifts of the Holy Spirit, the basic prayers (Pater Noster, Ave Maria, Credo, and Salve Regina), as well as in how to serve the Lord with each of the five senses. The bishops' position for these teachings, however, departed in one significant way from their thoughts regarding the sign of the cross. They instructed ministers to convey these teachings not only in Latin and Castilian but furthermore "to the Indians, *in their language*, so that they might be able to better know and retain [the teachings]."[54] For these particular teachings, the bishops appear to have intended that Europeans and creoles (Europeans born in America) receive instruction in Latin and Castilian while natives learn in their own languages. The bishops also may have intended that natives learn both in their own language as well as in a European language.

Montúfar and the other bishops thus drew a distinction between the languages that ministers should use for the sign of the cross and the languages for other essential teachings.[55] Why did they differentiate between the sign of the cross and other points of doctrine? The sign of the cross consisted of just a few words, and the crucial words—"Father, Son, and Holy Spirit"—referred to specific persons unknown in pre-Columbian religious traditions. The bishops, therefore, might have resisted using indigenous terms for these particular words. By using Latin and Castilian for the sign of the cross, they could emphasize the difference between the Christian God and indigenous deities.[56] The brevity of the sign of the cross also might have lent itself more easily to memorization than did other lengthier prayers and teachings.

Catholic theology, furthermore, put a high premium on ritual language (e.g., the sign of the cross, the parts of the Mass, and other sacramental rites). In order to retain the universality of its rites, the Church gave preference to its primary liturgical language (Latin). While several mendicant friars puzzled over the best way to *explain* the concept of the Trinity in Nahuatl, at least some of the same friars chose Latin when it came to *invoking* the Trinity. Both Spaniards and natives could use the same words: *In nomine patris et filii et spiritus sancti. Amen.*[57]

The bishops frequently recommended using more than one language in order to cultivate accurate knowledge about Christian teachings. They knew that many adults who sought to convert (here, they included Amerindians as well as Africans) received baptism without sufficient instruction.[58] To encourage instruction in Christian doctrine, the bishops proposed that every parish church assemble a display board summarizing the essential Christian teachings both in Castilian and in "the language of the *indios*" and place it in a central location so that these fundamentals of the Catholic faith "could be seen and read by all." Probably to assist the many individuals who could not read, the council encouraged all pastors to take time during the Mass to read aloud the contents of this display board.[59] Other records indicate that pastors largely did adhere to this practice.[60] By calling for the use of both languages, the bishops highlight once again that they did not actively seek to propagate one language over another. The bishops seem to have advocated the use of indigenous languages to a greater degree than Martín de Valencia did. Yet both Valencia and the bishops had common ground in that they attributed value to more than one language.

The Mexican bishops also mirrored Martín de Valencia in another way. Though they encouraged churchmen to use the local languages, the bishops expressed some suspicion regarding indigenous languages as used by natives. For instance, Montúfar and the bishops declared that natives could have neither sermons (*sermones*) nor catechisms (*doctrinas*) in their own languages unless a cleric or a religious with advanced knowledge of the given language first examined it.[61] The bishops' comments imply that some natives possessed illicit texts (i.e., without official approval from the viceroy and the Church), probably in manuscript form. The bishops had two concerns with these texts: not only that the natives might have misunderstood the content but also that the translation might have contained errors or gaps. While the bishops ordered the confiscation of sermons in the possession of Native Americans, they did not close the door on producing such texts in indigenous languages. They approved the distribution of "good" catechisms or sermons for the Amerindians, texts that they believed natives could understand and that had received approval by the appropriate authorities (to avoid falsification of content). The bishops took a similar stance when considering natives' use of traditional, indigenous-language songs: they could sing them as long as the relevant authorities had examined them to guard against profane content. Altogether, the bishops demonstrated suspicion regarding indigenous-language media, but they did not advocate the use of Castilian to the exclusion of native tongues.[62]

The bishops expressed concerns not only about indigenous-language texts but also regarding Castilian ones. They requested that all "suspicious" books be examined by Church authorities and, more specifically, that all those books "composed in our Castilian vernacular be shown and presented to us." Individuals who sold such books to natives, furthermore, "caused God a major offense."[63] The bishops' position implies that proficiency in Castilian among natives had grown significantly by 1555. Of primary interest here, though, the bishops do not seem to have preferred Castilian-language books over indigenous-language ones. Rather, they extended suspicion to books in both European and indigenous languages. Rather than propagate one language over another, the bishops seem primarily concerned with ensuring orthodoxy.

Similar to their concerns regarding translation and popular comprehension of doctrine, Mexico's bishops expressed worry over variation in religious instruction. In the fourth chapter of the council, the bishops noted that "All variety ought to be avoided because it can bring confusion in the catechesis and instruction of the *indios*." Recognizing the variety of methods for instructing the native peoples, the bishops ordered the production of two uniform catechisms, "the first one abridged, without gloss, containing all the things described above in the first constitution, and the other one containing a substantial exposition of the articles of faith, the commandments, the mortal sins, as well as the Our Father, and let them be translated into many languages and printed." That the bishops ordered multiple translations of the two catechisms is striking, for they desired to avoid variation at all costs. Here, they departed from Martín de Valencia, who viewed the existence of multiple indigenous languages as an impediment to church governance. The bishops expressed relatively less concern. That is not to suggest that they believed that translation did not affect the meaning of a text.[64] Instead, it seems that the bishops considered it possible to maintain the essential uniformity of doctrine in spite of the process of translation.[65] While both Valencia and the bishops acknowledged the value of having churchmen who used indigenous languages, the bishops seem less anxious about the multiplicity of native tongues.[66]

"IF THE MINISTER IS NOT PROFICIENT IN THE LANGUAGE . . .": CONTINGENCY PLANS AT THE SECOND PROVINCIAL COUNCIL (1565)

Approximately ten years after the First Provincial Council, Archbishop Montúfar convened the Second Provincial Council. Given that the Council of Trent (1545–63) had come to a close, Philip II ordered each archbishop in his kingdoms to convene a provincial council in order to implement the decrees from Trent. Compared to the ninety-three capitula produced at the first council, the second council left behind a shorter record, with twenty-eight capitula. The bishops developed a shorter document because they wished to reaffirm the first council, adding to and not replacing the previous capitula. Brevity aside, the second council further illuminates our understanding of language practices in the early colonial period.[67]

Like the bishops at the first council, the Mexican bishops in 1565 exhorted priests to learn the local languages: "For the conversion of the natives, it is necessary to know their languages, for without understanding them, [clerics can offer] neither effective catechesis nor the administration of sacraments. Thus, we order and command that all pastors put great diligence into learning the languages of their regions, and should they be negligent in this duty, they will be removed from their village and will not be sent to another." Although they reiterated the value of having clerics who know indigenous languages, the bishops at the second council made a slight change in their position this time around. They did not order all clerics to learn indigenous languages; instead, the bishops specifically referred to pastors. While the bishops now required language study of a marginally smaller portion of the clergy, they adopted more rigorous language, threatening to remove delinquent pastors and not reassign them.[68]

The bishops' repeated exhortations related to indigenous languages—as well as the threat of removing noncompliant pastors—should not be taken as suggesting that all or even most priests failed to learn indigenous languages. In fact, the opposite seems to be true. Recent research has indicated that in parishes where natives constituted the majority of the population, they did have priests who could function in an indigenous language. But not all indigenous languages were equal. Finding priests who knew Nahuatl or Otomi did not present a major obstacle. Many young men during the second half of the sixteenth century would have known Nahuatl, in particular. The indigenous communities that used less common languages—like Huastec or Chontal—were likely to struggle in obtaining a priest who could communicate in the local tongue.[69] It is plausible, therefore, that when the bishops insisted that pastors know indigenous languages, they actually were most concerned with providing competent pastors to the communities that spoke languages other than Nahuatl or Otomi. In finalizing the decrees of the council, therefore, the bishops demonstrated the geographical range of their concerns, establishing practices not only for the central valley of Mexico but for all their constituencies.

When they ordered pastors to study indigenous languages, the bishops seemed aware that they needed a contingency plan. Even if every pastor did learn a native tongue, he still might not have known the language of each of his parishioners. The bishops, therefore, expected that situations would arise in which the only cleric available might not know a person's language. Accordingly, the bishops made provisions for such cases. For instance, they allowed—in limited cases—a cleric to administer the sacrament of confession through an interpreter: "If the minister is not proficient in the language, we order that he visit the sick person with an interpreter and, through the interpreter, encourage [the sick person] to die well. If, by chance, the sick person asks for confession by interpreter, understanding that he is not required to do so but would take advantage of increased security for his conscience, the minister may in this case confess him via the interpreter, as long as the interpreter is a religious or a well-trusted Spaniard of good conscience." The notion of administering confession by an interpreter seems, of course, inimical to the confidential nature of the sacrament. For this reason, the cleric could only encourage—not oblige—the dying person to take confession. Despite the less-than-ideal nature of confession by interpreter, the Mexican bishops clearly wanted to have backup plans for when priests and Amerindians did not speak the same language.[70]

Although evidence suggests that priests who spoke Nahuatl and Otomi were relatively abundant compared to those who spoke Chocho or Tzeltal, for example, the bishops' record from the council still suggests a more general problem related to all indigenous languages. According to the bishops, clerics proficient enough to preach or hear confessions in native languages could be hard to find: "When the prelate, some vicars, or pastors and their parishioners ask and plead with clerics to go and preach or hear the confessions of the natives of the villages where they live, it is a highly meritorious and necessary duty to which they are accustomed; we beg and entrust them to do so, especially where the vicar or pastor does not know the language, for it is known that we do not have the abundance of ministers necessary for these needs."[71] The bishops had exhorted—and in some cases, required—priests to learn the local indigenous language. Some clerics, however, had learned it well enough only to teach (i.e., read) basic Catholic doctrine. Their minimal facility with the given language prevented them from using it to preach or administer the sacrament of confession. The bishops did not clarify whether this problem arose more frequently with regard to less common languages. It does seem that those clerics who did know a native language very well might receive requests to serve as itinerant priests, for not every parish would have someone with a high level of linguistic facility.

This reliance upon interpreters and itinerant preachers recalls another situation, which the bishops discussed in the first council, ten years earlier. At that meeting, the bishops present recommended that natives could provide instruction in Christian doctrine when priests were not available. The bishops called for "two or three well-instructed, trustworthy *Indios* to teach

Christian doctrine to children and to other individuals who do not know it."[72] While some contemporary sources did not explicitly acknowledge indigenous *doctrineros* (catechists), Mexico's bishops did so, thus suggesting that it was a widespread practice. In calling for natives to serve as teachers, the bishops sought a contingency plan in response to two challenges: first, they knew that many indigenous communities had infrequent access to a priest; second, the bishops expected that some priests would not comply with the order to learn native languages. The bishops, therefore, enlisted the help of indigenous church members in the hopes that as many indigenous people as possible would receive instruction, even if they rarely saw a priest. If the natives had a priest who did not know the local language, then the bishops wished to supplement the celebration of the Latin Mass with basic instruction in Christian doctrine by indigenous catechists. Therefore, when the bishops at the second council allowed for confession by interpreter and for itinerant preachers, they acted according to precedent. The leading figures of the Mexican Church already had experience in making recommendations and developing backup plans in case their ideals did not come to fruition.

Although the bishops encouraged priests to learn local languages, they also implied that clerics did not have to know an indigenous tongue in order to serve the natives. For instance, the bishops set the expectation that priests would celebrate Mass every day in the mornings so that the natives could participate: "We order that all those who have the duty of catechesis and of overseeing some native villages in our archbishopric and province celebrate Mass early in the morning in their assigned locale, so that the natives can listen to it and put themselves in the hands of God, and having heard the Mass, they can tend to their jobs and labors."[73] Despite the fact that only a small number of natives would have had training in Latin, the bishops still expected that Amerindians could participate meaningfully in something celebrated in a foreign language, listening and putting "themselves in the hands of God." Therefore, although the bishops consistently encouraged and often required priests to study indigenous languages, the individuals who did not comply still played a key part in the Mexican Church, whether by collaborating with interpreters or in celebrating the Latin Mass. Finally, by supporting the study of indigenous languages and celebrating the Mass in Latin, the bishops further encouraged the linguistic coexistence of New Spain.

"IN THE VERNACULAR TONGUE, IF NEED BE . . .": ADAPTING PRACTICES AT THE THIRD PROVINCIAL COUNCIL OF MEXICO (1585)

In 1585 Archbishop Pedro Moya de Contreras convened the Third Provincial Council. Several years had passed since the last council, and thus Moya wished to address new circumstances within the Mexican Church. The first two councils, furthermore, had not received official approval from the papacy. Compared to the two previous provincial councils, the third seems to have elaborated the most long-lasting set of guidelines for the Church in Mexico (the next provincial council would not take place until 1770).[74]

As significant as the Third Provincial Council would become, it was not the first time that Archbishop Moya would make a mark on the Mexican Church. About ten years earlier, he put his support behind implementing the Ordenanza del Patronazgo, or "Ordinance of Patronage." The 1574 royal document consisted of twenty-three articles, by which Philip II sought to restructure the Church in the Americas. Calling, in part, for the transfer of rural churches from mendicant friars to secular priests, the laws eventually gave the monarchy greater oversight over ecclesiastical matters. Though the friars remained influential, appointments to parishes now would be determined through a system of *oposiciones*, or competitive exams. Moya took the lead in implementing the exam system, undoubtedly with hopes that the initiative would lead to filling positions with well-qualified priests. The men who competed would have to demonstrate their knowledge in a variety of ecclesiastical matters, including moral theology, the administering of sacraments, and competence in an indigenous language.[75]

Just over a decade later, Moya convoked the Third Provincial Council. There, bishops simultaneously set out to evangelize the Americas while promulgating the decrees of the Council of Trent.[76] Taking Trent as their point of departure, though, by no means implied to churchmen that they were unequivocally imposing European norms on a New World Church. Accordingly, Juan Pérez de la Serna, a later archbishop of Mexico, wrote in 1622 that the decrees of the Third Council "corresponded to the doctrine of the ancient Church Fathers, conformed to the decrees of the holy councils and common law, and also were very much adjusted to the customs of this region and the condition of its people."[77] In taking into account the local conditions of Mexico, the bishops present at the council followed the precedent set by their predecessors and encouraged priests to use indigenous languages. Again, the bishops demonstrated a practical mind-set, advocating different languages depending on the situation.

The bishops at the Third Provincial Council affirmed much from the first and second councils. For instance, bishops continued to call for priests to preach in the indigenous languages: "for the Indians, Christian doctrine shall be delivered in their own mother tongue." While some scholars of colonial Mexico generally view the idealism of the early missionaries as waning in the late sixteenth century, bishops continued to call for instruction in the local tongues. The rule would vary, however, depending on the particular audience that Catholic ministers sought to evangelize.[78]

At the council, the bishops adopted a different strategy to foster the study of indigenous languages. The bishops at earlier councils had sustained their position by indicating that priests who did not study native tongues either would not serve the natives (first council) or would lose his position and not receive another (second council). At the third council, the bishops concluded that priests who study native tongues should receive benefits for the time they invested. In order to become a secular cleric, one normally needed to demonstrate a source of income. Men who knew an indigenous language, however, could receive the sacrament of Holy Orders without the usual requirement: "Weighing carefully how much need there is in this province for ministers well-versed in the mother tongue of the Indians, this synod determines that those who know some language of the Indians be promoted to Holy Orders, even if they have not obtained a benefice, assets, or a salary that suitably provide for their sustainment."[79] With knowledge of the local language, then, came privileged status. The bishops thus incentivized men to learn indigenous languages.

Just as the bishops at the third council continued to exhort priests to study local languages, they also maintained the previous support extended toward catechisms in native tongues. In line with prior practice in Mexico and with the Council of Trent, Moya de Contreras and the bishops required the translation of the catechism into the primary indigenous language of each diocese. In the decades following the council, members of different religious orders continued to produce indigenous-language catechisms and other doctrinal texts. These volumes contained several of the basic prayers and tenets of the Catholic faith, including but not limited to the Apostles' Creed, Salve Regina, Pater Noster, Ave Maria, and Ten Commandments, generally printed in Latin in one column and in the relevant indigenous language in another. These texts served as crucial aids to churchmen and to natives who instructed Amerindians in Catholic doctrine. Adults who presented themselves to receive the sacrament of baptism, in principle, had to recite in their own language at least the Pater Noster, the Apostles' Creed, and the Ten Commandments, as well as demonstrate some contrition for their sins. The catechism thus provided a foundation for studying Christian doctrine. By publishing these texts in indigenous languages, the bishops demonstrated their ongoing support for both the instruction and the recitation of basic doctrine in native tongues. By often including Latin and/or Castilian together with the relevant indigenous language, authors underlined the continued status of the Mexican Church as one that used multiple languages.[80]

The ideal of preaching in the languages of the people, however, did not extend to all the communities that inhabited Mexico. The bishops at the third council made some exceptions: they concluded that priests ought to use Castilian when teaching African slaves and the so-called Chichimec peoples. To provide a historical reference point for these policies, council leaders pointed to the twenty-fourth session of the Council of Trent:

> In order that the faithful people may approach the reception of the sacraments with greater reverence and devotion of mind, the holy Synod enjoins on all bishops, that [. . .] they shall first explain, in a manner suited to the capacity of those who receive them, the efficacy and use of those sacraments [. . .] by every parish priest; and this even in the vernacular tongue, if need be, and it can be conveniently done [. . .] in a catechism which the bishops shall take care to have faithfully translated into the vulgar tongue, and to have expounded to the people by all parish priests; as also that, during the solemnization of mass, or the celebration of the divine offices, they explain, in the said vulgar tongue, on all festivals, or solemnities, the sacred oracles, and the maxims of salvation.

The decree's reference to "the vernacular tongue" suggests that priests had to use the language of the people. Nonetheless, the delegates from Trent only *encouraged* the use of the vernacular "if need be and it can be conveniently done." Thus they allowed a loophole, as it were, for difficult situations.

Something about the Africans and Chichimecs, therefore, led the bishops to suggest a different approach.[81]

Why did the bishops wish to use the vernaculars of most indigenous communities yet not those of the Chichimecs or Africans? Taking their cue from the Nahuas, Spaniards viewed the Chichimecs as fierce, itinerant peoples; they only managed to achieve *some* level of peace with them in the early seventeenth century.[82] Given the difficulties that the Chichimec communities posed to the Spaniards, it seems likely that churchmen had a difficult time engaging with them, let alone learning their languages. Furthermore, "Chichimeca" functioned as a blanket term for individuals from several different groups (the principal ones were the Pames, Guamares, Zacatecos, and Guachichiles). Thus learning one language may not have helped churchmen to communicate with all the "Chichimecas."

The evangelization of African slaves seems to have posed similar problems. As the property of Spanish *encomenderos*, Africans generally had limited contact with missionaries. Furthermore, African slaves often did not live with other slaves who spoke their native languages. Thus learning one African language would not necessarily have enhanced communication with other African slaves in the same area. Therefore, for both the "Chichimecas" and African slaves, Mexican bishops considered Castilian as the most practical option for communication. Their discussion about how to approach these populations indicates that in 1585, Mexico's bishops followed their predecessors in attempting to meet the needs of all of their jurisdictions not only for the "core area" of the central valley but also for the peripheries of New Spain.

While Moya de Contreras and the other Mexican bishops generally called for preaching in indigenous languages, this approach applied largely to adults. To receive baptism, adults had to demonstrate at least that they could recite basic Catholic prayers in their own language: "This synod establishes that no pastor—whether secular or regular—bestow the sacrament of baptism to adults if beforehand they have not been instructed in the Catholic faith or have not at the very least learned in their own language the Lord's Prayer, the Apostles' Creed, the Ten Commandments of the Law, and show some sign of grief concerning their own sins." The bishops implied here that adult Amerindians would do better to go beyond the basic requirement of learning prayers in their own language. Perhaps the bishops hoped that the natives also would learn additional prayers in their own language, or maybe they viewed the memorization of the same prayers in Latin as a better practice. Nonetheless, reciting the fundamental prayers in their own language remained a licit practice. In a similar vein, the bishops indicated that "To use songs that bring back memory of their old history and of false religious practices shall never be permitted, with the exception that they may sing only those which are approved by their pastors and vicars." Indigenous songs, then, remained permissible as long as they contained no content that priests deemed redolent of native devotions. The council record also says nothing against translating Christian scripture into indigenous languages for use in singing. The Franciscan friar Arnaldo de Basacio (Arnaud de Bassac) apparently had "translated the epistles and gospels that are sung in church during the whole year." The Church's desire to use indigenous languages within a circumscribed space reveals, on the one hand, a desire to extirpate native devotions. On the other hand, it betrays a conviction that within the right context, Amerindian languages could become Catholic ones.[83]

Adults could use their native languages to demonstrate their Christian identity, but the bishops adopted a different approach for indigenous children. They expected these younger ones to learn Castilian: "The pastors of Indians—both seculars and regulars—ought to diligently pursue that schools be established in those cities, districts, or villages where they reside, so that the children of Indians may learn to read and write, receive instruction in Christian doctrine, and be taught the Spanish language. For [Spanish] is most helpful for their Christian and civil education." For the bishops in 1585, the purpose of teaching Castilian to native children lay primarily—if not exclusively—in facilitating their conversion to Christianity. They noted, accordingly, "When children have attained basic literacy, school teachers must strive to give them elementary instruction in doctrine and Christian customs." The bishops' decree on the subject of children's education, however, did not constitute an entirely new development. Rather, it mirrored a statement from the First Provincial Council, when the bishops indicated that instruction of children in reading and writing should not be taught apart from Christian doctrine. Still, the emphasis on learning Castilian seems stronger in the third council.[84]

The children who learned Castilian could provide important assistance to missionaries in evangelizing their parents through their own languages. One letter from a Jesuit in western Mexico indicated, "[The natives] go to church, singing 'Te Deum laudamus [We praise you, God].' When they eagerly pursue prayer during some space of time, the native boys, whom the Fathers brought with them to the service, teach their parents Christian doctrine in a brief declaration, through a sermon in the dialogical, vernacular style of the Indians." In this case, the children had learned an aspect of Christian doctrine from their Jesuit teachers and then imparted the same lesson to their parents. As speakers of both Castilian and their own language (in this case P'urhépecha), the children could serve as intermediaries between their parents and the Jesuits.[85]

In the last quarter of the sixteenth century, churchmen continued to rely on the assistance of natives as part of efforts to evangelize the indigenous communities of Mesoamerica. At the same time, however, they also proceeded with the production of new indigenous-language texts, providing additional aids to their fellow churchmen who sought to attain some facility with the local native tongues. Altogether, the bishops continued to encourage the use of indigenous languages, but they did so while calling for the use of Castilian in certain contexts (for Africans and Chichimecs, as well as all indigenous children).

CONCLUSION

In sixteenth-century Mexico, leading churchmen generally did not think about language in terms of a debate between two exclusive options: indigenous languages or Castilian. While churchmen did see themselves as part of a battle, pitting Christianity against indigenous "idolatry," they did not engage in a parallel conflict between European and native languages. It is true that Mexico's clerics largely advocated the study of native tongues, but their approaches were more complex. Given that concerns about language connected with a range of other issues—including theology, liturgy, race, and ethnicity—churchmen could not craft one or even a few fixed practices. Instead, because of the variety of language-related issues that arose, churchmen had to address specific problems first and then develop solutions that they considered appropriate to each situation. It probably is for this reason that the linguistic practices of the Church and Crown have seemed contradictory to many scholars. Churchmen could not separate language from other concerns, and thus they had to adopt a practical decision-making process that eludes binary categories. It seems highly plausible to suggest that this kind of flexible thinking characterizes ecclesiastical thought in other areas.[86] Mexico's churchmen often took each case as it came, and as a result, a uniform language policy did not take root in the sixteenth century. In fact, many would have thought it undesirable.

Catholic bishops desired uniformity of doctrine, as they noted at the Council of Trent and in the provincial councils of Mexico. Scholars have noted, accordingly, that the bishops failed to eliminate all or even most variations in belief and practice.[87] At the same time, it would be misleading to view the bishops and other Catholic authorities as searching for uniformity in all aspects of Catholicism. While they wished to proclaim the same *doctrine* worldwide, they allowed diverse external forms (e.g., language) for the *practice* of the faith. It seems, therefore, worth suggesting that the variation that scholars have described emerged partly from popular initiative and partly from Catholic authorities themselves.

The bishops at Mexico's provincial councils exhorted their fellow churchmen to study indigenous languages; at the same time, they acknowledged situations where other approaches might be necessary. Similarly, the Franciscan friar Martín de Valencia called for the introduction of Castilian among Amerindians, indicating that New Spain could become a "land of one language" if its pastors insisted for fifty years on having their parishioners learn Castilian. But even he valued the contributions made by other friars who facilitated the conversion of natives by learning indigenous languages. Valencia's original position, calling for the propagation of Castilian as the sole language of New Spain, seems an outlier among Mexico's most influential churchmen. When he acknowledged the value of studying native tongues, he shared ground with other leading clerics, making space for more than one language. Through a series of ad hoc decisions, churchmen encouraged a de facto coexistence between Castilian and indigenous American languages.

It was, therefore, not an accident or a contradiction that the Spanish Crown wanted churchmen to study indigenous languages *and* to instruct native peoples in Castilian. Variations on that outcome actually were desired by influential churchmen. The Crown seems to have taken its cue from them, incorporating this linguistic coexistence into the Laws of the Indies.

Given this line of thought, it seems appropriate to revisit the familiar conclusion that the Church served as a tool for the expansion of the Crown's power.[88] The Spanish monarchy indeed exercised authority over its churchmen. Still, it seems worthwhile to suggest that the Church and Crown also had a reciprocal relationship, especially concerning the formulation of plans for evangelization.

Why did Mexico's churchmen generally not prioritize the establishment of one language above all others? Why, as Shirley Heath asked several decades ago, did the conquistadors fail either "to perpetuate Nahuatl as the standard tongue" or "to introduce Castilian in its place"? The answer to the latter, as other scholars have suggested, probably lies in the fact that Europeans did not have the numbers to propagate Castilian successfully among the millions of Mesoamerica's native peoples.[89] The evidence discussed throughout this chapter suggests an additional part of the puzzle—namely, that many (probably most) sixteenth-century Europeans did not conceive of linguistic communication in terms of two exclusive options (i.e., Castilian or indigenous languages). Having lived in the Iberian peninsula, among or near people who spoke different languages (e.g., Arabic, Basque, Castilian, Catalan, Galician, Ladino), they would not have considered the simultaneous existence of multiple languages as unusual. Many sixteenth-century Iberians would have used one language (e.g., Castilian, Galician) for most day-to-day purposes, would have heard another at church (i.e., Latin), and could have heard yet another—or more—when they encountered people from other parts of Iberia or the Mediterranean.

When considering the decades that followed the initial contact between native Mesoamericans and Europeans, it is worth reconsidering the notion that Europeans debated over whether to communicate in one language or another. Instead, we might reflect on how premodern Europeans thought about communication. Though many national governments eventually would foster linguistic unity among their people, that goal may not have seemed so urgent for many of the individuals examined here. A monolingual, Castilian America indeed did appeal to a number of churchmen (and Spanish monarchs), but it did not become the leading priority of conversion efforts throughout the sixteenth century. Instead, many—if not most—churchmen sought the conversion of the natives with such zeal that no other agenda could trump their God-given task.

CHAPTER 5

CREATING A MULTILINGUAL NEW SPAIN, CA. 1550–1600

In 1770 Charles III called for the elimination of all Amerindian languages, ordering that Castilian serve as the sole language of the Spanish Americas: "Let all the different languages that are used in these territories be extinguished. Let only Castilian be spoken, as is ordered by repeated laws, royal decrees, and orders released on this issue."[1] When he did so, he cited precedent; in the past, "repeated" laws aimed to make Castilian the only language spoken throughout Spain's American territories. Charles thus drew a necessary link between supporting Castilian and extinguishing indigenous languages.

The eighteenth-century monarch, however, did not represent the views of his predecessors entirely accurately. In the sixteenth century, supporting Castilian could—and often did—go hand-in-hand with calling for the use of indigenous languages.[2] In the sixteenth century, the expansion of Castilian among indigenous peoples did, of course, lead to some decline of indigenous languages. But when Charles III explicitly called for Castilian to become the only language of the Americas, he did something different.

In the pages that follow, we will examine Philip II's views concerning the relationship between Amerindian tongues and Castilian. While he may have desired to see Castilian eventually become the primary or sole language of the Spanish Americas, Philip saw no need to take immediate action toward that end. Given that each of the first three provincial councils of Mexico took place during the reign of Philip II, we will examine how the king's views related to those of the bishops. Like them, Philip did not uphold Castilian over indigenous languages or vice versa. Instead, he found a way to support *both* the propagation of Castilian *and* the study of indigenous languages by clerics. In doing so, Philip followed the lead of the bishops, contributing to a multilingual Spanish America.[3] Examining Philip's views offers an opportunity to examine further the relationship between the Church and the Crown.

When the bishops and the Crown supported the extension of both Amerindian tongues and Castilian, they opened the door to several models of linguistic competence. The majority of this chapter explores how members of the religious orders viewed the use of indigenous languages. Specifically, did these churchmen "on the ground" think that all missionaries had to achieve fluency in an indigenous language? Did they posit other ideas? Existing scholarship has noted correctly that the friars generally supported the use of indigenous languages for evangelization.[4] Nonetheless, in calling for the use of native tongues, the friars described different ways of doing so.

Some friars considered indigenous languages as the foundation of the Mexican Church. A greater portion of churchmen, however, seems to have upheld the value of the local tongues while also making room for their confrères who had less training in indigenous languages. In exploring how the friars responded to orders from the bishops and the king, we will see that the Mexican Church found space for individuals across a range of linguistic abilities. Many used indigenous languages with skill, while others operated on a more limited scale.

This chapter brings together a number of sources. The correspondence of Philip II and documentation from his Council of the Indies offer insight into how royal officials approached the relationship between Amerindian tongues and Castilian. Understanding the degree to which priests and religious friars used the local tongues poses a difficult task, in part because much correspondence from sixteenth-century churchmen no longer exists. Given the source limitations, the discussion below cannot offer definitive conclusions. Still, through examining the prolegomena of several indigenous-language publications and a sixteenth-century account from the diocese of

Tlaxcala, we can attain suggestive information.[5] Though these sources often employ a formulaic structure, many contain unique insights related to the use of native Mesoamerican tongues.

"YOU HAVE MANY CLERICS . . . WHO DO NOT UNDERSTAND THE LANGUAGE": PHILIP II'S VIEWS

Existing scholarship has noted that Spanish monarchs of the sixteenth century alternated between promoting Castilian, on one hand, and promoting indigenous languages, on the other. Despite this vacillation, the most detailed work on language practices in colonial Mexico suggests that the monarchs' long-term vision ultimately favored Castilian as a language of empire.[6] Existing documentation from the reign of Philip II and from earlier Spanish monarchs complicates that conclusion.

In 1550 Philip's father, Charles I, sent a letter to Franciscans, Dominicans, and Augustinians, ordering them to teach Castilian to the Amerindians.[7] Only a few years earlier, Charles also encouraged the mendicant friars' work in learning indigenous languages. He sent a decree to Diego de Mendoza, his ambassador in Rome, asking, among other things, that the pope grant graces and indulgences to the religious who evangelized in native tongues. Charles also sent a similar letter directly to the pope.[8] Though Charles ultimately might have favored Castilian, he had not always clung to that position.

Mirroring his father as well as the Mexican bishops, Philip II exhorted churchmen in the Americas to use indigenous languages in order to preach to the natives. What exactly Philip considered as the proper place of native tongues in the Mexican Church can be confused by one notable incident concerning the study of indigenous cultures. This particular occurrence involved the Franciscan friar Bernardino de Sahagún.[9]

Sahagún left Spain and arrived in Mexico in 1529 with twenty other Franciscan friars, ready to preach to the native peoples. After several years in Mexico, his provincial (superior) Fray Francisco del Toral, commissioned Sahagún to write in Nahuatl anything that he considered useful for the Nahuas' conversion to Christianity. Sahagún assembled a team of indigenous Nahua nobles to record a compendium of all things related to the Nahua peoples, including their religious devotions. The result of this project, the

Historia general de las cosas de Nueva España, led to much controversy during Sahagún's lifetime. Sahagún and others among the Franciscans considered it a most worthwhile undertaking, one that could provide valuable information to facilitate conversion efforts. Some also suspected, however, that the project contributed to the preservation of traditional native beliefs and rites. Sahagún's *Historia general* forced churchmen and royal officials to revisit the already well-known question of how—if at all—they ought to tolerate indigenous customs among Amerindian Christians.[10]

When confronted with the controversy, Philip II ordered the confiscation and transfer of Sahagún's papers to Spain for examination by his Council of the Indies. In his April 1577 decree, Philip described Sahagún's motivations as good and zealous, but he concluded that his work should not circulate in any manner, whether in print or manuscript.[11] Some scholars have noted that Philip's order coincided with a decline in the study of indigenous languages by churchmen. That observation may be true, but it is worth noting that the Spanish monarch did not discourage clerics from studying native tongues. Accordingly, Philip added, "no one should write anything—in any language—related to the superstitions and way of life that these Indians used to have, because this is most appropriate for the service of our Lord God." Philip thus placed a cease-order on the circulation of Sahagún's work and any similar writing. The Spanish king considered writing about indigenous "superstition" and customs as wrong *in any language*.[12]

While Philip clearly took issue with the preservation of certain indigenous practices, there remains strong evidence demonstrating that his suspicion did not extend to Amerindian tongues themselves. Shortly after his decree addressing Sahagún's *Historia general*, Philip made an emphatic statement in support of churchmen using indigenous languages. In December 1578, a year and a half after the Sahagún decree, Philip II sent a letter to his bishops across the Americas, chastising them for appointing clerics who failed to use Amerindian languages adequately. He declared that although many churchmen had studied and used the local tongues, many others had not: "We know that although you have been told and ordered to not entrust the catechesis of Indian villages to persons who do not have a very good knowledge of the language of the people whom they are to instruct, you have many clerics in the said villages of your archbishopric who do not understand the language of the Indians in their care."[13] Disappointed with the clerics' linguistic training, Philip attempted to correct their behavior by imposing fines.

In response to Philip's efforts, some priests found ways to circumvent the penalties. In doing so, Philip argued that they compromised their responsibility to serve the native peoples. For example, "Some priests, aware of the monetary penalties imposed on those who do not know [the relevant local language], learn some words from confessors' manuals and then—without having made any other effort to understand the care that ought to be applied to a benefice and the good of the Indians' souls—provide [the natives] with confession, knowing neither how to make them understand the things of our holy Catholic faith, nor how to preach [the faith] to them, nor how to reprimand them for their vices and sins."[14] In Philip's eyes, the priests who did not learn a local language failed to comply not only with their linguistic duty. They had neglected a much more significant task: the salvation of souls. Disappointed, Philip concluded his letter with a plea: that "individuals who do not understand and know very well the language of the Indians" should not receive the responsibility of ministering to the natives.[15] Philip thus criticized not only the ordinary churchmen for their failure to study the local languages; he also admonished the bishops for failing to adhere to standards that had been in place for some time.

Philip's letter provides much insight into his stance regarding indigenous languages. His letter confirms that not only Church leadership but also the Crown encouraged clerics to learn indigenous languages. Like the bishops at the provincial councils, Philip insisted upon the importance of language learning, citing the need to attend to the spiritual welfare of the native peoples. Though he shared this value of indigenous-language study, Philip might have adopted more stringent standards than many Church leaders.

Some additional context will help illuminate the degree to which Philip advocated indigenous-language study by clerics. As noted in the previous chapter, the bishops at the second provincial council in 1565 had required indigenous-language facility of pastors. Documentation from the years following the council demonstrates that in many—if not most—cases, they found the staff that they needed. A 1571–72 report from the central Mexican city of Tlaxcala reveals that this diocese had forty-four secular priests serving more than fifty-nine thousand Amerindians.[16] Forty of those priests, just over 90 percent, received the classification of *lengua*, apparently able to use an indigenous language well enough to teach Christian doctrine, to preach, and to administer the sacrament of confession.[17] Among those forty priests, all of them knew Nahuatl (*lengua mexicana*), and eight—20 percent of the *lengua* priests—knew two languages. Francisco de Alfaro, Juan Larios, Luis de Peña, and Juan de Peñalver, for instance, had attained the status of *lengua* in both Nahuatl and Mixtec. Pedro Romero and Nicolás Méndez did the same in Nahuatl and Otomi; Cristóbal de Rivera in Nahuatl and Popoloca; and Alonso de Muñoz likewise in Nahuatl and Totonac. It is worth noting that these eight priests learned languages that had very little in common; each of the pairs above contained languages from different families.[18] Despite the bishops' substantial success in appointing priests who knew indigenous languages, Philip remained unsatisfied. He admonished the bishops, indicating that they had not done enough to ensure that priests who served the natives knew the relevant language(s).

In his 1578 letter, Philip mentioned that some priests had learned just a few words of an indigenous language in order to avoid penalties (fig. 4). If he was right, one might wonder how well the priests described in the Tlaxcala report actually knew the given language(s). Since not all the priests mentioned received the title of *lengua*, it is plausible that this status actually had real meaning. It seems that the linguistic shortcomings of the priests lay elsewhere. Philip might have known that while some priests had learned a native tongue, they had not learned all the languages of the particular people that they served. Francisco de Terrazas, for instance, was a *lengua mexicana*, serving the *altepetl* of Xicotepec and Papaloticpac. Of the 1,400 people assigned to him, many knew Nahuatl, but many also spoke Totonac or Otomi. Despite having a flock with three very different languages, the record notes that "all for the most part" understood Nahuatl, so they could receive doctrinal instruction in that language. Of the forty secular priests in Tlaxcala that knew Nahuatl, a total of fourteen (35 percent) served in communities where they could speak one of the local languages (Nahuatl) but not the other(s). Some native Mesoamericans knew Nahuatl as a secondary language and thus could communicate with their priest. Not all, however, understood Nahuatl. It is plausible, therefore, that when Philip chastised the bishops of Mexico, he criticized them only in part for the small number of priests who did not know any indigenous language. Philip's

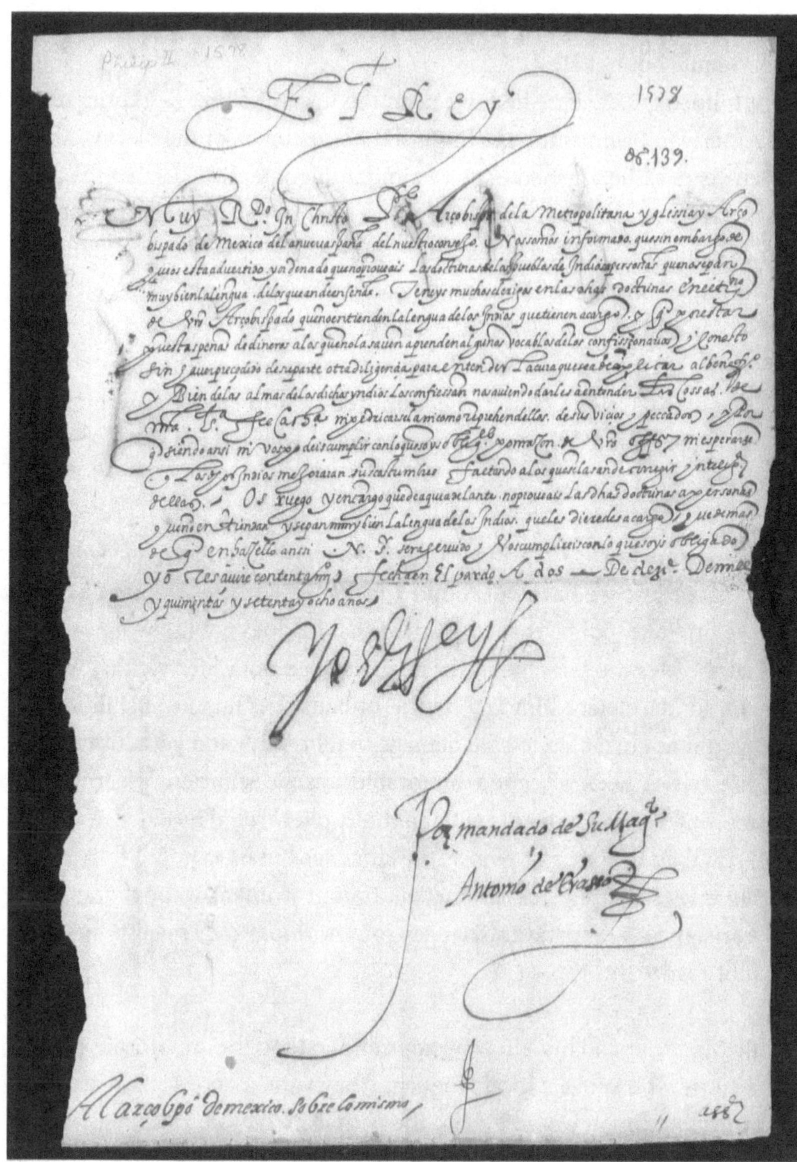

FIG. 4 | Philip II letter. Library of Congress, Washington, DC, Rare Book and Special Collections Division.

reproach might have had more to do with cases in which a priest knew one local tongue but not all.[19]

Philip's 1578 critique had not been the first time that he reprimanded his American bishops for the linguistic competence of the clergy. About eleven years earlier, he had issued a similar document, criticizing the bishops of the Americas for appointing clerics who did not know the language(s) of the people whom they served. In response to Philip's rebuke, Alonso de Montúfar, archbishop of Mexico, responded in November 1567, defending himself and his fellow bishops. He argued that they exercised great care in seeking men proficient in indigenous languages and that they considered it a most serious matter. He admitted that in a few cases, however, circumstances forced them to appoint a cleric who did not know the local language:

> If in some towns occasionally we put a cleric who is not a *lengua*, it is because we have not found a *lengua*. Alternately, sometimes we find one, but he is so unlearned that he does not know how to administer the sacraments, or he has such a poor lifestyle that we do not dare place him among the Indians. His linguistic abilities would not make up for the damage that he would do with his bad lifestyle. A cleric of a good, honorable lifestyle, sufficiently learned to confer the sacraments with an interpreter would produce more fruit than the one who knows the language but has a poor lifestyle. This is especially true among the Indian women, among whom resistance is rare and the danger so notorious. Your majesty may not realize this.[20]

While Montúfar and his fellow bishops understood the importance of finding a cleric who spoke a local language, they valued above all the example that the churchman would give to the people he served. Despite the occasional difficulties in finding a cleric who had both good character and linguistic proficiency, Montúfar wished to assure Philip that he and the bishops had the matter well in hand and that they understood the situation in Mexico to a degree that Philip did not.

Montúfar suspected that more lay behind Philip's criticism of the bishops than the king lacking the local knowledge possessed by the leaders of the Mexican Church. At the start of his discussion, Montúfar called

Philip's information "diabolical and hellish," coming from someone "who is not Christian."[21] In doing so, the archbishop suggested that he had an adversary among Philip's advisers, someone who might have knowingly provided false information, perhaps to impugn the work of Montúfar and/or one of his bishops. Altogether, Philip's exchanges with the American bishops in both 1567 and 1578 reveal that he valued a clergy proficient in indigenous languages and that he would, on more than one occasion, hold the bishops to their own rule.

Besides his strict standard for indigenous-language study, Philip's letter also illuminates his relationship with Church leaders. Philip allowed the bishops to initiate the decisions related to the administration of the Church. As the king, he affirmed their recommendations and attempted to lend greater authority to them. Once the bishops arrived at their conclusions, Philip appears to have made them his own.[22] That is, he did not merely affirm their decisions. Rather, he took the general substance of the bishops' orders and he tried to make sure that they upheld the standards that they developed.

Although Philip upheld and even surpassed the bishops' support for indigenous-language study, not everyone agreed with his approach. Some of Philip's advisers questioned the wisdom of the positions taken by the king and the bishops. In 1596, toward the end of Philip's reign, the Council of the Indies recommended making greater efforts toward propagating Castilian among the natives. Specifically, the council members desired that Amerindians speak Castilian themselves and that they receive doctrinal instruction in the same language.[23]

When the Council of the Indies recommended this increased emphasis on Castilian, it acted with some knowledge of past and current practices related to indigenous languages. Council members knew that the Church had taken measures to facilitate the use of indigenous languages in preaching. They knew that the Mexican bishops had sought both regular and secular clerics who could preach in the native languages. The Council also cited the professorships established in order to provide instruction to clerics who needed to study the local tongues.[24] They knew, furthermore, that the bishops had required pastors to know the relevant indigenous language. Having considered all these initiatives, the members of the council branded them as misguided or ineffective. The council concluded that these plans simply did not work; they had "never reached the level of perfection that was appropriate."[25] The council members attributed the failure of the plans to a number of causes, among them that an insufficient number of priests had learned indigenous languages.

These arguments resemble the information given to Philip approximately twenty and thirty years earlier, when he criticized the American bishops for not appointing enough priests who knew native tongues. Recall, however, that in 1567, Archbishop Montúfar suggested that someone had purposely given the king misleading information about the clergy's linguistic abilities. Considering these accounts at once, one might suspect that there existed in Iberia a cadre of royal advisers who disapproved of the American clergy's interests in indigenous languages. Apparently, the council members considered peninsular Spaniards—not "mestizos and creoles"—as the men "who are needed for the instruction of the Indians."[26] Given this bias in favor of peninsular culture, it seems plausible that as early as 1567, some of Philip's advisers had sought to clear the way for the increased use of Castilian by maligning the American clergy's efforts to use indigenous languages.

In general, the Council of Indies considered the entire project of learning native tongues as futile. They concluded, first and foremost, that indigenous languages could not properly convey Christian doctrine: "The principal and greatest concern is that [even] in the best and most perfect language of the Indians, the mysteries of the faith cannot be explained well and in their proper sense."[27] In contrast to the indigenous languages, the council viewed Castilian as "better known" (presumably, among clerics) and more "capable" of expressing Christian teachings.

Besides the supposed inadequacy of indigenous languages, the council cited other obstacles. Several mirrored the arguments made by Fray Martín de Valencia in the 1520s. They cited the wide variety of languages spoken in the Americas—in New Spain, Peru, and elsewhere—as a hindrance to the effective instruction of native peoples. They added that the traditional indigenous languages prevented the Amerindians from becoming civilized Christians: "preserving the language of the Indians poses an obstacle to their good instruction in doctrine and to guiding them in the ways of good customs and civil life that they ought to have." They added that the native languages led Amerindians to learn "about the traditional idolatry and superstitions of their ancestors." In contrast, should the natives learn Castilian, they would have far more ministers who could preach the Gospel to them and guide them on the path toward salvation. If they learned Castilian, council members indicated that Amerindians also would acquire the ability "to read books written in the Spanish language," which would provide them with "many important things for their edification and for knowing how to order and govern themselves like men of reason."[28] In short, learning Castilian would facilitate the evangelization and the acculturation of the natives.

For council members, the intensified propagation of Castilian seemed a far more suitable project than the continued study of indigenous languages. Though the council did not call explicitly for extinguishing the local tongues, their report identified no benefits in using those languages. The council seems to have desired at least the eventual abandonment of indigenous languages in favor of Castilian.

King Philip, however, did not embrace the approach suggested by the council. Responding to them, he wrote, "It does not seem appropriate to pressure [the Amerindians] to leave behind their native tongue. Rather, we could place teachers for those who voluntarily wish to learn the Castilian [language]. It shall be ordered that we uphold the rule of awarding the position of priest only to individuals who know the [language] of the Indians."[29] Philip may have attempted to reach a compromise between his own vigorous support of indigenous-language preaching and the council members' wishes. In one sense, Philip made a concession to the council when he agreed to provide Castilian-language teachers for native communities. Nonetheless, in doing so, he still adopted a different approach from the members of his council. Philip ordered that Castilian-language teachers should work only with the Amerindians who *voluntarily* sought instruction. Notably, Philip refused to pressure the natives to use Castilian, as the council members suggested.[30]

Philip II's positions with regard to indigenous languages and Castilian may have guided the language policies adopted by later monarchs. For example, his cautious support of Castilian-language instruction may have influenced Philip IV (r. 1621–65), who would back Castilian but by "the softest means" possible.[31] In upholding (and sometimes exceeding) the bishops' support of indigenous languages, Philip also may have contributed to the laws adopted in later years. For instance, his son Philip III (r. 1598–1621) required that pastors and other ministers of the Amerindians know the people's language.[32] These laws, in favor of both Amerindian tongues and Castilian, remained a part of the Laws of the Indies through at least the reign of Charles II (r. 1665–1700). Therefore, the multilingual approaches adopted in the sixteenth century remained influential—at least in theory—well beyond the reign of Philip II.

One might argue that Philip II's simultaneous support for both indigenous languages and Castilian suggests that he intended Castilian to become eventually the primary (if not the only) tongue of the Spanish Americas. Yet the fact remains that Philip II did not explicitly restrict the use of indigenous languages as he did with Arabic in Granada. In fact, at the time that he criticized Montúfar and the American bishops (1567), he more or less simultaneously restricted the use of Arabic among Moriscos. Philip's language policies appear to have only a minimal connection with the 1770 position taken by Charles III, who promoted Castilian and aimed to extinguish indigenous languages. Instead, Philip II seems to have had much more in common with his contemporary Mexican bishops, who seemed relatively comfortable with a multilingual Spanish America.

"READING WITH THE BOOK IN HAND": FRIARS AND INDIGENOUS-LANGUAGE AIDS

Philip largely upheld (and sometimes exceeded) the standards recommended by the Mexican bishops for using indigenous languages. In the New World, priests and religious also had to decide how to uphold the positions that the bishops set forth at the Mexican provincial councils. As we saw in the previous chapter, leading churchmen valued the use of indigenous languages for preaching to Amerindians, yet the same men differed in the degree to which they called for using the local tongues. In what follows, we will see that other priests and friars similarly espoused a range of positions when considering how to utilize the native tongues. The individuals examined in the following pages each faced different circumstances, given that they served distinct regions of Mexico. Despite their differences, their work in diverse regions was discussed and influenced by the bishops who met at Mexico's provincial councils.

Examining the publication of indigenous-language texts reveals that priests and religious in Mexico used the local tongues extensively. Between 1539 (the date of the first printed book in Mexico) and 1600, Mexican presses produced at least forty-five texts in a variety of indigenous languages. (For comparative purposes, Spanish churchmen authored approximately three printed Arabic-language books during the sixteenth century.)[33] This number would grow significantly if it included the many manuscript and print sources that have not survived. In the case of both print and manuscript sources, churchmen frequently—if not always—worked with indigenous collaborators, and sometimes those native writers produced their own manuscripts. Almost all the printed texts named a member of a religious order as the author. Of the extant titles, the Franciscans claimed over twenty; the Dominicans, more than ten; and the Augustinians, about five. A significant number of churchmen thus achieved a high degree of facility with an indigenous language.[34]

Who exactly authored these indigenous-language texts is a complicated question. The churchmen named as the authors sometimes built upon previously existing manuscripts, handed down to them within their religious community. They also benefited greatly from indigenous collaborators, though little information survives regarding these Mesoamerican intellectuals. Though the named authors usually did not work alone, I still refer to them as the authors, in keeping with contemporary European norms.[35]

The Dominican friar Francisco de Alvarado is one of the few religious authors who discussed the other individuals who contributed to his work. Alvarado lived among the Mixtecs, an umbrella name for several communities from Oaxaca, Guerrero, and Puebla.[36] In the prologue of his 1593 Mixtec dictionary, he cited his fellow Dominicans, noting "the majority is owed to the Fathers [priests] of this nation."[37] In the same document, Alvarado indicated that his predecessors and contemporaries provided a source of inspiration, for they had confronted the difficulties inherent in studying for Mixtec: "They conquered idolatry, which had reigned for so many years. They began to study an odd, barbaric language [. . .]. Others may say as much about other languages, but regarding Mixtec, I can say that besides its various errors it has traces of thought and study, which makes very admirable the work of the preachers and ministers who have been able to master it. [. . .] The holy conquerors of souls, sent to the Mixtec nation, undertook an enormous labor." The friars provided not only moral support and inspiration to Alvarado but also some practical assistance. Perhaps facing geographical or financial obstacles to printing their work, Dominicans of previous generations had compiled manuscript word lists in Mixtec.

Alvarado's superior arranged for him to receive these informal dictionaries so that he might put them together into a more comprehensive text to be used by other friars, "so that those who begin to study the language have an easy method, not as difficult as it has been up until now."[38] The book examiners confirm that Alvarado compiled the Mixtec dictionary "with the help and support of all the fathers of this nation, learned in this language."[39] Few books of a similar genre include such detail regarding the production of their content. Still, it seems plausible that other ecclesiastical authors worked in comparable circumstances.

Besides acknowledging his confrères, Alvarado indicated that the natives played an important part in the production of his Mixtec dictionary. "The Indians," he wrote, "are the best teachers that one could have for this task, and they have been the authors."[40] The official examiners of Alvarado's text also highlighted the crucial assistance they received from the Mixtecs. They "discussed the meanings of the words with the native Indians, as they were the most capable and experienced in this language."[41] When Alvarado referred to the Mixtecs as "the authors," he appears to have considered them not as the writers of the text but as the authorities behind it. The book examiners' words corroborate this sense, given that they turned to the Mixtecs regarding the appropriate usage of Mixtec words.

Formal, published works like Alvarado's dictionary did not serve as the only textual medium available to missionaries who sought to use indigenous languages. Although the printing press had existed in Mexico since 1539, missionaries throughout the colonial period also produced manuscript sermon collections and other indigenous-language texts. One of the most prolific authors of sixteenth-century Mesoamerica was the Dominican friar Domingo de Vico (1485–1555). His renowned Dominican brother, Francisco de Vitoria, compared Vico's extensive theological writings in various Mayan languages to the work produced by Thomas Aquinas in Latin.[42] During the sixteenth century, several manuscript copies of Vico's main work, *Theologia indorum* (Theology of the Indians), circulated in the Yucatan, at least in part to provide indigenous-language material for sermons. Vico also produced a Quiché-language grammar, Quiché-Kaqchikel dictionaries, and sermon collections—all in manuscript as well.[43] Vico's work never reached the printing press during his lifetime. After his death and well into the seventeenth and eighteenth centuries, others produced additional manuscript copies of his works. Other friars besides Vico produced manuscript texts in different indigenous languages, aiming to serve a similar purpose.[44]

This reliance on manuscripts rather than on printed texts may have occurred for a number of reasons. Two seem particularly worthy of consideration. First, the cost of printing sometimes dictated the way that an author produced a text. When writing his Mixtec catechism, the Dominican friar Benito Hernández noted, "I had thought about producing this catechism in both Castilian and Mixtec (as I have seen done with other languages), but then I decided against it, focusing instead only on Mixtec because if it were published in both languages, the book would be very large and very costly."[45] While the cost of printing encouraged the continued use of manuscripts, geographical obstacles may have proved even more decisive in the cases discussed above.[46] Many of these indigenous-language manuscripts circulated among clerics ministering to Mayan communities in the Yucatán peninsula, a region noted for its isolated nature. Because the printing press did not reach the Yucatán until 1813, the remoteness of the Yucatán from central Mexico probably proved a fundamental obstacle to producing printed catechetical texts. While the Franciscan Juan de Coronel did publish a Mayan-language catechism in Mexico City in 1620, other extant texts in Mayan languages have come down to us largely in manuscript.[47]

The kind of linguistic proficiency attained by Alvarado and Vico applied to many priests and religious. Friars from several religious orders published indigenous-language grammars and catechisms, but those authors constituted only one part of the clergy. One contemporary author noted that the friars "would not dare to preach in the language of the Indians until they had perfected it."[48] That assessment seems to have been an exaggeration. Most churchmen, of course, did not produce books in an Amerindian tongue, yet many still demonstrated linguistic competence. They managed to use Mesoamerican languages even if on a less sophisticated level.

While some churchmen viewed local languages as the foundation of successful efforts to convert the indigenous peoples, a greater number of priests and religious adopted a different view. Many churchmen valued the use of Amerindian tongues, yet they did not consider linguistic fluency as the sine qua non of converting the natives to Christianity. Instead, they found ways to support the study and use of the local, native tongues while also acknowledging that not every priest would become fluent. Thus at the same time as some churchmen skillfully used indigenous languages, others operated primarily in Castilian but still utilized the local tongues. Similar to the bishops and to Philip II, priests and religious helped foster a multilingual environment in Spanish America.

The Franciscan friar Alonso de Molina took a leading role in the early study of Nahuatl. Born in Spain, he had come to Mexico with his parents as a young child, around the time of the conquest. Through contact with other children, he quickly learned Nahuatl, "as though it were his native tongue."[49] Having learned of the boy's extraordinary ability, the Franciscan friars asked his parents to let him serve as an interpreter. After becoming a Franciscan himself, he published various bilingual texts (in Castilian and Nahuatl) over the course of the sixteenth century (fig. 5). His works include a dictionary, confession manuals in short and long formats, a grammar, and a catechism, all of which existed in multiple editions, used throughout the colonial period. Though he explicitly addressed some of his work to natives themselves, Molina's books probably found the most use among clerics aiming to prepare themselves for the pastoral use of Nahuatl.[50]

The abundance of Molina's published work in Nahuatl betrays his belief in its importance as a medium of communication between the Nahuas and Europeans. Nonetheless, Molina did not just let the existence of his work speak for itself. He described at length the significance of studying and using Nahuatl: "To declare the mysteries of our faith, it does not suffice to know the language in any old way; rather one must understand well the proper sense of the words and manners of speaking used by the natives. Indeed, when this preparation is lacking, it may occur that those who should be preachers of truth instead are preachers of error and falsehood. For this reason (among many others), the Holy Spirit was given to the apostles on the day of Pentecost, in many different languages, so that they would be understood by all." For Molina, ministers not only had to preach in the local people's language; they also had to use the people's idiom. This difficult task did not serve merely as a helpful aid in the conversion process. Instead, Molina considered preaching in idiomatic Nahuatl as fundamental to the conversion of the Nahuas, and he justified its importance by pointing to Christian scripture. For Molina, not only pastors but any cleric who would preach or administer the sacraments "had a great need of knowing this language."[51] Thus in discussing the importance of indigenous-language study, Molina not only mirrored the views of the bishops; like Philip II, he may have had even higher standards.

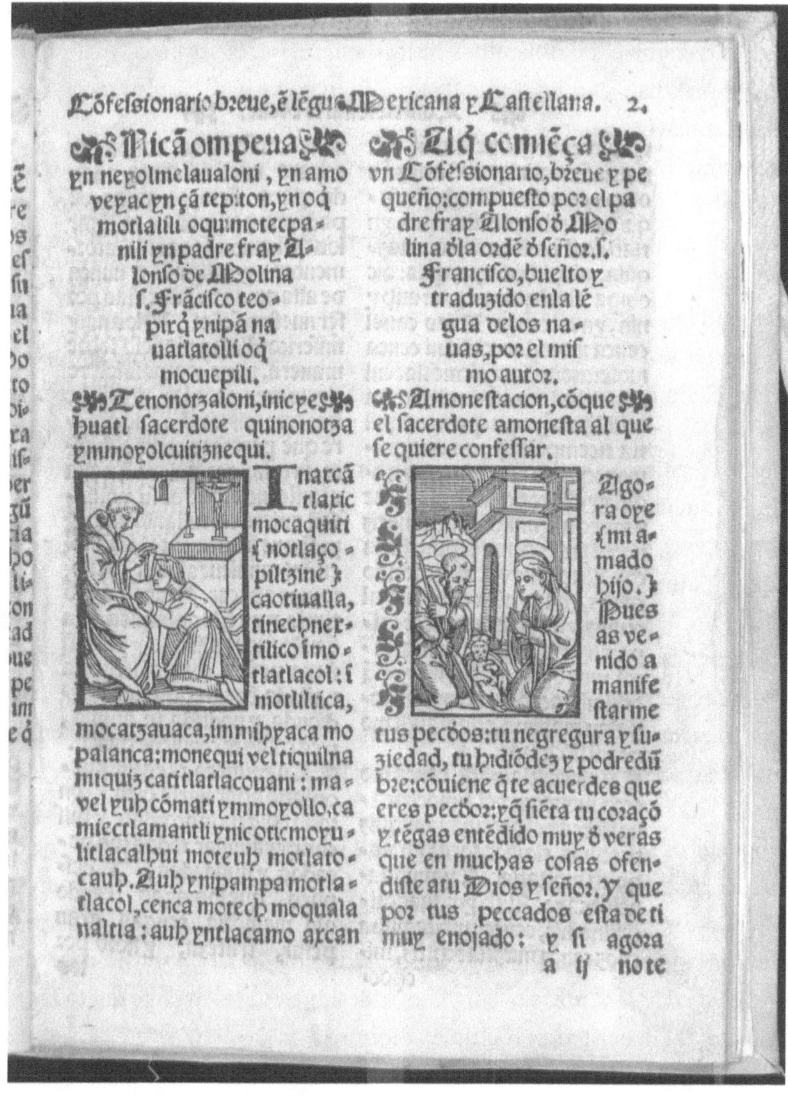

Cõfessionario breue, ẽ lẽgua Mexicana y Castellana. 2.

Nicã ompeua
yn neyolmelaualoni, yn amo
ueyac yn çã tepiton, yn oq̃
motlalili oquimotecpa-
nili yn padre fray Al-
lonso de Molina
f. Frãcisco teo-
pixq̃ ynipã na
uatlatolli oq̃
mocuepili.

Tenonotzaloni, inic yehuatl sacerdote quinonotza ymmoyolcuitizneq̃ui.

Inacca tlaxic mocaquiti {notlaço-piltzine} caotiualla, tinechhnextilico imotlatlacol: i motlilitica, mocatzauaca, immihyaca mopalanca: monequi vel tiquilnamiquiz catitlatlacouani: mavel yuh cõmati ymmoyollo, ca miectlamantli ynic oticmoyulitlacalhui moteuh motlatocauh. Auh ynipampa motlatlacol, cenca motech moqualanaltia: auh yntlacamo axcan

Aq̃ comiẽça
vn Cõfessionario, breue y pe
queño: compuesto por el pa
dre fray Alonso d Mo
lina dla ordẽ d señor. s.
Francisco, buelto y
traduzido enla lẽ
gua delos na-
uas, por el mis
mo autor.

Amonestacion, cõque el sacerdote amonesta al que se quiere confessar.

Agora oye {mi amado hijo.} Pues as venido a manifestarme tus peccados: tu negregura y suziedad, tu hidiõdez y podredũbre: cõuiene q̃ te acuerdes que eres peccador: y q̃ sienta tu coraçõ y tẽgas entẽdido muy d veras que en muchas cosas ofendiste a tu Dios y señor. Y que por tus peccados esta de ti muy enojado: y si agora a si no te

FIG. 5 | Alonso de Molina, *Confessionario breue en lengua mexicana y castellana.* Library of Congress, Washington, DC, Rare Book and Special Collections Division.

Although Molina vigorously exhorted other clerics to study Nahuatl, he did recognize the difficulties in this enterprise. He realized that not all churchmen had learned Nahuatl as children, as he had. He also recognized that Nahua vocabulary varied from one region to another and that Europeans wanted to explain concepts that sometimes did not exist in Nahuatl. Though he appreciated these obstacles, Molina did not waver in upholding Nahuatl as a fundamental tool in achieving the conversion of the natives. Nowhere in the relatively extensive prolegomena to his 1555 Nahuatl dictionary did he advocate or even acknowledge the possibility of using Castilian to preach to the Nahuas.[52] Instead, he provided several justifications for using Nahuatl, including additional references to Christian scripture and ancient Roman history. Therefore, although Molina acknowledged obstacles to learning Nahuatl, he remained firm in his expectation that his fellow churchmen had to take up that arduous task.[53]

Several other friars besides Molina produced books in indigenous languages, aiming to facilitate the study of the local tongues among their confrères. Like Molina, they often used the prolegomena to those texts as a space to advocate the use of indigenous languages. They did not always use the same reasons, go to the same length, or write the same genre of books.

In 1559, just a few years after Molina published his Nahuatl dictionary, his Franciscan brother Maturino Gilberti published the *Diálogo de doctrina christiana en lengua de Mechuacán* (Dialogue of Christian doctrine in the language of Michoacán).[54] Like Molina, Gilberti also wrote extensively. He specialized in P'urhépecha (also known as Tarascan), spoken widely in Michoacán, a western region of Mexico. Besides his *Diálogo*, Gilberti's publications in P'urhépecha include a grammar, a dictionary, a spiritual treatise, and a *cartilla para niños* (a small book designed to teach children to read). Some of them existed in multiple editions.

While Molina exhorted ministers to not speak the local languages "in any old way," Gilberti may have approached his fellow churchmen differently. In his *Diálogo*, Gilberti included "material to preach on every Sunday of the year."[55] The content that he offered included extended reflections in P'urhépecha on each of the Ten Commandments, as well as other fundamental facets of Christian doctrine. He did not, however, produce a text entirely in P'urhépecha. He included section titles and marginalia in Castilian, presumably to help the ministers to find the material they needed for a particular Sunday (fig. 6). Producing this text, Gilberti may have aimed

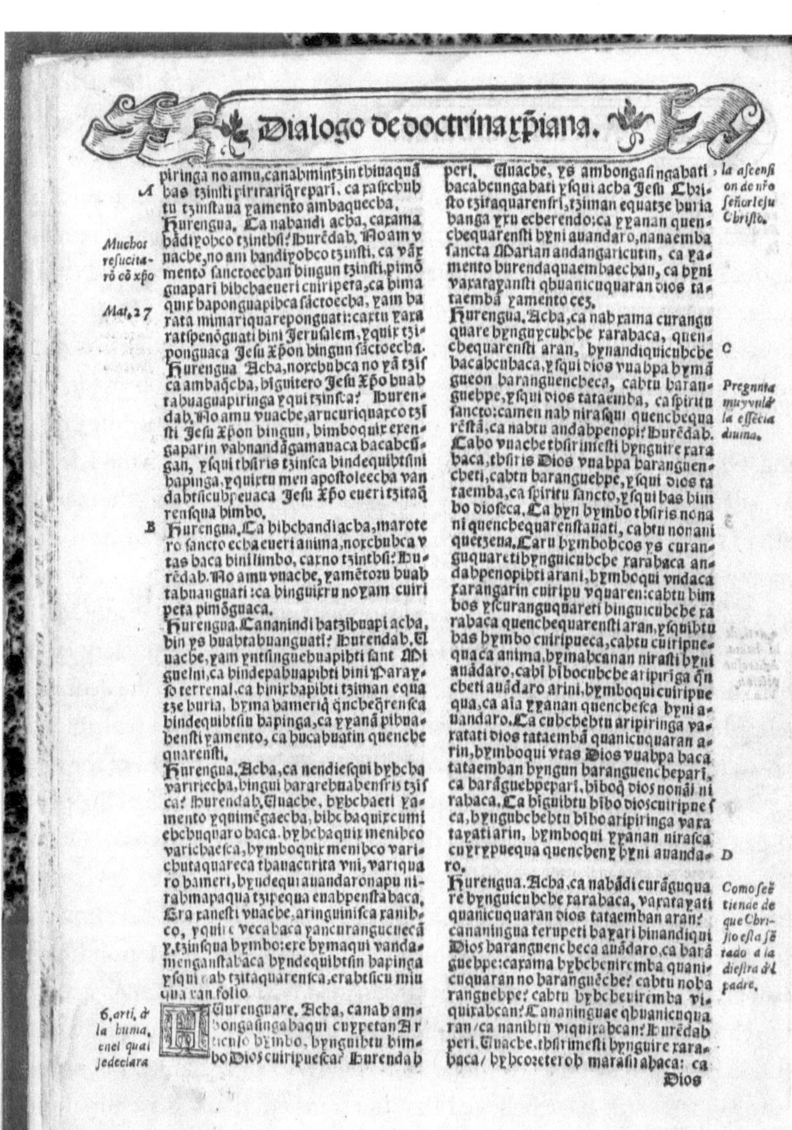
Dialogo de doctrina xpiana.

FIG. 6 | Maturino Gilberti, *Diálogo de doctrina christiana*. Courtesy of the John Carter Brown Library at Brown University.

to provide assistance to those ministers who had attained a limited knowledge of P'urhépecha. His audience may have consisted—at least partly—in ministers who could read the language but lacked the facility to produce an original sermon.

The two Franciscan friars, Gilberti and Molina, form an interesting comparison. Both authors utilized a combination of an indigenous language and a European language in their texts, and clearly, both wished to help other churchmen to use a local Mesoamerican tongue. Yet Molina did not provide extended reflections in Nahuatl for inclusion in sermons. He seems to have wanted to teach other clerics but was not willing to provide them with a crutch, so to speak, from which they could read directly while preaching. Gilberti, however, may have accepted that some clerics would acquire an advanced knowledge of indigenous languages and that others would attain more ad hoc abilities, perhaps consisting in learning to read a sermon written by someone else.

Gilberti may have differed from Molina in another way. While Molina explicitly addressed some of his work to natives (as well as to clergy), Gilberti may have envisioned his work for a narrower audience. In the dedicatory letter to his *Diálogo*, Gilberti wrote, "Such a necessary and fruitful work could not, and should not, be placed in the hands and tongues of the entire Christian *vulgus*."[56] Gilberti's support for using the languages of the people did not necessarily imply a belief that *all* people should engage with the full breadth of Christian doctrine. Instead, he believed that some people would have trouble understanding particular aspects of Christian teaching, thus further suggesting that he wrote his *diálogo* with preachers in mind. While Gilberti clearly attributed significant value to P'urhépecha as an instrument of religious instruction, he may not have considered the language as the fundamental solution to facilitate conversions to Christianity. Put another way, Gilberti may have believed that the translation and dissemination of doctrine solved some problems but created others.

Like Molina and Gilberti, the Dominican friar Benito Hernández also produced written work to help fellow churchmen to learn indigenous languages. Though perhaps not as prolific as Molina and Gilberti, Hernández did publish a catechism (*doctrina*) in Mixtec in 1568.[57]

In the dedicatory letter of his catechism, Hernández described his motivations for writing. He noted that priests in his territory had fled from the "dangerous and burdensome responsibility" (*tan pessada y peligrosa carga*) expected of them in the conversion of the local natives.[58] In this regard, Hernández concluded that "no other time had been like the present, especially in this land because of the lack of ministers." Perhaps in an effort to alleviate the burdens that caused these clerics to flee, Hernández produced his catechism: "After having worked in the diocese of Your Lordship for so many years, I decided to write a catechism in Mixtec (which is the province where I worked after having arrived in this land) so that the natives of this land might be better instructed, and those who are to preach to them can learn the language with greater facility and have at hand the things that they should preach. I know well that I could offer nothing more pleasing to Your Lordship, for you desire nothing so much as that which benefits your sheep." Hernández thus affirmed that indigenous languages would facilitate the instruction of the Mixtecs. In the catechism itself, he mirrored Gilberti by including lengthy discussions (*exposiciones*) in Mixtec on various fundamental topics of Catholic doctrine (e.g., the Ten Commandments, the seven sacraments, the virtues). Like Molina and Gilberti, Hernández hoped that his book would lead other missionaries to learn Mixtec well.[59]

Like Gilberti, Hernández may have had somewhat lower expectations than Molina. He "lived many years among the *Yndios*, [and] through much conversation, attained an understanding of their customs and ways of speaking." Not all priests and religious, however, attained a sophisticated ability to use an indigenous language, and Hernández knew it. He thus suggested that ministers might use his book to "have *at hand* the things that they should preach" (emphasis added), perhaps implying that some churchmen would read directly from the book while explaining doctrine. Elsewhere, Hernández confirmed his expectation that ministers should use his book especially if they lacked fluency in Mixtec: "For those who do not know the language very well, it seemed to me a great benefit to put in writing the most important and common ways of speaking used by the *Yndios* because knowing how to teach them the things of our faith in their own manner goes a long way." In describing his book, Hernández may have implied that churchmen could read directly from it while explaining doctrine and that they might use it to learn the "the most important and common ways of speaking" used by the Mixtecs. His suggestion of how other churchmen might have used his book may recall the kind of limited language use that Philip II would denounce as unacceptable in 1578.[60]

Hernández paralleled Molina and Gilberti when he acknowledged several obstacles regarding the communication of Christian doctrine to the Amerindians. For instance, he expressed concerns with the ways in which natives understood Christian doctrine translated into the local languages. Even though Hernández called for teaching the natives "in their own way," he noted that "because [Christian teachings] are so sophisticated and [the natives] so simple-minded, they still have difficulty understanding them even when expressed in their own way."[61] While some churchmen believed that natives understood well the explanations in these indigenous-language texts, Hernández disagreed.[62] Furthermore, Hernández's value of the native languages did not preclude him from characterizing the Amerindians as simple-minded (*baxos*) or of little capacity. Thus he did recognize that indigenous languages served as a more fruitful medium than Castilian for conveying Christian doctrine to natives. Like Gilberti, however, he may have thought that the local tongues alone did not provide the fundamental solution to the challenge of converting the natives.

The Augustinian friar Juan de la Anunciación also seems closer to Gilberti and Hernández than to Molina. A Granada native, who joined the Mexican Augustinians in 1554, Juan de la Anunciación wrote at least three works in Nahuatl: a catechism and two collections of sermons. Among the works printed in sixteenth-century Mexico, Juan de la Anunciación's first texts use *sermón* or *sermonario* within the volume's title (fig. 7). For the Augustinian friar, one's maternal language certainly served as the most effective medium for teaching doctrine, but especially at the earliest stage. Providing the Nahuas with instruction in their own language was "giving them the bread of the Holy Gospel in the smallest pieces possible, ensuring the good that is believed to come from the first digestion. [All this resulted] from teaching them the things of the faith in their own language, along with a few notes, from which longer, more extended thoughts may arise."[63] The Augustinian friar's comments indicate that he considered indigenous tongues especially useful in an early stage of conversion. After this "first digestion," the initial period of instruction in Nahuatl, he may have envisioned exposing the most well-educated Nahuas to works in Castilian or (more likely) Latin, allowing them to study the "longer, more extended thoughts" of esteemed Christian intellectuals, such as St. Augustine of Hippo or other Church fathers. In general, Juan de la Anunciación commended the clerics who contributed to the production of Nahuatl texts; he considered their

SERMONARIO.
EN LENGVA
MEXICANA, DONDE SE CON-
TIENE (POR EL ORDEN DEL MISSAL
NVEVO ROMANO,) DOS SERMONES
en todas las Dominicas y Festiuidades principales de todo el año:
y otro en las Fiestas de los Sanctos, con sus vidas, y Communes.
CON VN CATHECISMO EN LENGVA MEXICANA
y Española, con el Calendario. Compuesto por el reuerendo padre
Fray Iuan de la Annunciacion, Subprior del monaste-
rio de sant Augustin de [illegible]

DIRIGIDO AL MVY REVERENDO PADRE
[illegible]stro fray Alonso de la vera cruz, Prouincial de la [illegible]
Hermitaños de sant Augustin, en esta nueua España.
EN MEXICO, por Antonio Ricardo. M. D. LXXVII.
Esta tassado en papel en [illegible]

FIG. 7 | Juan de la Anunciación, *Sermonario en lengua mexicana*. Courtesy of the John Carter Brown Library at Brown University.

efforts "undoubtedly" beneficial for both ministers and the natives under their care. But his emphasis on using Nahuatl at the earliest stage of conversion efforts (as opposed to calling for a more general use within the Mexican Church), may suggest a different position compared to Molina. The two friars may not have supported the use of Nahuatl to quite the same extent.

While Gilberti and Hernández may have departed implicitly from Molina's standards of language learning, Juan de la Anunciación made an explicit divergence. When addressing linguistic facility, he wrote, "For the one who does not have fluency in the Mexican language, which is necessary to be able to preach, I do not consider it unsuitable (if his desire is appropriate, hoping to benefit souls and not to be ostentatious) that he seek to learn how to read it very well. For with the book in hand, he can help himself to preach the doctrine that he wishes."[64] Juan de la Anunciación thus produced his book not only for the busy minister who knew Nahuatl but lacked the time to write sermons; he wrote it also for the churchman who lacked fluency in Nahuatl. Even without knowing the language well, a minister could learn to read it and thus preach while reading from a book. The thoughts of Maturino Gilberti, Benito Hernández, and Juan de la Anunciación, friars of distinct orders, writing in different regions of Mexico, suggest that it was not uncommon for missionaries to use a language even when they had not mastered it.

Altogether, these friars viewed indigenous languages simultaneously as an opportunity and as a challenge. Although many ministers—if not most—considered Amerindian tongues as an advantage in conversion efforts, they did not hesitate from highlighting the shortcomings associated with using the same indigenous languages. For instance, the Dominican Hernández advocated the use of Mixtec while concurrently describing the natives as *baxos*. The evidence considered above thus suggests that attempting to categorize Mexican churchmen as either "pro-indigenous" or "anti-indigenous" would fail to appreciate the complexity of their attitudes toward Native American communities. In a similar vein, these friars also suggest that membership in a given religious order did not lead necessarily to significant differences in attitudes toward indigenous languages. Accordingly, one Franciscan (Gilberti) seems more similar to an Augustinian (Anunciación) and a Dominican (Hernández) than to his fellow Franciscan (Molina).[65]

Finally, while one might advocate the use of indigenous languages, that support did not entail a belief that all ministers of the Church had to use the language fluently. Many churchmen went to some length to expand the study and use of indigenous languages while also making room for clerics to use the same languages on a more limited basis. The large number of these indigenous-language aids and the fact that many of them existed in multiple editions suggests widespread use. Sixteenth-century New Spain probably had many churchmen whose primarily language remained Castilian but who managed to use indigenous languages to varying degrees, thus contributing to a situation in which both Castilian and indigenous tongues retained important roles.

CONCLUSION

Nearly five hundred years have passed since the arrival of Hernando Cortés and his band of conquistadors. Despite the current predominance of the Spanish language in Mexico and nearly all of Central America, millions of inhabitants of this region speak an indigenous language at present. Though many indigenous languages face extinction, several remain viable. Nahuatl, for instance, has over one million speakers today, and the Mayan language family has more.[66] Their continued use undoubtedly attests to the persistence of many indigenous peoples to retain the languages of their ancestors.[67]

Another part of the explanation, I submit, is found in the ways that European Christians approached language in the sixteenth century and beyond. In general, Spanish religious leaders sought many ways to encourage the use of indigenous languages within the Church. While Church authorities generally did not seek to preserve indigenous tongues for their own sake, the evidence strongly suggests that officials of the Church and Crown still contributed to the ongoing use of Amerindian languages.

While Spanish authorities encouraged churchmen to use indigenous tongues, they also contributed to the propagation of Castilian. Though Philip II wished that all clerics would use Amerindian languages at an advanced level, the reality was different. Countless churchmen—fluent in one or more native tongues—helped their confrères to acquire a kind of ad hoc linguistic proficiency. Many clerics did not use the languages at a sophisticated level, but they might have been able to read a prepared sermon or perhaps teach basic elements of Christian doctrine in an Amerindian tongue. This kind of language use, which the sources suggest was common, laid the groundwork for a multilingual Spanish America, where many churchmen acknowledged the value of indigenous languages while still operating in and thus propagating their native Castilian.[68]

From the view of Charles III, writing in 1770, the Crown had consistently ordered that Spanish alone be spoken in the Americas. But that had not been the case in the sixteenth century. Some individuals did desire to see Spanish spoken more often. The expansion of Spanish, however, did not necessarily mean the exclusion of native tongues.

CONCLUSION

In 1580 the Spanish Crown ordered the establishment of professorships in New Spain's most widely spoken indigenous languages. The question of whether to have Arabic professorships also arose in sixteenth-century Spain. In 1587 King Philip II called an assembly of Church and Crown officials to discuss the religious instruction of Valencia's Moriscos. He also asked Archbishop Juan de Ribera to hold another assembly on the same topic, in order to confirm the findings of the king's group. Both assemblies considered whether the city of Valencia ought to have a professorship of Arabic. Everyone present agreed that such a position "was in no way appropriate." The same assemblies decided that religious instruction should be offered to the Moriscos in Castilian and Valencian.[1]

This anecdote raises several important questions that guide this book: How did Catholic churchmen on both sides of the Atlantic compare in terms of language practices? Why did the Spanish Church and Crown view Amerindian languages and Arabic differently? To what extent did Castilian Spanish serve as a language of empire? Finally, what broader conclusions can we draw from learning about the language practices of the Spanish Church and Crown? The pages that follow provide an overview of the book's findings and attempt to shed additional light on these key questions.

Did the Spanish Church have a language policy? A transatlantic comparison of language policies and practices in Spain and Mexico reveals similarities and differences. This book has emphasized that the Spanish kingdoms had no universal language policies in the sixteenth century; instead, practices varied, sometimes significantly, from one place to another. Despite those differences, the Catholic Church did have some general rules regarding language. These practices translated from Europe to America. For instance, in the Mass, Latin served as the official language across the Spanish kingdoms.[2] Latin also had a privileged status when it came to the Bible. While the Council of Trent did not require Latin as the language of the Bible, vernacular Bibles—whether in a Romance or an Amerindian language—were the object of suspicion in both Spain and the Americas.

Latin, however, did not have pride of place in all contexts. Though the Mass prioritized Latin, there remained room for the vernaculars. For instance, the Council of Trent encouraged all priests to explain basic Catholic teachings in the vernacular during the Mass. Priests could do so either through a sermon or by reading from a catechism; in this way, the vernaculars found their way into the Mass both in Spain and in the Americas. Furthermore, when the Mexican bishops called for the translation of basic catechisms into indigenous languages, they followed recommendations made at the Council of Trent and in Spain. The Mexican bishops also mirrored their peninsular contemporaries by regulating printed texts, requiring that the bishop approve both short catechisms and lengthier texts (such as sermons) in indigenous languages.[3] The Mexican bishops also resembled some churchmen who worked among the Moriscos. In calling for the use of indigenous languages for preaching and some of the sacraments, they paralleled the relatively few Spanish clerics who called for some use of Arabic. On both sides of the Atlantic, most Church leaders considered the vernaculars as ideal for communicating *basic* doctrine to people who had little knowledge of Christianity. To this end, catechisms and interpreters served as ideal aids. But the vernaculars (whether Iberian or Amerindian languages) became potentially problematic when used for books that contained more complex material.

In comparing language practices across the Atlantic, the differences are equally illuminating, if not more so. Several did not transfer from Iberia to America. The status of indigenous languages in the Mexican Church stood in sharp contrast to the place of Arabic in the peninsular Church.

Sixteenth-century Mesoamerican natives experienced no linguistic restriction like the 1566–67 order directed at Granada's Arabic-speaking Moriscos.[4] Also, the number of churchmen that used indigenous languages dwarfed the number of Arabic-speaking priests in Iberia. Though the monarchy sometimes criticized the clergy's indigenous-language skills, the fact remains that Mexico was home to a vast number of linguistically competent churchmen.

Other differences stand out. While Mexico's bishops made explicit mention of the Council of Trent in their provincial councils, they made relatively few, if any, references to the Moriscos.[5] The bishops were not the only Church leaders to forego comparisons between Moriscos and Amerindians. When looking for points of comparison for their efforts to convert Amerindian peoples, some churchmen—such as José de Acosta—looked beyond the Moriscos to alternate points of reference, like the ancient Samaritans.[6] Given that many clerics considered the Moriscos as resistant to Christianity, drawing a link between the Amerindians and Spain's Islamic communities probably seemed a negative association.

Because many of Mexico's clerics came from Iberia, they undoubtedly drew on past experiences when they attempted to instruct the indigenous peoples in Christian doctrine. While they made efforts to implement the standards from the Council of Trent, they also made adjustments to accommodate their new locations. The Mexican archbishop Juan Pérez de la Serna (1613–27) probably summarized the mentality of many churchmen when he noted that local church practices "corresponded to the teachings of the ancient fathers and conformed to the decrees of the holy councils and common law" and also "adapted to the customs of the region and the lifestyle of its inhabitants."[7] American churchmen clearly drew on collective knowledge from the "old world." Following this line of thought, it seems reasonable that their experiences with Spain's Islamic communities would have served as a model for their encounter with America's native peoples.[8] But as Pérez de la Serna's words suggest, churchmen could not simply take European practices and apply them in a new place; adjustments had to be made. Thus the differences were perhaps as significant as the continuities, as the previous chapters have shown. Particularly with regard to language, Mexican churchmen adopted notably different practices relative to their counterparts who worked among Muslims and Moriscos.

The European Church thus influenced the new American Church in significant but limited ways. Looking from the other direction, it remains unclear to what extent the Church in the Americas exerted a reciprocal influence upon Europe. Spanish authorities knew about important developments in the Americas, as seen above in their discussion of language professorships. That Spanish authorities decided against a professorship of Arabic in Valencia suggests the following: Church and Crown leaders appreciated the complexity of each particular context and considered language practices as situation-specific. Although clerics shared some methods in approaching Amerindians and Moriscos, they viewed the two populations as vastly different. Churchmen on both sides of the Atlantic drew on ecumenical, or church-wide, councils, such as Trent. Diocesan synods—like that of Guadix (chapter 2)—or provincial councils—like those of Mexico (chapter 4)—often discussed local problems. As such, their recommendations might but did not necessarily influence churchmen in other geographical areas. Each province and each diocese had unique concerns, and for this reason, the Council of Trent allowed variation in language practices.[9] This context enables us to begin to comprehend how the Spanish Church and Crown could restrict the use of Arabic in Granada (1566–67) at precisely the same time as they pushed the use of indigenous languages in the Americas.

Why did Arabic not take root as a language of religious instruction in the sixteenth-century Spanish kingdoms, especially when Christians in other parts of the world *did* use it?[10] For centuries, the Church had recognized that the languages of the people served as the ideal medium for preaching, confirming this principle at the Fourth Lateran Council in 1215. By that logic, it would seem obvious that the Spanish Church should have used the vernaculars to preach to all peoples. Why did the Spanish Crown and Church vigorously encourage priests to study Amerindian languages but not Arabic?

The answer seems to rest in understanding how Spaniards perceived each broad population. Islamic communities posed a distinct challenge in Spanish evangelization efforts. Unlike Native Americans, Muslims had exercised political sovereignty over Spanish Christians for well over seven hundred years, beginning in 711 and ending in 1492. Muslims also, for the most part, had not converted to Christianity. It would be misleading to describe Spain's Moriscos as uniformly antagonistic to the Crown and the Catholic Church; a relatively small but significant number of Moriscos embraced Christianity, with some becoming loyal servants of the Crown. Still, that group remained a minority. Thus many Catholic clerics viewed the Moriscos as a lost cause, exceedingly difficult if not impossible to convert. Perhaps for similar reasons, efforts to establish formal programs of Arabic study appear to have failed during the central Middle Ages. For most Spanish clerics, the study of Arabic and its use for religious instruction would entail considerable efforts that probably would not bring about the desired conversions. Clerics seem to have resisted Arabic because they lived in societies with a recent memory of Islamic rule, they had directly experienced or at least heard about failed efforts at conversion, and they also had a keen awareness of a formidable Islamic polity in North Africa. During the eight decades that followed the completion of the *Reconquista*, Christians in Granada and Crown authorities frequently expressed concern about not only the possibility of rebellion by Granada's Islamic communities but also a potential Ottoman invasion. Arabic thus suffered by association.[11]

Officials of the Spanish Church and Crown might have resisted using Arabic for another reason, related to its sacred status as the language of God within Islam.[12] Philip II may have been thinking of precisely this point in 1566 when he wrote, "Through this language, they retain and conserve the memory of their ancient and dangerous sect and life."[13] Given the extraordinary religious significance that Muslims attached to Arabic, it seems likely that many Spanish churchmen believed that translating Christian doctrine into Arabic posed a risk, potentially reminding neophytes of their Islamic past.

By the start of the seventeenth century, many officials of the Church and Crown considered the religious instruction of the Moriscos an insurmountable challenge. During the sixteenth century, only a small number of clerics managed to use Arabic for the religious instruction of Moriscos. Across the Atlantic, a very different scenario developed: unprecedented numbers of Catholic churchmen threw themselves into preaching and translating Christian doctrine into Amerindian languages.

One might say that the fate of Amerindian languages and Arabic was the opposite of what seems logical. After several centuries of interaction, Spanish Christians and Muslims had abundant opportunities to learn each other's languages. It would seem that language should not have been an obstacle to communication. Yet it was. Mesoamerica, conversely, was home to an immense variety of languages, many of which pertained to entirely distinct linguistic families. Europeans and Mesoamericans encountered one another for the first time in the sixteenth century. Despite having no previous experience with one another, they engaged in a vastly more fruitful dialogue. How did that seemingly improbable outcome become a reality?

The answer seems to be that effective communication depended not just on learning languages. More importantly, communication rested on how peoples perceived one another. Christians and Muslims had a long history. A previous generation of scholarship emphasized peaceful coexistence and cultural exchange in the medieval Spanish kingdoms.[14] More recent scholarship has reminded readers of the friction that sometimes characterized relations between Muslims and Christians.[15] Why Catholic churchmen largely failed in evangelizing Spain's Moriscos may be less a question of linguistic difference and more a matter of historic tensions.

To many, Spain's Islamic communities seemed firmly resistant to Christianity. But they would perceive Amerindian peoples differently. To Christopher Columbus, for example, the native peoples of the Caribbean seemed to represent a new hope for the Spanish monarchy and for Catholic Christendom, more generally. In a 1493 letter to Luis de Santangel, Columbus wrote that the native peoples he encountered "have neither iron, nor steel, nor arms, nor are they competent to use them, not that they are not well-formed and of handsome stature, but because they are timid to a surprising degree."[16] Columbus did not compare the people whom he saw explicitly to Muslims. It would not be a stretch to imagine that the comparison occurred to him and to his contemporaries. In the Caribbean, Europeans had encountered a "timid" people who allegedly posed no threat of political domination over the Spaniards. To Columbus and many Europeans, the natives could not have been more different from Muslims.

Columbus also noted that the natives seemed to live according to Christian virtue. He added that they "never refuse anything that they possess when it is asked of them; on the contrary, they offer it themselves, and they exhibit so much loving kindness that they would even give their hearts; and, whether it be something of value or of little worth that is offered to them, they are satisfied." From Columbus's perspective, the natives had shown such openness—as well as eagerness in accepting humble European "gifts"—that he considered them ideal candidates for Christianity. Their potential as Christians must have become obvious to Columbus, who added, "They are not acquainted with any kind of worship, and are not idolaters; but believe that all power and, indeed, all good things are in heaven." To Columbus, they lacked religion but seemed inclined to it. America thus must have seemed a model ground to propagate Christianity.[17]

Columbus, of course, did not represent all Europeans who would go to the Americas, and he only saw a limited number of indigenous communities. Still, the idealism (or paternalism) that pervades his observations helps to understand the men who would sail to America in the hopes of bringing the Gospel to new peoples. To many European churchmen, Amerindians must have seemed the inverse of the Islamic communities of Spain.

Was Castilian Spanish a language of empire? Some did make that case. As discussed in chapter 4, Fray Martín de Valencia called for the propagation of Castilian during the early years of New Spain, hoping that the newly conquered territory could become "a land of one language." During his time as a missionary, however, he also acknowledged the valuable contributions that his brother Franciscans made by learning indigenous languages. The archbishops Alonso de Montúfar and Pedro Moya de Contreras went further than Valencia—each in their own way—by encouraging and incentivizing the study of indigenous languages by priests. Both archbishops also made room for Castilian as a language of Catholicism among Mesoamerican natives. Mexico's churchmen thus supported both indigenous languages and Castilian to varying degrees.

Given that Mexican churchmen often taught Castilian to indigenous children, one may conclude reasonably that they aimed for Castilian to become eventually the primary language of Mesoamerican natives. That may be true to some extent, and if so, one might surmise that churchmen in Mexico only supported indigenous languages as a temporary measure, similar to what Martín Pérez de Ayala and others did with Arabic in Iberia.[18] As the previous chapters have shown, however, the similarities only go so far; there were important differences between attitudes toward Amerindian languages and Arabic. Ayala, as seen in chapter 2, called for Arabic sermons but allowed churchmen to preach with an interpreter or to appoint someone to preach. In the Americas, none of the first three provincial councils explicitly allowed preaching through an interpreter or delegating the task. Sixteenth-century Mexico also produced several collections of indigenous-language sermons, more than enough for every Sunday and feast day of the year. Spanish churchmen, however, did not print any such text in Arabic. Relative to Arabic, indigenous languages received far more enthusiasm from Spanish churchmen. It seems unclear, therefore, that Mexican churchmen viewed indigenous languages as a temporary instrument, to be superseded by Castilian Spanish.

Overall, there is much to suggest that Spanish officials did not make the propagation of Castilian a priority. As shown in chapter 1, many churchmen sought to circumscribe the use of Castilian, instead pushing Latin as a superior (or perhaps safer) medium for complex books of prayer and certainly for Christian scripture. Returning to the 1587 assemblies on Valencia's Moriscos (recounted above), it bears noting that officials of the Spanish Crown and Church advocated offering instruction in Castilian *and* Valencian. Thus they only went so far in their desires to convert Moriscos into Spanish Christians; for the leading men gathered at those assemblies, religious conversion did not have to walk hand-in-hand with the Castilian language. Castilian Spanish, of course, would become the second most widely spoken native language in the world. Nonetheless, that possibility probably seemed very distant, if not impossible, among many sixteenth-century churchmen. To them, the multilingual world of medieval Spain—with its use of Arabic, Basque, Castilian, Galician, Ladino, and other tongues—must have seemed much more realistic.

Finally, what broader conclusions can we draw from learning about the language practices of the Spanish Church and Crown? A key theme of this book is diversity: in languages, in ways of thinking about language, and in approaches to using language. Why do these differences matter?

Perhaps they should not surprise us. As the eminent historian Sir John H. Elliott has written, the immense diversity of the Spanish Crown made it "a fragmented monarchy," a vast complex of different pressure groups and interests. It had only a few common elements to bind it together: the king, Catholicism, the king's officials, and the king's subjects.[19] At the level of Crown politics, historians have long been aware of diverse interests and factions.

Thanks to relatively recent scholarship, we are now more conscious of diversity on a broader, social level. Historians no longer consider easy divisions, such as Christian and non-Christian or missionary and heathen, as useful ways to describe the people whom they study.[20] To ask, for instance, whether Moriscos were Christian or Muslim is to ask the wrong question. Neither category could do justice to the broad spectrum of beliefs and practices that historians have uncovered.

Among the clergy, however, we often fall short in looking for diversity. Scholars still have a limited awareness of difference among the clergy, in part, because of the "black-and-white" categories that these historical people often used in writing about their work. For instance, when the Mexican archbishop Juan Pérez de la Serna commented on the work of earlier churchmen in Mexico, he used stark contrasts, describing his predecessors as coming "from the most productive ground of the Catholic Church: the most fertile land of Spain." The place where they arrived, however, was "a sterile territory, of vast solitude." To replace "the darkness of idolatry," the "most holy men" took on the work of "planting, cultivating, and propagating" the Christian faith.[21] The archbishop's words suggest that churchmen thought about the world in oppositional categories, such as Christian versus idolatrous and fertile versus sterile. But that assessment is only part of the picture. In the same page of the same letter, Archbishop Pérez de la Serna also discusses the need to observe the "teachings of the ancient fathers" while also accommodating "the customs of the region and the lifestyle of its inhabitants."

The Mexican archbishop's letter reveals a paradox that I contend was characteristic of sixteenth-century Spanish churchmen: though they often thought and wrote about the world in oppositional terms, they simultaneously demonstrated an ability to accommodate different customs and lifestyles. They wrote about extirpating idolatry, but in practice, they made room for many aspects of local cultures. To put it simply, churchmen could be "black-and-white," but when it came to reaching out to real people, they were much more subtle.

Just as historians balk at stark oppositions, such as Christian and non-Christian or missionary and heathen, this book suggests that asking whether Spanish authorities prohibited or propagated a particular language is to ask the wrong question. Each part of this book has highlighted the careful positions taken by churchmen in different parts of the Spanish kingdoms. When considering the use of the vernaculars, many—if not most—churchmen utilized a practical, situation-specific approach. Neither the Crown nor the Church made comprehensive prohibitions or endorsements of any language.[22]

Facing so-called heretics, infidels, and pagans, churchmen insisted on the truth of Catholicism. Nevertheless, their resolve often did not translate into fixed, intransigent expectations for how to propagate their faith. Recognizing the important differences between one context and another, early modern churchmen developed a highly pragmatic way of thinking in order to facilitate conversions.

In the Spanish kingdoms, scholarship often has considered religious leaders in a dualistic framework: those who sympathized with reform and those who opposed it; those who sought to educate the people and those who wished to keep them ignorant; those who saw the vernaculars as an opportunity and those who feared them. However, the leaders of the Spanish Church do not fit clearly into these categories. Instead, they adopted surprisingly intricate positions when considering how to communicate Christianity to Spanish subjects. The complexity of their views is evident in the ways that they discussed language practices. Those subtle differences played no small part in shaping the diverse landscape of religious belief and practice in the Spanish world.

Historians know only part of the reason the sixteenth-century Spanish kingdoms witnessed such a diversity of religious practices "on the ground." The common people, who made up the vast majority of the Church, upheld countless interpretations of the Christian message. But in investigating the highly complex world of early modern global Christianity, scholars of Spanish and Latin American history must operate on the conviction that diversity existed not only among the masses but also, crucially, among officials of the Catholic Church.

We must leave behind a widespread modern assumption if we wish to understand the diverse language practices espoused by Catholic authorities and the gap between institutional agenda and the practices on the ground. That assumption, made famous in the Protestant Reformation, is that the written and spoken word constitute the fundamental and best way for people to learn about religion. To be sure, sixteenth-century Catholic churchmen viewed preaching in the vernaculars as a fundamental part of catechesis. But it was not the only or the most fundamental element. Some churchmen did not know the language of their flock—or did not know it well—and still found ways to encourage conversion.

As the second chapter has shown, Jesuits relayed admiration for the Arabic preaching of Juan de Albotodo. But his Jesuit brothers offer equal, probably greater, emphasis on the work done by other men who spoke only Castilian. The sources suggest that Arabic preaching offered just one of multiple options for Spanish churchmen to approach Islamic communities. Preaching in Castilian also made a positive impact.

The first bishops of Mexico City, Guatemala, and Oaxaca similarly indicated to King Charles I that sermons may not have been the key to the conversion of the American natives: "We confirm, Your Majesty, that the Natives are edified very much by devoted service, ceremonies, and ornate artwork, perhaps even more than by sermons." Thus in the minds of many clerics, the combination of vivid artwork, the fragrant smell of incense, the sense of inclusion in a community, and the example of a pious, Christ-like cleric together could prove a more powerful force for religious conversion than preaching alone.[23]

Few churchmen fixated on the vernaculars as the absolute foundation for the communication of Catholic doctrine to the common people. That we consider the vernaculars and the spoken word an obvious need perhaps says more about modern literacy than it does about sixteenth-century religious practices.

APPENDIX

Linguistic Abilities of Franciscan Friars in Sixteenth-Century New Spain

While the list here is extensive, it is not exhaustive. It was compiled primarily by using the index included in the García Icazbalceta edition of Gerónimo de Mendieta's *Historia eclesiástica indiana*. Even if this list did contain every Franciscan friar mentioned by Mendieta, it still would not account for the many friars who used indigenous languages to a limited degree (e.g., reading from a catechism).[1]

Name	**Description of linguistic abilities (Mendieta)***
Ayora, Fr. Juan de	"provincial que fué de Michoacan, entre otros tratados, dejó uno impreso en lengua mexicana, del Santo Sacramento del altar."
Baptista, Fr. Juan	"estos [los últimos veinte capítulos del *Contemptus mundi*] tradujo de poco tiempo acá Fr. Juan Baptista, que al presente es guardian del convento de Tezcuco, y todos cuatro libros los ha corregido y limado de muchos vicios que tenían, por descuido de los escribientes que los habían ido trasladando, y los tiene muy á punto para imprimir." (551)
Bassacio, Fr. Arnaldo	"escribió muchos y muy copiosos sermones, y de muy escogida lengua, y tradujo las epístolas y evangelios que se cantan en la Iglesia por todo el año, todo lo cual se estima en mucho."
Betanzos, Fr. Pedro de	"supo mejor que otros la lengua de los indios [de Guatimala] (que es muy bárbara y dificultosa de pronunciar), y en ella compuso arte y vocabulario" (385)
Beteta, Fr. Antonio de	"excelente lengua de los indios [tarascos]" (378)
Bononia, Fr. Miguel de	"supo cinco lenguas diferentes de indios, y en ellas predicó y convirtió á muchos" (378)
Castro, Fr. Andrés de	"primero evangelizador de la nación matlazinga, hizo en aquella lengua arte y vocabulario, doctrina y sermones." (552)
Cisneros, Fr. García de	"Compuso también Fr. Garcia de Cisneros otros sermones predicables" (550)

Name	Description of linguistic abilities (Mendieta)*
Daciano, Fr. Jacobo	"Fué el primero que administró á los tarascos el santísimo sacramento de la Eucaristía, y supo muy bien aquella lengua y la mexicana." (378)
Dávila, Fr. Alonso	"Aprendió también en breve tiempo (demas de la mexicana) la lengua totonaca, con celo de ayudar á aquellos naturales" (716)
Escalona, Fr. Alonso de	"escribió muchos y muy buenos sermones, de que se han aprovechado y aprovechan hoy dia los predicadores, así de dominicas como de santos, y también escribió sobre los mandamientos del Decálogo." (551) "siendo guardian el siervo de Dios Fr. Luis de Fuensalida, comenzó á deprender la lengua mexicana. Y como tenia tenacísima memoria y deseo de la saber para poder aprovechar á la salud de tantas almas, en breve tiempo salió con ella y la supo muy bien, y en ella hizo sermones que han aprovechado á muchos predicadores de los indios mexicanos, porque hasta entonces no había otros con que se aprovechar los que aprendían la lengua, los cuales se tradujeron en la lengua achí ó de Guatemala. Juntó en la mesma ciudad de Tlascala cuasi seiscientos niños, y enseñóles a leer, escribir, cantar y la doctrina cristiana." (668)
Fuensalida, Fr. Luis de	"fue servido el Señor de darles lengua para poder hablar y entenderse razonablemente con los indios. Los primeros que salieron con ella fueron Fr. Luis de Fuensalida y Fr. Francisco Ximenez." (224–25)
Gante, Fr. Pedro de	"compuso una copiosa doctrina, que anda impresa" (550)
Gaona, Fr. Juan de	"fué muy primo en la lengua mexicana, y en ella compuso admirables tratados, aunque de ellos no quedó memoria, sino solo de unos diálogos o coloquios, que andan impresos, de la lengua mas pura y elegante que hasta ahora se ha visto, y otro de la pasión de nuestro Redentor; los demás supe que por desgracia se quemaron." (550–51)
Garrobillas, Fr. Pedro de las	"fué muy diestro en la lengua indiana [tarasca]" (378)
Gilberti, Fr. Maturino	"En la lengua tarasca [que es la de Michoacan] ninguno le hizo ventaja, y en ella compuso una obra de mucha doctrina." (378) "compuso y dejó impreso en la lengua tarasca (que es la de Michoacan) un libro de doctrina cristiana, de marca mayor, en que se contiene todo lo que al cristiano le conviene entender y saber para su salvación." (552)
Gómez, Fr. Francisco	"esencial religioso y muy buena lengua de aquella tierra [Guatimala]" (669)

Name	Description of linguistic abilities (Mendieta)*
Herrera, Fr. Alonso de	"compuso en provecho y lengua de estos naturales un sermonario dominical y *de Sanctis*." (550)
Jiménez, Fr. Francisco	"Entre [los doce que primero vinieron] el que primero puso en arte la lengua mexicana y vocabulario" (550)
Lagunas, Fr. Juan Baptista de	"provincial que también fué de Michoacan, escribió en lengua tarasca, y dejó impresos, la arte y doctrina cristiana." (552)
Molina, Fr. Alonso de	"Este fué el primero que sirviendo de intérprete á los frailes dió á entender á los indios los misterios de nuestra fe, y fue maestro de los predicadores del Evangelio, porque él les enseñó la lengua" (220) "fué el que mas dejó impreso de sus obras, porque imprimió arte de la lengua mexicana, y vocabulario, y doctrina cristiana mayor y menor, y confesionario mayor y menor ó mas breve, y aparejos para recebir el Santísimo Sacramento del altar, y la vida de nuestro padre S. Francisco. Fuera de esto tradujo en la mesma lengua los evangelios de todo el año y las horas de Nuestra Señora, aunque estas se recogieron por estar prohibidas en lengua vulgar. Tradujo también muchas oraciones y devociones para ejercicio de los naturales, porque aprovechasen en la vida espirtual y cristiana." (551)
Motolinía, Fr. Toribio	"hizo luego una breve doctrina cristiana Fr. Toribio Motolinia, la cual anda impresa" (550)
Olmos, Fr. Andrés de	"fué el que sobre todos tuvo don de lenguas, porque en la mexicana compuso el arte mas copioso y provechoso de los que se han hecho, y hizo vocabulario y muchas otras obras, y lo mesmo hizo en la lengua totonaca y en la guasteca, y entiendo que supo otras lenguas de chichimecos, porque anduvo mucho tiempo entre ellos." (550)
Oroz, Fr. Pedro	"se deben gracias por lo mucho que en esta lengua otomí ha trabajado, y no menos en la mexicana, en la cual tiene compuestos unos copiosos sermonarios, que placiendo á Dios, preso saldrán á luz." (552)
Palacios, Fr. Pedro de	"excelente lengua otomí, hizo en ella un catecismo ó doctrina cristiana, y también un arte para aprenderla, la cual corrigió y amplió después el padre Fr. Pedro Oroz" (552)
Parra, Fr. Francisco de la	"[Betanzos] compuso arte y vocabulario, y después un Fr. Francisco de la Parra la perficionó, añadiendo cuatro ó cinco letras, ó por mejor decir caracteres, para mejor pronunciar aquella lengua, porque no bastaban los de nuestro *a*, *b*, *c*." (385)
Rengel, Fr. Alonso	"hizo una arte muy buena de la lengua mexicana, y en la mesma lengua hizo sermones de todo el año, y también hizo arte y doctrina en la lengua otomí" (550)

Name	Description of linguistic abilities (Mendieta)*
Ribas, Fr. Juan de	"compuso un catecismo cristiano y sermones dominicales de todo el año: un *Flos Sanctorum* breve, y unas preguntas y respuestas de la vida cristiana" (550)
Rodríguez, Fr. Luis de	"tradujo los proverbios de Salomón de muy elegante lengua, y los cuatro libros del *Contemptus mundi*, salvo que del tercero libro faltaban los últimos veinte capítulos" (551)
Romanones, Fr. Juan de	"compuso muchos y elegantes sermones y otros tratados, y tradujo muchos fragmentos de la sagrada Escritura." (551–52)
Sahagún, Fr. Bernardino de	"hizo arte de la lengua mexicana y unos sermonarios de todo el año, unos breves y otros largos, y una postilla sobre los evangelios dominicales, y otros muchos tratados de escogidísima lengua. Y como hombre que sobre todos mas inquirió los secretos y profundidad de esta lengua, compuso un Calepino [que así lo llamaba él] de doce ó trece cuerpos de marca mayor, los cuales yo tuve en mi poder, donde se encerraban todas las maneras de hablar que los mexicanos tenían en todo género de su trato, religión, crianza, vida y conversación." (551)
San Francisco, Fr. Juan de	"compuso un sermonario bien cumplido y de muy buena lengua, y unas colaciones llenas de santos ejemplos, muy provechosas para predicar á los indios" (550) "Y súbitamente se le manifestó que le era concedida por don del cielo la lengua mexicana (que es la mas general), y luego otro dia siguiente comenzó á predicar en ella con grande admiración de los naturales, y en ella compuso un muy cumplido sermonario y unas colaciones de diversas materias, llenas de maravillosos ejemplos, en muestra de la merced que Dios le había hecho en manifestarle aquella lengua para que predicase sus misterios" (656)
San Miguel, Fr. Juan de	"famosa lengua [tarasca] y excelente predicador" (378)
Tembleque, Fr. Francisco de	"Aprendió la lengua mexicana para confesar á los indios y aunque no se dispuso á predicar en ella con el aparato acostumbrado, leia por el libro á los indios la doctrina ó sermón que le parecía convenirles, porque leia expeditamente su lengua." (697)
Toral, Fr. Francisco de	"obispo que fué de Yucatan, supo primero que otro alguno la lengua popoloca de Tecamachalco, y en ella hizo arte y vocabulario, y otras obras doctrinales." (552) "Supo también la mexicana." (788)
Villalpando, Fr. Luis de	"el primero que supo la lengua de aquella tierra [Yucatan] y que hizo arte y vocabulario en ella" (382)

* When the reference does not mention a specific language, it seems understood that Mendieta generally referred to Nahuatl ("la lengua Mexicana").

NOTES

INTRODUCTION

1. The broad term "Islamic community" refers here not only to Muslims but also to *Moriscos* (i.e., baptized individuals of Islamic descent and sometimes their children, even if not baptized). Though eastern Christians had spoken Arabic for centuries, Philip and some leading churchmen linked the language with Islam.

2. Here and throughout the book, my references to "the Spanish Church" or to "Spanish religious leaders" include both clerics and the Spanish monarch. Given that the monarchy exercised significant influence over the Church in Spain, I often refer to the king as part of "the Church" or as a "religious leader."

3. I resist using "language policy" throughout this book. The term implies a certain coherence that did not exist in the sixteenth-century Spanish kingdoms. What one might describe as the language policy of the Church and Crown actually consisted of a scattered set of references in a range of documents. Neither the Church nor the Crown had a unified policy, so to speak. Instead, individual authorities developed ad hoc practices, suited to specific situations. Clerics' use of several different language practices arguably contradicts the famous statement made by Spain's foremost Renaissance grammarian, Antonio Nebrija, who called language an instrument of empire. See Nebrija, *Gramática castellana*. See also Pastor, *Apologias de la lengua castellana*, cited in Burke, *Languages and Communities*, 18.

4. I use "multilingual" here in the simple sense of describing something that contains many languages.

5. On "interior missions" in Spain, see Rico Callado, "Misiones interiores," 109–29.

6. See Sandoval, *Treatise on Slavery*, 44–45. Learning Amerindian languages did not present quite the same challenge. European clerics could learn indigenous languages in the Americas through contact and collaboration with members of native communities.

7. For an introduction to the historiography on Afro-Mexicans, see Vinson, "Afro-Mexican History," 1–14. Vinson notes that colonial travel writings described Africans as having a corrupting influence on society in New Spain. Thus it may be that missionaries generally lacked facility with African languages for another reason, beyond the obstacle of slave masters limiting contact between priests and Africans: some clerics might have believed that the evangelization of Native Americans constituted a worthier effort than a campaign directed at Africans, who as people of the Old World had, in theory, already had a chance to embrace Christianity and rejected it.

8. On the languages of medieval Jews, see Gallego, "Languages of Medieval Iberia," 118–19. On the study of Hebrew scripture, see Thompson, *Strife of Tongues*. On vernacular Bibles in Spain, see Fernández López, *Lectura y prohibición*.

9. Wiegers, *Islamic Literature*, 1. Vernacular Arabic (*algarabía*) differed from

the classical Arabic of literary and religious texts.

10. Campbell, *American Indian Languages*, 156–69. See also McQuown, "Indigenous Languages," 501. Cited in Campbell, *Historical Linguistics*, 157.

11. Though "Morisco" referred to a new Christian of Islamic descent, they encompassed a wide range of religious identities. On the use of Arabic and Castilian among Granada's Moriscos, see Coleman, *Creating Christian Granada*, 66–67.

12. See the appendix for the names of several sixteenth-century Franciscan friars who learned Amerindian languages.

13. García-Arenal, "Religious Identity," 495–528. See also El Alaoui, *Jésuites, Morisques et Indiens.*

14. See, for example, Burkhart, *Slippery Earth*; Coleman, *Creating Christian Granada*; and Domínguez Ortiz and Vincent, *Historia de los moriscos*. For a detailed examination of the religious and intellectual history of sixteenth-century Spain highlighting initial interest in Renaissance humanism followed by a decline, see Bataillon, *Erasme et l'Espagne*. For a revision of this history, see Homza, *Religious Authority*.

15. In this vein, some of the notable work in English includes Bilinkoff, *Ávila of Saint Teresa*; Christian, *Local Religion*; Coleman, *Creating Christian Granada*; Ehlers, *Between Christians and Moriscos*; Kamen, *Spanish Inquisition*; Nalle, *God in La Mancha*; Poska, *Regulating the People*; and Schwartz, *All Can Be Saved.*

16. See, for example, the work of Ginzburg, *Cheese and the Worms*, originally published in Italian in 1976. Ginzburg's work influenced an entire field of study known as microhistory, examining the day-to-day lives of "common" men and women who for years were considered either lost to history or not worthy of close study as individuals. Ginzburg and many other scholars have used records such as Inquisition trials as windows into the lives of these individuals. For another influential examination of religious history "from below," see Delumeau, *Catholicism Between Luther and Voltaire*, originally published in French in 1971.

17. For a survey that emphasizes continuity in the postconquest period of central Mexico, see Lockhart, *Nahuas After the Conquest*. Among the many excellent works that have revised traditional views of European-indigenous relations and appreciated both European and indigenous contributions to colonial Latin American societies, see, for example, Burkhart, *Slippery Earth*; Clendinnen, *Ambivalent Conquests*; Gruzinski, *Conquest of Mexico*; MacCormack, *Religion in the Andes*; Restall, *Maya World*; and others. For a survey of some of these works and others, see Wasserman-Soler, "Language and Communication," 491–502.

18. For instance, when addressing the trial of the Spanish primate and archbishop Bartolomé Carranza, even the most recent and revisionist studies of the Inquisition take little interest in the theological justifications for the trial, insinuating that the institution's leaders had only personal and political reasons for their actions. Accordingly, Lu Ann Homza has noted, "The best scholarship on the matter insists that there were no substantial theological reasons for Carranza's prosecution." Homza, *Spanish Inquisition*, 194. For examples, see Tellechea Idígoras, *Arzobispo Carranza* and Kamen, *Spanish Inquisition*. With little work in English, scholarship on inquisitors themselves remains largely the domain of Spanish, French, and Italian scholars. For more on this gap in Spanish historiography, see Lynn, *Between Court and Confessional*. Other recent studies on the Inquisition include Galván Rodríguez, *Inquisidor General*; Moreno, *Invención de*

la inquisición; Pastore, *Vangelo e la spada*; Rodríguez Besné, *Consejo de la Suprema Inquisición*; Pérez Villanueva and Escandell Bonet, *Historia de la Inquisición*; and Bethencourt, *L'Inquisition à l'époque moderne*. Studies of specific tribunals include Dedieu, *L'administration de la foi*; and García-Cárcel, *Herejía y sociedad*.

19. García-Arenal, "Moriscos e indios," 153–75. For similar themes, see Garrido Aranda, *Organización de la Iglesia*; Garrido Aranda, *Moriscos e indios*; and El Alaoui, *Jésuites, Morisques et Indiens*. According to Garrido Aranda, the first to bring to light the possibility of continuity between the *Reconquista* and the conquest of America was Sánchez Albornoz, *España*.

20. Among these works are Broggio, *Evangelizzare il mondo*; Clossey, *Salvation and Globalization*; and El Alaoui, *Jésuites, Morisques et Indiens*.

21. Concerning language, El Alaoui notes that Catholic churchmen in America accomplished the ambitious goal of using indigenous languages for evangelizing the native peoples. In Spain, they abandoned the parallel effort of using Arabic among the Moriscos. El Alaoui, *Jésuites, Morisques et Indiens*, 165. He also sees similarities between the Crown's policy for the Moriscos and its approach in America, noting a shift from Arabic and indigenous languages to advocating Castilian. El Alaoui, *Jésuites, Morisques et Indiens*, 13–14.

22. The closest work is Heath, *Telling Tongues*. Heath's work focuses on Mexico, primarily in the postindependence period.

23. Garrido Aranda recognizes some important differences between Moriscos and Amerindians, noting for instance that the former had some exposure to Christianity while the latter had none prior to 1492. Nonetheless, he concludes that the individuals who led the evangelization of Moriscos and indigenous peoples had "more or less homogeneous mentalities." Garrido Aranda, *Moriscos e indios*, 30–31. El Alaoui, similarly, argues that the Jesuits in Spain and in America used the "same methods, adapted to the idiosyncrasies of each people" (*Jesuites, Morisques et Indiens*, 301).

24. These findings counter claims that the evangelization of Native Americans occurred largely through Hispanization. See, for example, García-Arenal, "Religious Dissent," 901; and Garrido Aranda, *Moriscos e indios*, 25–26, 61.

25. The life and work of the saint and biblical scholar continue to interest modern scholars. A few recent English-language monographs include Cain and Loessl, *Jerome of Stridon*; Lifshitz, *Name of the Saint*; and Williams, *Monk and the Book*.

26. For the recommendations made at the councils, see *Disciplinary Decrees*, ed. H. J. Schroeder, Fourth Lateran Council, Canons 9 and 11. On language study in medieval Aragon, see Vose, *Dominicans, Muslims and Jews*, 104–15.

27. Several years before the publication of Luther's New Testament, Desiderius Erasmus had called for the translation of scripture into the vernacular. See Erasmus, "Paraclesis." Prior to the sixteenth century, medieval reformers such as Peter Waldo, John Wycliffe, and others had advocated similar goals.

28. *Council of Trent*, ed. Waterworth, Fourth Session, Decree Concerning the Edition, and the Use, of the Sacred Books.

29. One famous vernacular Bible is the Douay-Rheims version, a Catholic translation of the Latin Vulgate into English. Its first edition of the New Testament dates to 1582. See *Vulgate Bible*, ed., Edgar and Kinney. In Spain, however, Inquisition authorities looked with more suspicion on the translation of the Bible into the vernacular. On Spanish attitudes toward Christian scripture in the vernacular, see Fernández López, *Lectura y prohibición*.

30. *Council of Trent*, ed. Waterworth, Twenty-Fourth Session, Decree on Reformation, chapter 7.

31. The topic of vernacular scripture has been discussed in detail elsewhere. Fernández López, *Lectura y prohibición.* See also Nesvig, "Epistemological Politics," 165–201.

32. Febvre and Martin, *Coming of the Book*, 182.

CHAPTER 1

Selections of this chapter are published in Wasserman-Soler, "True Threat." The chapter title uses "Spanish" to refer to the Castilian language. Residents of the sixteenth-century Spanish kingdoms had other Romance vernaculars besides Castilian, including Catalan, Galician, Ladino, and Valencian. Arabic and Basque also had many speakers, though Arabic posed a different problem, examined in chapters 2 and 3.

1. On the infamy of the Carranza trial and selections from the original sources, see Homza, *Spanish Inquisition*, 194. On Valdés's prohibition of vernacular texts, see González Novalín, *Inquisidor general Fernando de Valdés*, 274–75.

2. In addition to the 1559 Index, Valdés published in 1554 an edict prohibiting various Bibles. Madrid, Archivo Histórico Nacional (cited hereafter as AHN), Inquisición, Legajo 4426, n. 32. The impulse to produce vernacular religious aids for people without formal education also occurred in Catholic areas outside of Spain. See, for example, the work of Eliano, *Doctrina christiana*. Eliano's work was translated into several languages.

3. Dalmases, "San Francisco de Borja," 64. Quoted in Kamen, *Spanish Inquisition*, 123.

4. On the popularity of Granada's book, see Whinnom, "Problem of the Best-Seller," 189–98. On the life of Granada, see Huerga, *Luis de Granada*; and for Carranza, see Tellechea Idígoras, *Arzobispo Carranza*; and Jericó Bermejo, *Bartolomé Carranza de Miranda.* Jericó Bermejo notes, however, that neither his work nor Tellechea Idígoras's is a biography of Carranza. For Ávila, see Roldán-Figueroa, *Ascetic Spirituality*; and John of Ávila, *Audi, Filia.* On Borja, see Ryan, *Jesuita secreto.*

5. While the revised edition of Granada's book did not find a place on subsequent versions of the *Index librorum prohibitorum*, the original edition of his book remained prohibited. For the Spanish Index of Prohibited Books, see Martínez de Bujanda, *Index des livres interdits.*

6. Ginzburg, *Cheese and the Worms*; Nalle, *Mad for God.*

7. Many recent works of Spanish historiography—too many to mention—fall into this category, but perhaps the most renowned is Kamen's *Spanish Inquisition*, published originally in 1965 and revised most recently in 2014.

8. For more on inquisitors, see Lynn, *Between Court and Confessional*; Lynn, "Was Adam the First Heretic?," 184–210; and Edwards, *Torquemada and the Inquisitors.*

9. Kamen, *Spanish Inquisition*, 132–33.

10. Pinto Crespo, *Inquisición y control ideológico*, 19–21, 25–26, 293.

11. See, for example, Rawlings, *Spanish Inquisition*; and Kamen, *Spanish Inquisition.*

12. Huerga, *Luis de Granada.*

13. For a transcription of the 1525 Edict, see the appendix in Márquez, *Alumbrados*, 273–83. On the alumbrados, see Hamilton, *Heresy and Mysticism*; Huerga, *Historia de los alumbrados*; Márquez, *Alumbrados*; and Fowler, "Illuminating the Empire." The charges made against the alumbrados in later years did not exactly match the ones made in the early to mid-sixteenth century.

14. On Granada's support of the Jesuits, see Huerga, *Luis de Granada*, 96–97.

15. Huerga, *Luis de Granada*, 139, 148–50. See also Kamen, *Spanish Inquisition*, 88–89, 112; and Kamen, *Philip of Spain*, 314.

16. For the work in question, see Carranza, *Comentarios*. On personal enmity as the reason for prohibiting Carranza's work, see Kamen, *Spanish Inquisition*, 160–61; and Kamen, *Disinherited*, 122–23. On Carranza's efforts in Tudor England, see Edwards and Truman, *Reforming Catholicism*.

17. On Carranza's critique of Valdés, see Pastore, *Vangelo e la spada*, 229–44. See also Tellechea Idígoras, *Arzobispo Carranza*. For Carranza's argument on the necessity of episcopal residence, see Carranza, *Controuersia de necessaria residentia*. Carranza's critique of Valdés and Valdés's response are available in Tellechea Idígoras, *Fray Bartolomé Carranza*. See documents 9, 11, 12, and 13. On Carranza and the influence of jurists in the Inquisition, see Tellechea Idígoras, "Dos documentos inéditos," 525–44. Cited in Pastore, *Vangelo e la spada*, 229.

18. Pastore, *Vangelo e la spada*, 229–34.

19. Carranza's catechism had a place on the 1559 Index, and Cano died in 1560. On the life of Melchior Cano and a wealth of related primary source material, see Sanz y Sanz, *Melchor Cano; cuestiones fundamentales*; and Caballero, *Sr. D. fray Melchor Cano*. On the college of San Gregorio de Valladolid, see Arriaga, *Historia del colegio*. On Carranza's ecclesiastical nominations, see Kamen, *Spanish Inquisition*, 160. On Carranza's positions at the Colegio de San Gregorio, see Jericó Bermejo, *Bartolomé Carranza de Miranda*, 50.

20. Tellechea Idígoras, *Fray Bartolomé Carranza*, vol. 1, documents 12–13. Carranza also noted that Valdés supported Cano's finances and ambitions.

21. For the argument that Valdés sought to regain his political standing, see Martínez Millán, *Felipe II*, 64. On Valdés's support of Philip's military efforts, see González Novalín, *Fernando de Valdés*, 288. On Philip's agreement with Inquisitor Valdés, see Kamen, *Philip of Spain*, 73.

22. For the Roman portion of Carranza's Inquisition trial, see Tellechea Idígoras, *Proceso romano del Arzobispo Carranza*. On the conflict between the Inquisition and the papacy, see Kamen, *Inquisition and Society*, 158. On Philip's relationship with Carranza, see Kamen, *Philip of Spain*, 152.

23. On literacy in sixteenth-century Spain, see Nalle, *God in La Mancha*, xvi. On Inquisition concerns about foreign religious texts, see AHN, Inquisición, libros 574–75. An examination of Libro 575 of the Suprema (the register of notable issues and provisions for the years 1555 to 1567) reveals documents that attest to the transmission of heterodox religious writings from Germany and the Low Countries to Spain. While Libro 574 (1540–55) includes no mention of the need to exercise vigilance especially over German or Dutch books, between 1555 and 1567 the Suprema produced at least five provisions referring specifically to texts coming to Spanish ports from either Germany or the Low Countries. The Suprema instructed local tribunals to produce edicts requiring both the confiscation of these books and the punishment of those who brought them to Spain. While the Suprema directed local tribunals to prohibit owners from importing books from Germany and the Low Countries until the Inquisition had examined and approved them, there are indications that efforts to suppress the propagation of German and Dutch heresies were unsuccessful. Documents from the 1555 to 1567 period indicate that the required edicts had not been produced by some local tribunals and that heterodox books had moved beyond the ports and into Spanish bookstores. On Spanish Protestant communities, see Thomas, *Represión del protestantismo*.

24. Carranza, *Comentarios*, 1:136, 433 (on faith without works); 1:182 (on clerical

mediation); 2:166–67, 186 (on the dignity of the seven sacraments); 2:175 (on ecclesiastical defense of ceremonies); 1:136; 2:105 (on mocking Church ceremonies); 1:550–51 (on keeping the spirit and letter of the law).

25. Carranza, *Comentarios*, 1:106.

26. Jedin, *History of the Council*, 2:67–72; Carranza, *Comentarios*, 1:120–21.

27. Carranza, *Comentarios*, 1:114–15; Cano, "Censura," 536.

28. Carranza, *Comentarios*, 1:114–15.

29. Ibid., 1:126.

30. Cano, "Censura," 536–37.

31. Carranza, *Comentarios*, 1:115; Cano, "Censura," 536–37.

32. Lea, *Inquisition of Spain*, 3:489. Substantial scholarship exists regarding Inquisition attitudes toward women's religious practices. See, for example, Giles, *Women in the Inquisition*. See also Francisca de los Apóstoles, *Inquisition of Francisca*; Kagan, *Lucrecia's Dreams*; and Weber, *Teresa of Ávila*. On Inquisition practices toward the "uneducated," see, for instance, Ginzburg, *Cheese and the Worms*, and Nalle, *Mad for God*.

33. Unlike the case of Carranza, no official Inquisition censure exists for Granada's *Libro de la oración*. Melchior Cano does, however, mention Granada's book briefly within his censure of Carranza's *Comentarios*. Based on Inquisition concerns with Carranza's work, as well as other Inquisition documents, we can assemble a set of concerns that Inquisition authorities probably identified in Granada's work.

34. Cano, "Censura," 597.

35. Ibid.; Luis, *Libro de la oración*, 15; Eimeric, *Directorium Inquisitorum*, 230–31. For translations of his work, see *Manuale dell'Inquisitore*, ed., Cammilleri; and *Manuel des inquisiteurs*, ed., Sala-Molins.

36. Luis, *Libro de la oración*, 255; Márquez, *Los Alumbrados*, 274.

37. Luis, *Libro de la oración*, 320; Cano, "Censura," 597.

38. Luis, *Libro de la oración*, 27; Cano, "Censura," 593, 597.

39. On prayer's power to transfigure souls, see Luis, *Libro de la oración*, 23. On reaching all good through prayer, see pp. 254–55. On "the perfect prayer," see p. 299. On the "democratizing" of mental prayer, see Oberman, *Harvest*, 341.

40. González Novalín, *Fernando de Valdés*, 274.

41. Cano, *De locis theologicis*. For a Spanish translation, see Cano, *De locis theologicis*, ed. Belda Plans.

42. Cano, *De locis theologicis*, 21. See book 2, chap. 6.

43. Cano, *De locis theologicis*, 29. See book 2, chap. 8.

44. Cano, "Censura," 536; Belda Plans, *Lugares teológicos*, 225.

45. Belda Plans, *Lugares teológicos*, 229. Related to Cano's point on the insolence of the heretics, see Cano, *De locis theologicis*, 364. See book 12, chap. 6.

46. Cano, *De locis theologicis*, 365. See book 12, chap. 6.

47. Lea, *Inquisition of Spain*, 3:437–51.

48. Kamen, *Spanish Inquisition*, 114. See also Lea, *Inquisition of Spain*, 490.

49. Martínez de Bujanda, *Index des livres interdits*, 6:879–80.

50. Kamen, *Spanish Inquisition*, 115.

51. AHN, Inquisición, legajo 4436, n. 35.

52. AHN, Inquisición, legajo 4426, n. 26. The Spanish Inquisition had three tribunals in the Americas (in present-day Mexico, Peru, and Colombia). Because the Inquisition did not have a tribunal in Hispaniola, Angulo may have corresponded directly with the Crown regarding Inquisition affairs on the island. He also may have served under the jurisdiction of another Inquisition official but wrote to Philip in order to settle a dispute.

53. AHN, Inquisición, legajo 4436, n. 39. *Licenciado* could refer to a lawyer or to a university graduate in general. Montoya received word of the "three substances"

problem from the Dominican friar Alonso de Sepúlveda.

54. AHN, Inquisición, legajo 4444, n. 13.

55. AHN, Inquisición, legajo 4436, n. 56. The title given in the document is presumably not the actual title, since the book was available only in Italian.

56. AHN, Inquisición, legajo 4444, n. 9. Curiel may have been a censor of the Inquisition, but the sources do not make it clear.

57. Carranza, *Comentarios*, 1:114.

58. Homza, *Spanish Inquisition*, 221–31. The instructions include protections for defendants who might have been the victims of retaliation by either common men or inquisitors themselves.

59. The fact that Quiroga exonerated Louis of Granada, John of Ávila, and Francis Borgia (three among the most prominent names included on the 1559 Index) but not Bartolomé Carranza highlights the more politicized nature of the Carranza case.

60. Martínez de Bujanda, *Index des livres interdits*, 5:634.

61. Thomas, *Represión del protestantismo*, 377. See also Kamen, *Spanish Inquisition*, 110–11.

CHAPTER 2

Selections of this chapter are published in Patricia Giménez-Eguibar and Daniel I. Wasserman-Soler, "*La mala algarabía:* Church, Monarchy, and the Arabic Language in 16th-Century Spain," *Medieval History Journal* 14, no. 2 (2011). For comments on this chapter, I am grateful to the participants of the 2013 meeting of the Pre-Modern Spanish History Association of the Midwest (PSHAM), held at the University of Notre Dame: Pam Beattie, Jeff Bowman, Grace Coolidge, Remie Constable, Tom Devaney, Karen Graubart, Encarnación Juárez, John Moscatiello, Maria Pluta, Bretton Rodriguez, Gretchen Starr-Lebeau, Valentina Tikoff, Belén Vicéns, and Kristy Wilson Bowers.

1. Coleman, *Creating Christian Granada*, 181–84. Alpujarras refers to a region in the present-day provinces of Granada and Almería. Although it is a mountainous area, the mountains themselves are called not the Alpujarras but the Sierra Nevada. I thank Encarnación Juárez for making this distinction.

2. Domínguez Ortiz and Vincent, *Historia de los moriscos*, 32. For a study of the individuals who favored the conservation of the Arabic language in Spain, see García-Arenal, "Religious Identity of the Arabic Language." On Ignacio de las Casas's methods of catechizing the Moriscos, see El Alaoui, *Jésuites, Morisques et Indiens.*

3. *Capitulaciones para la entrega*, ed. Garrido Atienza. See also Harvey, *Muslims in Spain*, 25.

4. Coleman, *Creating Christian Granada*, 83–84. For more on Talavera, see Iannuzzi, *Poder de la palabra.* On Talavera's support of persuasion over force, see Talavera, *Catholica impugnacion del heretico libello.* On Talavera's Ávila, see chapter 3 in Salomons, "1492 Reconsidered."

5. On this final point, see Garrido Aranda, *Organización de la Iglesia*; Garrido Aranda, *Moriscos e indios*; and Coleman, *Creating Christian Granada*, 2–3.

6. Talavera requested that his confessor, Pedro de Alcalá, produce an Arabic dictionary and grammar. In the book, Alcalá implied the existence of other Arabists who could have helped him in the production of the text but did not. See Alcalá, *Arte para ligeramente saber*, carta al lector. On Talavera's priests and interpreters, see García-Arenal, "Religious Identity of the Arabic Language," 500. For a translation of Núñez Muley, see Núñez Muley, *Memorandum*, 79. For the original text, see Garrad, "Original Memorial," 214–15. On Talavera's support for prayer in Arabic, see Núñez Muley, *Memorandum*,

80–81. See also Garrad, "Original Memorial," 215–16. On Talavera's methods of catechesis, see Talavera, "Instrucción del Arzobispo de Granada."

7. García-Arenal, "Religious Identity," 499–501.

8. Talavera, "Instrucción del Arzobispo de Granada."

9. Talavera, *Cartilla y doctrina en romance*. Records indicate that Talavera's cartillas may have circulated in Granada as early as 1498. Juan Varela also published them in Granada in 1508, and Jacobo Cromberger followed in Seville in 1512. If the cited texts survive, they are extremely rare. Wilkinson, *Iberian Books*; see also the website of the Universal Short-Title Catalog, http://www.ustc.ac.uk.

10. On Muslim dress and food, see Coleman, *Creating Christian Granada*, 63. On the new cathedral, see p. 88.

11. While Ayala encouraged the use of the language for sermons and confession, Talavera also permitted Arabic-language prayer books and books of psalms, as noted above.

12. Alcalá, *Arte para ligeramente saber*.

13. On Cisneros, see García Oro, *Cisneros* and others by the same author; see also Rummel, *Jiménez de Cisneros*. On the start of crypto-Islam in Spain, see Harvey, *Muslims in Spain*, 27–31.

14. Bernabé Pons and Rubiera Mata, "Lengua de mudéjares y moriscos"; García-Cárcel, "Estudio crítico del catecismo"; and García-Arenal, "Religious Identity." See also El Alaoui, *Jésuites, Morisques et Indiens*, 193, 202–16 and Coleman, *Creating Christian Granada*, 125, 176.

15. Núñez Muley, *Memorandum*, 80. See also Garrad, "Original Memorial," 215–16. I thank Claire Gilbert for highlighting the fact that printers continued to produce Alcalá's work well after the Cisneros visit. On the sixteenth-century works of Alcalá, see Wilkinson, *Iberian Books*; see also http://www.ustc.ac.uk.

16. The argument here parallels David Coleman's thesis that the creation of Christian Granada was not an event but a process. Coleman, *Creating Christian Granada*, 1.

17. Ibid., 37–40.

18. Ibid., 87.

19. Ibid., 119–20. Cf. Harvey, *Muslims in Spain*. Harvey argues that the assembly largely ignored the abuses of Moriscos.

20. Granada, Archivo de la Catedral de Granada, Reales Cédulas Carlos V, Libro 2, año 1526: fol. 70, published in Gallego y Burín and Gámir Sandoval, *Moriscos del reino de Granada*, doc. 31. I thank Patricia Giménez-Eguibar for pointing out this emphasis in the decree.

21. On the prohibition of Muslim names, see Granada, Archivo de la Iglesia Catedral de Granada, Reales Cédulas Carlos V, Libro 2, año 1526, fol. 70, published in Gallego y Burín and Sandoval, *Moriscos*, doc. 31. On the suspension of the edict, see Harvey, *Muslims in Spain*, 104–6 and Lea, *Moriscos of Spain*, 217–18.

22. Coleman, *Creating Christian Granada*, 87, 120–21.

23. Ibid., 90, 126–27.

24. Ibid., 127–28.

25. Torres Palomo, "Don Martín de Ayala," 510–13 and Torres Palomo, "Bartolomé Dorador y el árabe," 14–17. Cited in Garrido García, "Uso de la lengua árabe," 123–37. Ayala later would publish a bilingual Arabic-Castilian catechism as archbishop of Valencia; see chapter 3.

26. On Granada, see Coleman, *Creating Christian Granada*, 15. On Guadix, see Garrido García, "Guadix y su tierra," 74.

27. Madrid, Archivo Histórico Nacional (hereafter AHN), Consejos, Legajo 50.805, Caja 2, Constituciones sinodales de Guadix (hereafter "Synod of Guadix"). In prolegomena to the decrees of the Synod of Guadix, see the section entitled "Que se guarde en todo y por todo el sacro Concilio de Trento." On the Arabic requirement, see

fol. 2r. Cf. *Council of Trent*, ed. Waterworth, Twenty-Fourth Session, Decree on Reformation, chapter 7.

28. Pérez de Ayala, *Doctrina christiana, en lengua arauiga*. See the letter (epístola) at the start of the text. Chapter 3 includes further information on Ayala's work as archbishop of Valencia.

29. AHN, Consejos, leg. 50.805 (box 2), fol. 2v. The record of the Synod of Guadix is also available in print: Gallego y Burín and Gámir Sandoval, *Moriscos del reino de Granada*. It should be noted that although Ayala did not require the weekly delivery of sermons, his recommendation of having them on several important days throughout the liturgical year would have marked a substantial improvement from the pastoral situation in some parts of Spain during the previous century. For example, Lea once noted that the 1473 Council of Aranda required priests to celebrate Mass at least four times a year and bishops to celebrate Mass at least three times a year. See Lea, *History*, vol. 1, book 1, chap. 1, p. 10. Lea cites Valera, *Memorial de diversas hazañas* (Biblioteca Nacional de España, MS 1210).

30. *Council of Trent*, ed. Waterworth, Twenty-Fourth Session, Decree on Reformation, chapter 7. The emphasis is mine.

31. Although a sermon every week may not have been the norm in Spain, it does seem to have been the case in parts of Mexico, where some churchmen composed sermon collections for every Sunday of the year. Sermon collections from sixteenth-century Mexico include Juan de la Anunciación, *Sermonario en lengva mexicana*. The prolific Franciscan friar Maturino Gilberti authored a manuscript collection of sermons in P'urhépecha ("Sigvense vnos breves sermones en la lengua de Michuacan para cada domingo del año," Codex Ind 4), housed in the John Carter Brown Library. Cited in Gilberti, *Thesoro Spiritual*, ed. Márquez Joaquín. Bernardino de Sahagún also composed a collection of sermons, and while it focused on sermons for feast days, it included a total of fifty-four sermons, thus averaging approximately one per week. Sahagún, *Psalmodia Christiana*.

32. *Council of Trent*, ed. Waterworth, Twenty-Fourth Session, Decree on Reformation, chapter 7.

33. AHN, Consejos, leg. 50.805 (box 2), fol. 12.

34. Ibid., fols. 12r, 36v, 38r, and 67v.

35. Ibid., fols. 5v–6r. I thank Belén Vicéns Saiz for her comments on this translation and several of the following passages.

36. Ibid., fol. 22r.

37. Coleman, *Creating Christian Granada*, 145–49. On Guerrero, see also Herreros González, *Pedro Guerrero*; López Martín, *Imagen del obispo*; and Marín Ocete, *Arzobispo don Pedro Guerrero*. The archbishop of Granada should not be confused with another Pedro Guerrero, who served as bishop of Ugento (Italy) from 1599 to 1613.

38. Coleman, *Creating Christian Granada*, 145–53.

39. Ibid., 155.

40. AHN, Clero-Jesuitas, Libro 773, p. 3. In my experience, when documents refer to teaching reading or writing without specifying a language, then Castilian is implied.

41. Archivum Romanum Societatis Iesu (hereafter ARSI), Hispania 95, fol. 140r. Alfonso Ruiz to Diego Laínez, 31 August 1557. "Fuera de los p[adr]es ya dichos otro p[adr]e que sabe Arabigo ha continuado los sermones en arabigo en el albaizin que es el lugar donde estan los moriscos con mucho feruor, y aunque es comu[n]mente una gente muy endurescida, hase sentido mucho p[ro]uecho." In this context, "fervor" *might* refer to either religious piety or some kind of rebellious stirring. Covarrubias's 1611 *Tesoro de la lengua castellana* only offers "fervoroso, el fogoso, ferviente." Alfonso Ruiz's letter does not mention the

Arabic-language preacher by name, but it would appear to be Juan de Albotodo, whom several other letters acknowledge as the Arabic-language preacher of the Albaicín. Ruiz identifies this preacher as a primary influence in the story of two Moriscos who became very devout to Christianity and, in a July 1557 letter from Francisco de la Torre, describes the story of the same Moriscos, mentioning Albotodo as the influential preacher.

42. ARSI, Hispania 95, fol. 120r, Francisco de la Torre to Diego Laínez, 30 July 1557. Alfonso Ruiz narrates the same events in his August 1557 letter, cited above. According to Covarrubias's 1611 *Tesoro de la lengua castellana*, "Arrepe[n]tida sinifica [*sic*] algunas vezes la mugger Perdida, q[ue] conocie[n]do su yerro se arrepie[n] te, y se buelve a Dios: y de arrepe[n]tidas ay Monesterios de gra[n] Religio[n], y penite[n]cia en España, y en toda la Christiandad."

43. ARSI, Hispania 96, fol. 370r, NN, Granada to Laínez, 30 Jun 1559.

44. ARSI, Hispania 95, fol. 239v. We might wonder, though, whether Albotodo experienced such popularity among the prison community because of his knowledge of Arabic and his compelling nature as a preacher or rather because Islamic prisoners came to him with the hope that conversion to Christianity might bode well for them in the eyes of local authorities. This possibility did not escape the minds of contemporary Jesuits. One letter in 1563, for instance, relates the story of a prisoner whom the Jesuits did not wish to baptize because they suspected ulterior motives: "She asked for baptism [. . .] but because they believed that she did it only to leave the prison, they did not wish to baptize her then. After a few days, her illness became much worse and she told them to baptize her because she was dying and to do whatever they wanted with her because she only wanted to die a Christian. Then, they baptized her and took her to a hospital, where she lived for twenty days afterward, in great pain and without sleep. She would not go to sleep because she could not. She did not stop uttering the name of Jesus." ARSI, Hispania 100, fol. 128r. The inclusion of this woman's story and her requests for the sacraments may indicate merely that the Jesuits knew of potential objections to their methods of catechesis and that they eagerly sought to procure support for their work. However, it may also reveal that—unlike many campaigns to instruct Islamic communities in Christian doctrine—the Jesuits in the Albaicín employed methods that at least some Moriscos found persuasive.

45. ARSI, Hispania 98, fol. 155r, Pedro Navarro to Laínez, 29 Apr 1561: "Incepta autem est enarrari doctrina christiana mauris recens conversis in vinculis detentis sua vulgari lingua, quod deo optimo Maximo duce deinceps frequenter fiet, quidam in fratribus[?] qui discunt arabicam linguam ut dictum est, auspicatus est doctrinam christianam arabice interpretari, Alius pr[a]eterea pater festis diebus in plateam quondam contendit et colligens quos illic invenit et brevem oratiunculam habens, inde doctrinam canentes ad quamdam ecclesiam ducit ubi eos doctrina[m] christianam docet." The Jesuit brothers mentioned here did not include Albotodo, who was a priest ("father"). After mentioning the brothers who studied Arabic, Navarro's letter also refers to a priest ("Alius [. . .] pater") who "spoke passionately in the street on feast days, assembling those who came there and having a brief prayer. From there, he led them, reciting doctrine, toward a certain church where he taught them Christian doctrine." Navarro's letter is unclear whether this Jesuit actually preached in Arabic. While his inclusion of the anecdote immediately following the discussion of Arabic preaching may suggest that he did use their language, Navarro

may also have just included him in the letter as one of the number of preachers engaging in catechesis—regardless of language. Worthy of note in Navarro's letter is his choice of words in describing the intentions of the aforementioned Jesuit brother. In utilizing the relatively uncommon verb *auspicari* (i.e., to take signs, seek omens, make a ceremonial start, portend, begin favorably), Navarro may have wished to underline that preaching in Arabic constituted no small feat, as it certainly was not a widely practiced approach, owing perhaps to two main reasons: first, the difficulty of mastering a foreign language (especially one outside of the Romance family) and second, using that language for a different religious purpose than that with which its speakers were familiar.

46. Chapter 5 demonstrates, in part, that some ministers who lacked fluency in Amerindian languages nonetheless learned to read prepared texts (e.g., sermons, manuals for administering the sacraments) and thus were able to use the indigenous languages on a basic level. Because Martín Pérez de Ayala's bilingual catechism contained Arabic written in Roman letters, clerics who lacked fluency in Arabic still might have used the bilingual text to instruct the Moriscos in basic doctrine (e.g., the Our Father, the Ten Commandments).

47. Coleman, *Creating Christian Granada*, 159. For Ruiz's letter, see ARSI, Hispania 95, fol. 140. For the letter to Laínez, see ARSI, Hispania 96, fol. 370r. The reference to Bautista implies that he delivered sermons in Castilian because the following line refers to the Arabic-language sermons of Albotodo.

48. Roa, *Historia*, 155. For more details on the Jesuit apostolate to the Moriscos, see Medina, "Compañía de Jesús." See also *Historia del Colegio*, ed. Béthencourt and Olivares.

49. Roa, *Historia*, 156–57.

50. Ibid., 156.

51. See, for instance, Coleman, *Creating Christian Granada*, 156, and Álvarez Rodríguez, "Casa de la Doctrina," 231–46.

52. ARSI, Hispania 100, fol. 127v, Pedro Navarro to Laínez, 30 Apr 1563. The claim that Morisco parents wanted their children to attend the Jesuit school seems surprising given that an overwhelming number of contemporary sources describe Spain's Islamic communities as evincing a strong aversion to Christianity. Can we know if Morisco parents actually wanted their children to attend Jesuit schools or if Jesuit correspondents merely exaggerated the truth in order to concoct a tale of success? Examining other contemporary sources can help illuminate the question. Over the course of the sixteenth century, Church and Crown authorities held several assemblies and councils to discuss the religious conversion of Islamic communities and how to provide instruction in Christian doctrine, especially for Valencia's Moriscos. The next chapter will discuss the assemblies of 1587, 1591, and 1595, but prior to those *juntas*, as they were called, authorities held other meetings in 1525, 1548, 1564, 1567–68, and 1573. In many cases, the individuals present (generally bishops, Inquisition officials, and/or Crown officials) used a similar reason to justify their coming together: plans for the instruction of the Moriscos had not been properly executed in the past. Why, one wonders, did they continue to meet if the same problem(s) of catechesis remained? I submit that their motivation to continue addressing the same fraught subject lay—at least in part—in their knowledge of some successful efforts to catechize the Moriscos. The work of the Jesuits in the Albaicín around midcentury appears to be one example. Indeed, Archbishop Juan de Ribera's almost exclusive reliance upon Jesuits in sixteenth-century Valencia may underscore the notion that authorities outside of Granada

considered the Jesuits of Granada as relatively effective in their apostolate among the Moriscos. On Ribera's reliance upon the Jesuits, see Robres Lluch, *San Juan de Ribera*, 403. Though Jesuits encountered much opposition within the Church, contemporaries outside of the Society appear to corroborate the claims of success made in Jesuit letters.

53. Roa, *Historia*, 156.

54. *Historia del Colegio*, ed. Béthencourt and Olivares, 187–88. The eulogy of Albotodo's fellow Jesuit, Jerónimo Mur, by contrast, includes several references to his fluency in Arabic. ARSI, Historia Societatis Iesu 177, vol. 2, no. 93, fol. 201. I thank Claire Gilbert for providing this information.

55. ARSI, Hispania 96, fol. 370r.

56. Ibid., fol. 370v. The rhetoric in this letter, comparing Granada's Islamic community to the Indies and characterizing it as a new conquest, highlights the distinctive nature of the Jesuit effort to catechize the Moriscos. The Crown, as well as many secular and regular clerics, expressed much more interest in the catechesis of Native Americans than in the Moriscos, as chapters 4 and 5 will demonstrate. But a number of Jesuits—perhaps because of their enthusiasm as a new religious order—seem to have viewed the simultaneous campaigns more as parallel efforts. On the similarity between approaches advocated by the Jesuits José de Acosta for the New World and Ignacio de las Casas for the Moriscos, see El Alaoui, *Jésuites, Morisques et Indiens*. Whether the hope that Morisco children would teach Arabic to Jesuits actually transpired remains unclear and probably unlikely, given the paucity of references to Arabic-speaking Jesuits (other than Albotodo).

57. ARSI, Hispania 98, fol. 281v, Pedro Navarro to Laínez, 30 Aug 1561. While Navarro's use of *morisquitos* may convey condescension, I have chosen not to reflect this interpretation in my translation, using instead a more literal definition (Morisco boys). Part of a newly established religious order, the Jesuits who worked among the Moriscos lived in Granada for a relatively short period (approximately ten years). They assumed the task of catechizing a people who some Catholic clerics believed impossible to convert. Given the Jesuits' status as a new and energetic religious order, their relatively short time working with Spain's Islamic communities, and their active choice to adopt a challenging mission, I am inclined to think that Navarro would not have intended to convey condescension toward the Moriscos. For the second passage, see ARSI, Hispania 100, fol. 127v, Pedro Navarro to Laínez, 30 Apr 1563.

58. ARSI, Hispania 100, fol. 127v, Pedro Navarro to Laínez, 30 Apr 1563.

59. Their 1565 recommendation applied to the archdiocese of Granada and not to Spain as a whole. This regional difference may have allowed Valencia's archbishop, Martín Pérez de Ayala, to publish his Castilian-Arabic catechism in 1566.

60. O'Malley, *Trent*, 196–97, 259–60.

61. Coleman, *Creating Christian Granada*, 147–48, 179–80. Coleman suggests that the recommendation to prohibit Arabic signifies a shift in Guerrero's pastoral approach. Guerrero abandoned "the versatile approach of his friend and advisor John of Ávila." In this line of thought, his earlier work had included modest reform through visitations; collaboration with the Jesuits; and support for the colleges of Santa Catalina and San Cecilio as training grounds for future priests. Following his return from Trent, Guerrero appears to have changed, in no small part, as a result of battles waged at the Council of Trent.

62. Many of the sources from the 1565 Provincial Council of Granada are available in print: Marín Ocete, "Concilio provincial de Granada," 23–178. For the

quoted passage, see Simancas (Spain), Archivo General de Simancas (hereafter A.G.S.), Estado, Leg. 148: Doc. 113, fol. 1v. When examining the original source, the reader cannot help but notice the interesting use of *algaravía*, *arábigo*, *romance*, and *alxamía*. Algaravía and arábigo both refer to Arabic. The first term, however, refers not only to Arabic but also to an unintelligible language, confused shouting by many people, a poor manner of speaking, or a state of disarray. The use of *algaravía* seems to highlight two things: first, to the untrained ears of many Spanish Christians, Arabic sounded confusing, and second, the use of *algaravía* over *árabe* conveys a pejorative tone, perhaps underlining a belief that Arabic was less linguistically sophisticated than Castilian. Why both terms appear in the document remains unclear. One could argue that the bishops sought primarily to do away with the Moriscos' vernacular Arabic, as opposed to a more literary Arabic. See García-Arenal and Rodríguez Mediano, "Sacred History, Sacred Languages," 138. Additionally, the 1526 decree (to which the bishops refer) appears to have used *árabe* to refer to Arabic, while the 1567 decree used *algaravía* on more than one occasion, perhaps indicating an increased level of frustration on the part of authorities in later years. Finally, what distinction—if any—the bishops intend by referring to both *alxamia* and *romançe* remains unclear.

63. A.G.S., Estado, Legajo 148, Doc. 132. While the bishops at Granada addressed the linguistic medium for teaching doctrine, they did not specifically address sermons or the use of Arabic interpreters.

64. Ibid., Doc. 113, fol. 2v.

65. Ibid., Doc. 113, fol. 1r.

66. AHN, Clero-Jesuitas, Libro 773, p. 3. See also Medina, "Compañía de Jesús," 71. For more on Guerrero's relationship with the Society of Jesus, see López Martín, "Arzobispo de Granada," 453–98.

67. Coleman, *Creating Christian Granada*, 181–82; Medina, "Compañía de Jesús," n. 323. The Jesuits' efforts did indeed continue after the 1567 decree, though not for long, given the Morisco expulsions.

68. A print copy of the decree is available in Madrid, Biblioteca Marqués de Valdecilla, Universidad Complutense de Madrid, BH DER 36 (3): fol. 6r. The manuscript decree is available in the Archivo General de Simancas. A.G.S., R.G.S., 1566, 11, 17. Cited in *Los Moriscos: Españoles Trasterrados*.

69. Madrid, Biblioteca Marqués de Valdecilla, Universidad Complutense de Madrid, BH DER 36 (3): fol. 6. A careful reading of the passages above reveals that Philip did not explicitly prohibit the use of Arabic for preaching. Rather, the decree focused on language use among the Moriscos, thus suggesting that Philip viewed Arabic as dangerous not only because of the language's association with Islam but also because of the particular individuals who spoke it. Put another way, Arabic presented a greater danger when spoken by the Moriscos than when employed as a tool by Christian preachers and interpreters. Albotodo may have continued to deliver Arabic sermons after the decree. At least one source counts his sermons as one of the Jesuit ministries that continued until 1569, when the Jesuits left Granada, following the expulsion of the Moriscos from that kingdom. See AHN, Clero-Jesuitas, Libro 773, p. 3.

70. For the translation used here, see Núñez Muley, *Memorandum*, 92. For the original passage, see Garrad, "Original Memorial," 221. For a modern argument taking its departure from Núñez-Muley, see García-Arenal, "Religious Identity."

71. Guadix (Spain), Archivo Histórico Diocesano, caja 83, legajo 11, pieza C, fol. 1v. For the transcribed document, see Garrido Garcia, "Uso de la lengua árabe," 134–36.

72. At the time of the Arabic prohibition, a large portion of Granada's Moriscos knew Castilian to varying degrees. The fact that many already had started to adopt the language may have served as another reason many churchmen thought it unnecessary to attempt to use Arabic, thus adding a practical dimension to their stance.

CHAPTER 3

Selections of this chapter are published in Patricia Giménez-Eguibar and Daniel I. Wasserman-Soler, "*La mala algarabía:* Church, Monarchy, and the Arabic Language in 16th-Century Spain," *Medieval History Journal* 14, no. 2 (2011).

1. Navarra met with Martín de Córdoba y Mendoza, O.P., the recently appointed bishop of Tortosa (1560–74), Inquisitor Miranda, and the duke of Maqueda, the viceroy and captain general of Valencia. Arigita y Lasa, *Señor Don Francisco de Navarra*, 292–301. See also Boronat y Barrachina, *Moriscos*, 1:229–30. For documentation of the assembly, see García-Arenal, *Moriscos*, 110–11.

2. García-Arenal, *Moriscos*, 110–11.

3. Bernabé Pons and Rubiera Mata, "Lengua de mudéjares y moriscos," 599–632. On the culture of derision toward Moriscos, see García-Arenal, "Religious Dissent," 888–920.

4. AHN, Inquisición, libro 936, fols. 18r, 68v–70v.

5. AHN, Inquisición, libro 937, fols. 28r, 71r, and 316v–17v.

6. AHN, Inquisición, libro 937, fols. 316v–17v.

7. Ehlers, *Between Christians and Moriscos*, 18–21.

8. Pérez de Ayala, "Discurso de la vida." Among the few sustained studies of Ayala is Miralles, *Concepto de tradición*.

9. Pérez de Ayala, *Doctrina christiana, en lengua arauiga*. Austria and Ramírez de Haro, *Instructions*. Austria served as bishop of Brixen (Italy), 1526–38; archbishop of Valencia, 1538–44; and bishop of Liège (Belgium), 1544–57. During part of his term as archbishop of Valencia, he was also coadjutor bishop of Liège. Ramírez de Haro served as apostolic commissioner for the reform of the Moriscos in Valencia prior to various episcopal appointments; Charles V named him as bishop of Orense, 1537–39; Ciudad Rodrigo, 1539–41; Calahorra y La Calzada, 1541–43; and Segovia, 1543–49. For a discussion of the religious instruction of Spanish Islamic communities during the first half of the sixteenth century, see Ducharme, "De Talavera a Ramírez."

10. It is worth noting that one should not make a stark distinction between clerics and Moriscos, for some clerics, such as the Jesuits Juan de Albotodo and Ignacio de las Casas, were Moriscos.

11. Austria and Ramírez de Haro, *Instructions*, fol. 2v.

12. Ibid.

13. Pérez de Ayala, *Doctrina christiana*, fols. 2r and 4r. Here, Ayala's inclusion of Arabic responses for the Mass seems particularly noteworthy, given that the Council of Trent emphasized the vernaculars for religious instruction but gave pride of place to Latin as a liturgical language. Trent did not, however, indicate that the Mass had to be celebrated in Latin; instead, it emphasized "the ancient usage" in each church.

14. Pérez de Ayala, *Synodus diocesana valentiae*, 71. See the final chapter, "Confirmatio constitutio Synodalium Reuerendiss. F. Tho. de Vilanoua Archiepiscopi Valentini." A transcription of the constitutions from Villanueva's synod can be found in Iranzo, *Sinodales de Santo Tomás*. On the life of Tomás de Villanueva, see Llin Cháfer, *Santo Tomás de Villanueva*, as well as other works by the same author. See also Peraita, *Gobernar la república interior*; and Back, *Pelican*. Villanueva is the relatively

little-known patron of Villanova University in Philadelphia. Thanks to Carmen Peraita for the references regarding Villanueva.

15. Madrid, Archivo Histórico Nacional (hereafter AHN), Consejos, Legajo 50.805, Caja 2, "Constitucion.x.Que los que se baptizaren de los nueuos Christianos, se pongan nombres de sanctos o sanctas que honrra la sancta madre iglesia."

16. Their shared ground supports the argument made by Benítez Sánchez-Blanco that the Spanish Crown had a more-or-less consistent "Morisco policy" during the reigns of Charles V and Philip II. Benítez Sánchez-Blanco, *Heroicas decisiones*, 421.

17. Pérez de Ayala, "Discurso de la vida," 237.

18. Ibid.

19. Toledo (Spain), Sección Nobleza del Archivo Histórico Nacional (hereafter SNAHN), Osuna, C. 419, D. 476. I thank Claire Gilbert for making these sources known to me.

20. SNAHN, Osuna, C. 419, D. 476.

21. Elliott, *Imperial Spain*, 236–41.

22. It is worth underlining that Doménech says "we have tried in Sicily to find someone who could *read* the Arabic language." He may have referred to reading in a broader sense of knowing a language, yet his words may well indicate that he and others would have put to work even a Jesuit who only had reading knowledge of Arabic. Such a possibility is indeed conceivable, for—as the case of Mexico will reveal—the Church and its various religious orders often produced texts in different tongues with the expectation that ministers would use them even if they lacked proficiency in the given language. For instance, some churchmen in Mexico held that reading knowledge of Nahuatl provided sufficient qualification to read Nahuatl sermons during the Mass. On another note, it is also worth highlighting Doménech's point that "everyone had a strong desire" for some Jesuits to learn Arabic. He was speaking, presumably, about Jesuits in particular, who seem to have had more enthusiasm for Arabic study than other Spanish churchmen.

23. It seems odd that Doménech did not think of Juan de Albotodo, the Morisco Jesuit who worked in Granada's Albaicín and preached in Arabic. According to Ignacio de las Casas, however, Albotodo knew the language well enough to speak, but he did not know how to read it. See El Alaoui, "Ignacio de las Casas," 334. Interestingly, Las Casas made similar comments regarding Mur's abilities.

24. For the Doménech letter, see Rome, Archivum Romanum Societatis Iesu, Hispania 99, fol. 278v. For a brief contemporary commentary on the life of Jerónimo Doménech, see Ribadeneira, *Obras escogidas*, 604–5. See also O'Malley, *First Jesuits*, 36 and Medina, "Compañía de Jesús," 3–136.

25. Ehlers, *Between Christians and Moriscos*, 21, 30–35.

26. Ibid., 80–89.

27. Ibid., 90–103.

28. Ibid., 106–12.

29. The inquisitor general and archbishop of Toledo, Gaspar de Quiroga, led the proceedings. The men present with him included officials of both the Church and the Crown: Micer Simón Frigola, of Philip's royal council and vice chancellor of the Council of Aragón; Don Diego Fernández de Bobadilla, count of Chinchón and Philip's superintendent and treasurer for the Crown of Aragón; Micer Sapena, regent of the Council of Aragón; Fray Diego de Chávez, royal confessor; Don Francisco de Rivera, bishop of Segovia; Don Juan de Zúñiga, of the Inquisition's general council (the *Suprema*); Don Jerónimo Corella, of the order of Santiago; and Mateo Vázquez, secretary for Philip and the Suprema.

30. London, British Library (hereafter BL), MS Egerton 1,511. fol. 109v–11v. The record from the meeting suggests that every member agreed on the decision to

use Castilian or Valencian, possibly including the individual who initially supported instruction in Arabic.

31. Aldrete, *Del origen y principio*, I, XIII. Cited in Oliver Asín, *Historia de la lengua española*. El Alaoui, "Ignacio de las Casas," 317–39.

32. BL, MS Egerton 1,511, fol. 249v.

33. Though the Jesuit Doménech advocated the study of Arabic, sources do not indicate that he knew it himself. Other participants at Ribera's assembly included Don Pedro de Zárate, from the Valencian tribunal of the Inquisition; Micer Vicente Vidal, of Valencia's civil tribunal; Micer Gabriel Marchet, officer of the bishop of Tortosa; the Dominican fray Justiniano Antist; the Franciscan fray Francisco de Molina; and the Augustinian fray Gregorio Satorre. See BL, MS Egerton 1,511, fols. 246, 251r, and 252v–53v.

34. BL, MS Egerton 1,511, fols. 111r, 249v–50r. On indigenous-language professorships in Mexico, see Pérez Puente, "Creación de las cátedras públicas," 45–78. Although it had been decided that such a position should be created in Mexico, it apparently did not come to fruition in the sixteenth century.

35. BL, MS Egerton 1,511, fol. 110.

36. SNAHN, Osuna, C. 1913, D. 12.

37. For examples of these cases, see AHN, Inquisición, libros 936–37. At the next assembly, in 1591, Valencian authorities revisited the topics of the Moriscos' language and dress, arriving at a slightly different conclusion than the 1587 meetings. They decided to make an accommodation for Orihuela, a suffragan diocese of Valencia. In Orihuela, Arabic dress would be prohibited, as the local bishop had become aware that many women continued to use it. On the subject of language, however, they made no further revisions.

38. BL, MS Egerton 1,511, fol. 246v. Some individuals did acquire sufficient knowledge of Arabic to work as translators outside of primarily ecclesiastical contexts. See, for example, Gilbert, "Transmission, Translation, Legitimacy and Control." See also Gilbert, "Politics of Language."

39. Madrid, Biblioteca Nacional de España (hereafter BNE), MS 10388, fols. 95 and 106r.

40. BNE, MS 10388, fols. 104 and 110. For more detail on the catechism, see García-Cárcel, "Estudio crítico del catecismo"; see also Giménez-Eguibar and Wasserman-Soler, "*La mala algarabía*," 229–58.

41. BNE, MS 10388, fols. 95r and 106v–7r.

42. BNE, MS 10388, fol. 100r. We may wonder why the Moriscos asked for instruction in Catholic doctrine; the background of these particular Moriscos, however, remains unclear. It is possible that they had learned of the 1582 recommendation of expulsion (postponed by Philip II) and wished to defend themselves from any future, similar decision.

43. BNE, MS 10388, fol. 107v.

44. Benítez Sánchez-Blanco, *Heroicas decisiones*, 325–28.

45. London, BL, MS Egerton 1,511, fol. 145r. See also García-Cárcel, "Catecismo," 161–68.

46. Pérez de Ayala, *Catechismo para instruccion*, 1, 6.

47. Ibid., 6–7. It is particularly interesting that the catechism includes an Arabic interpreter given that Philip II specifically had requested that the Moriscos receive instruction in Castilian and Valencian. Boronat y Barrachina, *Moriscos*, 1:660. The presence of the Arabic interpreter in the catechism, thus, suggests that Ribera considered this measure licit within a program that prioritized Castilian and Valencian.

48. Ehlers, *Between Christians and Moriscos*, 108. In the catechism, the disciple is called a "Moor," translated here as "Muslim." It is worth noting, however, Ribera used "Moor" on many occasions to describe the Moriscos.

49. Ibid., 124–25.

50. Pérez de Ayala, *Catechismo para instruccion*, 3v.

51. For Philip's letter, see Boronat y Barrachina, *Moriscos*, 1:660. For Ribera's preface, see Pérez de Ayala, *Catechismo para instruccion*, 2v.

52. Pérez de Ayala, *Catechismo para instruccion*, 3. On the argument that Dorador inspired the Arabic-speaking cleric, see Torres Palomo, "Don Martín de Ayala." See also Torres Palomo, "Bartolomé Dorador y el árabe." Both works are cited in Garrido García, "Uso de la lengua árabe," 128–29.

53. Valencia, Archivo del Real Colegio Seminario de Corpus Christi (hereafter ARCSCC), I-7-8-12.

54. For an overview of Las Casas's views regarding the Moriscos, see El Alaoui, "Ignacio de las Casas," 317–39. For the quoted passages, see pp. 320 and 322. For more on Las Casas, see El Alaoui, *Jésuites, Morisques et Indiens*. On the Jesuits' work among the Moriscos, see Medina, "Compañía de Jesús," 3–136.

55. ARCSCC, I-7-8-273. "Se ha de considerar que estos viven entre [Christ]ianos, y los mas dellos hablan muy bien nuestro vulgar, y visten como nosotros, siendo tan moros en la ley como los del Reyno de Valencia." The document identifies no speaker, but because it comes from the Corpus Christi collection, it is possible that Ribera is the author.

56. ARCSCC, I-7-8-274.

CHAPTER 4

The bulk of this chapter is published in Daniel I. Wasserman-Soler, "*Lengua de los indios, lengua española:* Religious Conversion and the Languages of New Spain, ca. 1520–1585," *Church History* 85, no. 4 (2016). I would like to thank Sarah Rivett, Claire Gilbert, Ed Gray, Mayte Green-Mercado, Sean Harvey, Daniel Hershenzon, and Josh Piker for their extensive comments on an earlier version of this chapter.

1. *Recopilación de leyes*, Lib. 1, Tit. 13, Ley IV–V. Philip III issued law four in March 1619; Philip IV issued law five in March 1634. Though seventeenth-century monarchs promulgated these specific laws, earlier monarchs had made similar, apparently contradictory efforts. See Lodares Marrodán, "Contradictoria legislación lingüística americana."

2. Ricard, *Conquête spirituelle du Mexique*. See also Ricard, *Conquista espiritual de México* and Ricard, *Spiritual Conquest*. For a summary of many responses to Ricard, including work by Louise Burkhart, Inga Clendinnen, Serge Gruzinski, and Tzvetan Todorov, see Wasserman-Soler, "Language and Communication," 491–502. For more recent work, involving indigenous-language sources, see Restall, "History of the New Philology," 113–34; and Schwaller, ed., "A Language of Empire," Special issue of *Ethnohistory* 59:4 (2012): 667–790. The latter volume includes contributions by Mark Z. Christensen, Laura E. Matthew, Martin Nesvig, Caterina Pizzigoni, Sergio F. Romero, John F. Schwaller, Robert C. Schwaller, and Yanna Yannakakis.

3. Heath, *Telling Tongues*, 1. See also Heath, *Política del lenguaje en México*. The subject of royal legislation related to language arises frequently, as important contextual information, in the extensive scholarship related to evangelization in sixteenth-century Mexico. It has not been examined as a subject of study in itself since Heath's work. It also should be noted that Heath's book emphasizes the postindependence period of Mexico.

4. Christensen, "Use of Nahuatl," 691–711. See also Schwaller, "Expansion of Nahuatl," 675–90.

5. Heath, *Telling Tongues*, 15–18, 27, 36. See also Christensen, "Use of Nahuatl," 691–92; Schwaller, "Expansion of Nahuatl,"

675–77; and Balleriaux, *Missionary Strategies*, 51.

6. Nesvig, "Epistemological Politics," 165–201. See also Burkhart, *Slippery Earth*, 5.

7. Pérez Puente, "Creación de las cátedras públicas," 45–78. Fluency in indigenous languages continued to be a desirable skill for Mexican priests throughout the eighteenth century as well. At the same time, the Crown and the Church intensified efforts to instruct natives in Spanish, especially during the second half of the century. Their attempts, however, met with some opposition both from churchmen as well as from indigenous communities. Taylor, *Magistrates of the Sacred*, 95–96, 334–40.

8. Heath, *Telling Tongues*, 36. See also King, *Roots of Identity*, 45–47.

9. Heath, *Telling Tongues*, 36–37. Heath argues that, although the Spanish Crown had a long-term vision favoring Castilian, in practice it "alternated between proclaiming Spanish as the language of empire and promoting indigenous languages as the instrument of conversion."

10. Giménez-Eguibar and Wasserman-Soler, "*La mala algarabía*," 239.

11. The translation of Christian doctrine into indigenous languages often has been described as an accommodation of local cultures. Alan Durston, however, has argued that in sixteenth- and seventeenth-century Peru, translation did not lead necessarily to accommodation. He notes that the Spanish Church in Peru does not stand out for its use of accommodation, especially given that churchmen embarked on far more radical experiments in China and India. Although churchmen used Quechua extensively, they followed more of a *tabula rasa* approach than one of accommodation. Translation and accommodation, therefore, should not be seen as synonymous. Durston, *Pastoral Quechua*, 13–14. Durston's point, however, has limited applicability across the Americas, as he notes, given that Mesoamerica accommodated far greater linguistic and terminological diversity than the Andes (303).

12. Just a few of the many distinguished works in this field include Burkhart, *Slippery Earth*; Clendinnen, *Ambivalent Conquests*; Gruzinski, *Colonisation de l'imaginaire*; Lockhart, *Nahuas After the Conquest*; MacCormack, *Religion in the Andes*; Restall, *Maya World*; and Terraciano, *Mixtecs of Colonial Oaxaca*. Within the last ten to twelve years, another wave of scholarship has continued to examine the ways in which indigenous peoples shaped the societies in which they lived. See, for example, Christensen, *Nahua and Maya Catholicisms*; Matthew, *Memories of Conquest*; Pizzigoni, *Life Within*; Sarreal, *Guaraní*; Sigal, *Flower and the Scorpion*; Tavárez, *Invisible War*; and Yannakakis, *Art of Being In-Between*. The question of how to characterize the religious history of Latin America (e.g., "syncretic" vs. "hybrid") has provoked a lasting debate. For a helpful summary of some important contributors to this discussion, see Román and Voekel, "Popular Religion."

13. A classic example is Burkhart, *Slippery Earth*, which describes a flourishing dialogue between friars and Nahuas, ca. 1536–76. For the late colonial period, the magisterial study is Taylor's *Magistrates of the Sacred*, examining the contributions of both "priests and parishioners" to the Mexican Church.

14. In the words of one essential work, they were "hopelessly quixotic." Burkhart, *Slippery Earth*, 3, 11.

15. For Mexico, see Ricard, *Spiritual Conquest*. On the Philippines, see Rafael, *Contracting Colonialism*, 3–4, where he offers a critique of De la Costa, *Jesuits in the Philippines* and Phelan, *Hispanization of the Philippines*.

16. On the Nahuas, see Burkhart, *Slippery Earth*, 184–89. On the Maya, see Hanks, *Converting Words*, 368–69. On the Philippines, see Rafael, *Contracting*

Colonialism, 11. See also Garrido Aranda, *Moriscos e indios*, 58.

17. Scholarship related to Mexico's second and third archbishops—Alonso de Montúfar and Pedro Moya de Contreras—is not extensive, which is striking given that each man served as archbishop for more than fifteen years during the heavily studied sixteenth century. As of May 2019, the online catalogs of the Library of Congress and Biblioteca Nacional of Mexico reveal only one English monograph on Montúfar: Lundberg, *Unification and Conflict*. Alberto Carrillo Cázares has translated Lundberg's work into Spanish. See Lundberg, *Unificación y conflicto*. The same catalogs indicate just one other book-length study of Montúfar in Spanish: Ruiz Gutiérrez, *Fray Alonso de Montúfar*. The only English monograph on Moya de Contreras is Poole, *Pedro Moya de Contreras*. Carrillo Cázares also has translated Poole's work. See Poole, *Reforma católica y poder real*. In Spanish, see also Sánchez Rodríguez, *Pedro Moya de Contreras* and Icaza Dufour, *Pedro Moya de Contreras*.

18. Scholars of colonial Mexico know well that bishops often struggled to exercise their authority over influential mendicant friars. For that reason, it is worth noting that the records of Church councils did not necessarily become the point of departure in the everyday practices of the mendicant friars (Dominicans, Franciscans, and Augustinians), who have formed the basis of a robust historiography in colonial Latin American studies. Still, the provincial council records provide insight into the ideas of leading churchmen from both the mendicant orders and the secular clergy. Members of the mendicant orders attended the councils, and at the opening of the first provincial council, three of the five bishops present were mendicant friars. For more information about the individuals who attended the first and second councils, see Lundberg, *Unification and Conflict*, 81.

19. See, for instance, Cervantes, *Devil in the New World*, 2–4.

20. Díaz, *Conquest of New Spain*, 216. For an overview of the so-called Aztecs, see Nichols and Rodríguez-Alegría, eds., *Oxford Handbook of the Aztecs*. See also Clendinnen, *Aztecs*.

21. James Lockhart has noted that "city" or "town" probably is the best general English translation of *altepetl*. The Spanish *pueblo*, however, more accurately describes the Nahua concept because it suggests not just an urban location but also a group of people. Lockhart, *Nahuas After the Conquest*, 15.

22. This discussion is indebted to Lockhart, *Nahuas After the Conquest*, 1, 14–27. See also Smith, "Aztec Empire."

23. On Spaniards who learned Nahuatl, see Schwaller, "Expansion of Nahuatl." On the limitations of Nahuatl and Philip's changing stance, see Heath, *Telling Tongues*, 26. For a survey of the wide range of Mesoamerican indigenous languages, see Campbell, *American Indian Languages*, 156–69.

24. Díaz, *Conquest of New Spain*, 63–65, 85–87; Campbell, *American Indian Languages*, 156–69.

25. Cervantes, *Devil in the New World*, 12–13.

26. On the friars' influence in early Mexico, see Ricard, *Spiritual Conquest*, 4–5. Scholars have challenged much of Ricard's work, particularly with regard to his thesis that Mexico's native peoples experienced a "spiritual conquest." Nonetheless, his monograph remains foundational for the study of Mexico's early history, especially the roles played by the friars. This chapter primarily considers churchmen from religious orders (i.e., regular clergy). On the secular clergy of colonial Mexico, see Schwaller, *Church and Clergy*. See also Schwaller, *Catholic Church in Latin America*.

27. For some references to the relationships between friars and native peoples, see Ricard, *Spiritual Conquest*, 245–47, 288–90. See also Clendinnen, *Ambivalent Conquests*, 55–56. On the friars in resolving disputes, see Mills and Taylor, eds., *Colonial Spanish America*, 86–89; on the hospitals built under the auspices of the Church, see Ricard, *Spiritual Conquest*, 155–61.

28. On diabolism in New Spain, see Cervantes, *Devil in the New World*, 15. For one example of complaints issued against Franciscan friars, see Madrid, Archivo Histórico Nacional (hereafter AHN), Diversos, Colección Documentos de Indias, #25, n. 2. For a famous, well-documented case from the Yucatán, see Clendinnen, *Ambivalent Conquests*, especially pp. 129–93. For an excellent overview of the substantial and growing literature on the inquisitions and extirpation trials in New Spain, see Chuchiak, *Inquisition in New Spain*. See also Tavárez, *Invisible War*; Don, *Bonfires of Culture*; Nesvig, *Ideology and Inquisition*; Greenleaf, *Mexican Inquisition*; and Chuchiak, "In Servitio Dei," 611–46. The activity of New Spain's inquisition paled in comparison with that of its counterpart in Iberia. See Chuchiak, *Inquisition in New Spain*, 7.

29. For the Tlaxcala report, see "Relación del distrito y pueblos," in *Epistolario de Nueva España*, vol. 14. Without naming specific individuals, the report from Tlaxcala suggests that Indians would read (i.e., teach) the central tenets of Christian doctrine to their peers. The source frequently names a specific priest who would fulfill that role in each community. In some instances, however, the record names no specific teacher but still says that doctrine was read to the Indians. The use of the passive voice suggests the presence of a native catechist whom the author of the report wished not to name, perhaps to avoid conflict with other officials who might object to the idea of an indigenous teacher. On native peoples as assistants to (or associates of) clergy, see Christensen, *Nahua and Maya Catholicisms*, 16–17. For requests for more clergy, see AHN, Diversos, Colección Documentos de Indias, #23, n. 15; #24, n. 73; #25, n. 36. On indigenous interpretations of Catholicism, see Megged, *Exporting the Catholic Reformation*; Burkhart, *Slippery Earth*; and Christensen, *Nahua and Maya Catholicisms*.

30. For the reference to Cortés's chaplain, see Catholic Church, *Concilios provinciales*, 12. On the limited success of the first missionary efforts, see Heath, *Telling Tongues*, 7–8.

31. The most famous example of these interpreters is Doña Marina, also known as Malintzin or La Malinche. The sixteenth-century conquistador Bernal Díaz wrote a very brief account of her story. See Díaz, *Conquest of New Spain*, 85–87. For a more recent detailed study, see Townsend, *Malintzin's Choices*. On the Franciscans' early use of interpreters, see Mendieta, *Historia eclesiástica indiana*, 224–26. On the use of interpreters in Mexico during the early years after the European arrival, see Heath, *Telling Tongues*, 9–10. For a study of several individuals who served as interpreters and cultural intermediaries in the colonial Americas, see Karttunen, *Between Worlds*.

32. Primera Junta Apostólica de Mexico, 1524 (in *Concilios provinciales*, 3–4).

33. Madrid, Biblioteca Nacional de España, VITR/26/9. Pedro de Gante, *Catecismo de la doctrina Cristiana*. See also Resines, *Catecismos pictográficos*. Recently, Louise Burkhart has called into question the widely accepted conclusion that pictographic catechisms originated in sixteenth-century evangelization efforts in Mexico. Burkhart, "'Little Doctrine,'" 167–206.

34. Mendieta, *Historia eclesiástica indiana*, 197–202. On the historical organization

of the Franciscans in Extremadura, see García, "San Francisco de Asís," 759–80.

35. Mendieta, *Historia eclesiástica indiana*, 201–2.

36. Here, Mendieta clearly valued the contributions of Valencia, whom he said did more than the others despite having limited knowledge of indigenous languages. Earlier, however, Mendieta called indigenous languages "the most necessary instrument and medium for preaching the holy Gospel [to the Indians] and for teaching them the Christian life" (550). See also Mendieta, *Historia eclesiástica indiana*, 584.

37. Primera Junta Apostólica de México, 7–8.

38. Brain, "Aprendizaje de lenguas indígenas," 280, 294–95.

39. My use of "devotions" here and elsewhere is indebted to Tavárez, *Invisible War*, 3–4. He argues that "devotions"—as opposed to "idolatry" or "religion"—better highlights the diversity of indigenous practices. "Idolatry," he adds, implies that native peoples saw themselves as engaged in a war against Christianity, which he considers a distortion of reality.

40. Cervantes, *Devil in the New World*, 34–35.

41. Mendieta, *Historia eclesiástica indiana*, 550.

42. Some of the frustration here may have originated in the fact that many priests at midcentury lacked adequate theological training. The first provincial council record notes, "we have found some priests who do not know the basics of Christian doctrine." *Concilios provinciales*, 108.

43. On New Spain as a "land of one language," see Primera Junta Apostólica de México, 8. Valencia's emphasis on Spanish may have distinguished him from Domingo de Betanzos, the provincial of the Dominicans in New Spain. Betanzos ordered that "the friars who worked among the Indians had to learn their languages in order to preach to them and instruct them appropriately." Dávila Padilla, *Historia de la fundación*, 64. Still, a sharp distinction between Valencia and Betanzos (or between the early Franciscans and early Dominicans) would not be appropriate. As the rest of this section will demonstrate, Valencia also valued the use of indigenous languages, and many of his confrères studied them with energy.

44. AHN, Diversos, Colección Documentos de Indias, #22, n. 22, fols. 2v–3r. An original copy of this letter is available at Chicago's Newberry Library, MS Ayer 1539. "Report of a council meeting of bishops and priests in Mexico City to discuss their ministry to the Indians," 2r. The following eighteenth-century transcription with largely the same wording also exists: "Carta original de los ill[ustrisi]mos señores obispos de Mexico, Goatemala, y Oaxaca, sobre la ida al Concilio General, y piden sobre distintos puntos, así de Diezmos, como otros para la buena Planta, y permanencia de la Fé en este Nuevo Mundo" (1537), 3–4. In *Apendice á los concilios primero y segundo mexicanos* (1770).

45. AHN, Diversos, Colección Documentos de Indias, #22, n. 14.

46. While Valencia did not explicitly say that he viewed the use of indigenous languages as temporary, several clerics in Spain supported the use of Arabic as a temporary measure, looking to the eventual religious and linguistic assimilation of Islamic communities. See Giménez-Eguibar and Wasserman-Soler, "*La mala algarabía*."

47. Similar to Valencia, Gerónimo de Mendieta would praise the linguistic abilities of his confrères, but he also expressed his concern that the use of both Spanish and indigenous languages had created an impediment to the conversion of the native peoples. See Mendieta, *Historia eclesiástica indiana*, 552–53.

48. As of May 2019, the Library of Congress online catalog lists no English-

language monograph of Juan de Zumárraga's life. The most recent Spanish biography is Zavala, *Fray Juan de Zumárraga*. Besides other Spanish biographies from the first half of the twentieth century, see García Icazbalceta, *Don Fray Juan de Zumárraga*. A few recent historians have examined specific, though important, aspects of Zumárraga's work: for his role in the controversy related to the Virgin of Guadalupe, see Poole, *Our Lady of Guadalupe*; for his role in the infamous Indian inquisitions, see Greenleaf, *Zumárraga*; on his work related to early catechisms, see Gil, *Primeras doctrinas del nuevo mundo*.

49. On Montúfar, see Lundberg, *Unification and Conflict*. The meeting convened by the Franciscan friar Martín de Valencia in 1524 differs in important technical ways from the meeting held in 1555 by the Dominican friar Alonso de Montúfar. As the archbishop of Mexico, Montúfar called not just a meeting but a provincial council, an assembly in which bishops vote on issues related to their archdiocese (the archdiocese of Mexico at the time included the dioceses of Chiapas, Guatemala, Mexico, Michoacán, Oaxaca, and Tlaxcala). Another different kind of meeting is a diocesan synod, in which one bishop serves as the only voter and lawgiver. Martín de Valencia, for example, could not have convened a provincial council or a synod because he was not a bishop. Bishop Juan de Zárate of Oaxaca died while at the council.

50. Concilio Primero, 1555 (in *Concilios provinciales*, 36).

51. Concilio Primero, 1555, Cap. LX, 133. It might be argued that, in referring to the "lengua de los indios" (singular) here and elsewhere, the bishops meant Nahuatl. However, if they meant to say Nahuatl, they might have said "la lengua mexicana," as several contemporary churchmen did. Furthermore, John F. Schwaller has argued convincingly that the sixteenth-century Mexican Church actually did not lack priests who knew Nahuatl, but it did have a shortage of priests who knew other, less widely spoken languages, such as Matlatzinca or Huastec. See Schwaller, "Expansion of Nahuatl," 678–79. Given Schwaller's research, it seems more likely that the requirement here that ministers learn the "lengua de los indios" actually means something like "the language of the land," implying that ministers needed to know the language of the specific people they served, not that the ministers needed to know Nahuatl.

52. Concilio Primero, 1555, Cap. I, 39.

53. The commandments of the Church are distinct from the more well-known Ten Commandments of the Hebrew Scriptures, which also are mentioned here. The former included fasting at the times identified by the Church, paying tithes, going to confession once a year, and receiving communion at Easter.

54. Concilio Primero, 1555, Cap. I, 39–41.

55. The bishops elaborated somewhat on their language choices. For teaching the sign of the cross, they noted that using Latin and Castilian would help the faithful "to better *use and learn*." For the long list of other teachings, they stated that using Latin, Castilian, as well as native tongues would help parishioners "to better *know and retain*." It is possible that the bishops purposely chose these different words to describe the results of using distinct languages. They may have wished to suggest that using indigenous languages would aid in moving beyond memorization and onto a deeper comprehension of the teachings.

56. Accordingly, the Dominican friar Domingo de la Anunciación included the sign of the cross in Latin in his catechism, though he also provided more detailed explanations of it in Nahuatl. See Domingo de la Anunciación, *Doctrina xpiana*, 4v–8v. Published in dialogue format, the text included one column in Castilian and another in Nahuatl. When the time came

for the master to teach the disciple the words of the sign of the cross, Fray Domingo included it in Latin on both sides of the text (5r).

57. On Latin as a liturgical language, see *Council of Trent*, ed. Waterworth. See Session 22, Doctrine on the Sacrifice of the Mass, chapter 8. On the diversity of approaches taken in explaining and translating the concept of the Trinity, see Tavárez, "Naming the Trinity," 21–47.

58. Concilio Primero, 1555, Cap. I, 42–43.

59. The bishops suggested reading the contents of the display board especially during the weeks that preceded the celebration of Easter. Concilio Primero, 1555, Cap. I, 41.

60. "Relación del distrito y pueblos," in *Epistolario de Nueva España*, vol. 14.

61. Because the text mentions sermons together with catechisms and makes references to translation and inspection by a learned cleric, I believe that the reference to "sermones" concerns not spoken sermons but written texts.

62. On approved catechisms and sermons, see Concilio Primero, 1555, Cap. LXIX. For a useful overview of the different kinds of religious texts that circulated in colonial Mexico, see chapter 2 of Christensen, *Nahua and Maya Catholicisms*. On indigenous songs, see Concilio Primero, 1555, Cap. LXXII. These policies (esp. the one regarding the use of indigenous songs) remind us of Hernando de Talavera, the archbishop of Granada, and indicate that his attempts to use Islamic songs were not entirely unique.

63. Concilio Primero, 1555, Cap. LXXIV, 149–50.

64. Montufar and two other bishops (Tomás de Casillas of Chiapas and Martín Sarmiento de Hojacastro of Tlaxcala) were mendicant friars and thus had confreres engaged deeply in linguistic work. Furthermore, by the time that the 1555 Provincial Council met, translation work had been under way for decades in a variety of indigenous languages. Thus it seems unlikely that the bishops would have underestimated the challenges of translation.

65. Recent erudite work by Mark Christensen, for instance, partially bears out this discussion. He has argued that Nahuatl and Maya religious texts, "all preached Catholicism to be sure but different versions of Catholicism." See Christensen, *Nahua and Maya Catholicisms*, 3. Despite these "different versions," Christensen notes, "generally speaking, most texts—even unofficial ones—prescribed similar translations of the basic doctrines, including the Decalogue, the Lord's prayer, and the Creed" (123). Though the texts generally agree on the key tenets, Christensen aptly suggests that Maya and Nahua natives probably understood some of those core teachings, such as baptism, in very different ways given their distinctive cultural heritages.

66. Concilio Primero, 1555, Cap. IV, 45.

67. Lundberg, *Unification and Conflict*, 94–95. Also present at the Second Provincial Council were Fr. Tomás de Casillas, bishop of Chiapas; Fernando de Villa Gómez, bishop of Tlaxcala; Fr. Francisco del Toral, bishop of Yucatán; Fr. Pedro de Ayala, bishop of New Galicia; and Fr. Bernardo de Albuquerque, bishop of Oaxaca. The Council of Trent, the most significant council in the early modern Catholic Church, took place partly as a reaction to the criticisms of Martin Luther and other reformers and partly in response to generations of internal calls for renewal. The delegates at the council initiated a wide range of revisions, many of which aimed to reform the clergy. See O'Malley, *Trent*.

68. Concilio Segundo, 1565, Cap. XIX, 199. The pastor differs from the normal parish priest mainly in that the pastor holds administrative authority over the parish. That said, the distinction between a pastor and a parish priest probably did not matter for much of New Spain. Most

people probably had just one priest (their pastor), and many would only have seen him occasionally. A report from the diocese of Tlaxcala attests to the fact that priests regularly traveled from one village to another, with upward of one thousand and even two thousand people assigned to one priest. "Relación del distrito y pueblos," in *Epistolario de Nueva España*, vol. 14.

69. The information in this paragraph is indebted to Schwaller, "The Expansion of Nahuatl," 679.

70. Concilio Segundo, 1565, Cap. V, 191. It is worth noting here that if the interpreter were not religious, the bishops preferred a "well-trusted Spaniard" and not just a person of any background. Probably because Spaniards came from a long Christian heritage, a "well-trusted Spaniard" seemed more dependable than someone who had converted relatively recently. Other churchmen also discussed alternative methods of administering the sacrament of confession. For a later source, see Fray Juan Bautista, *Advertencias para los confesores*. He would indicate that confession could, in the absence of an interpreter, be administered to a dying person through sign or body language.

71. Concilio Segundo, 1565, Cap. VII, 192.

72. Concilio Primero, 1555, Cap. LXVI, 141.

73. Concilio Segundo, 1565, Cap. VIII, 192–93.

74. Poole, *Pedro Moya de Contreras*, 154–55.

75. Schwaller, "Ordenanza del Patronazgo," 253–74. See also Padden, "Ordenanza del Patronazgo," 333–54.

76. Like the Council of Trent (1545–63), which promulgated teachings that would remain influential for the Catholic Church as a whole until the First Vatican Council (1869–70), scholars recognize the Third Provincial Council of Mexico as having a similarly long-lasting impact. See Poole, *Pedro Moya de Contreras*.

77. Catholic Church, *Concilio III provincial mexicano*. The reader can find the source in the council publication preceding the record of the council itself. The relevant passage is on page 4 of the section entitled "Pastoral del Illmo. Serna."

78. For the bishops' affirmation of the previous councils, see *Concilio III provincial mexicano*, Titulus II (De Constitutionibus), De Auctoritate Decretorum et Publicatione eorum, Cap. I (Decreta praecedentium Synodorum abrogantur), 26–27. On the use of native languages, see *Concilio III provincial mexicano*, Titulus I (De Summa Trinitate, et Fide Catholica), De Doctrina Christiana Rudibus Tradenda, Cap. III (Cura Parochorum in tradenda et explananda Doctrina), 16–17. The following chapter will show that at least some members of the Council of the Indies eventually would consider the project of indigenous-language study futile. Churchmen in New Spain, however, generally seem not to have shared this attitude.

79. *Concilio III provincial mexicano*, Titulus IV (De Aetate, et Qualitate Ordinandorum et Praeficiendorum), De Titulo Beneficii aut Patrimonii, Cap. I (Nullus clericus secularis ad ordines admittatur, nisi beneficium habeat), 42–43. See also Schwaller, "The Expansion of Nahuatl."

80. On the production of catechisms, see *Concilio III provincial mexicano*, Titulus I (De Summa Trinitate, et Fide Catholica), De Doctrina Christiana Rudibus Tradenda, Cap. I (Doctrina Christiana uniformiter doceatur ad normam Catechismi Concilii Auctoritate dispositi), 15. In making this statement, the Mexican bishops followed the Council of Trent, ed. Waterworth, Twenty-Fourth Session, Decree on Reformation, chapter 7. See *Council of Trent*, ed. Waterworth. Prior to the Third Council, Archbishop Moya de Contreras ordered the publication of the following catechism: Vargas, *Doctrina*

christiana, muy vtil. Among the many later catechisms are Vergara, *Cartilla de la doctrina cristiana*; Molina, *Doctrina cristiana traducida*; Ledesma, *Tres catecismos*; and Coronel, *Doctrina christiana.* On the requirements for receiving baptism, see *Concilio III provincial mexicano*, Titulus I (De Summa Trinitate, et Fide Catholica), De Sacramentis Doctrinae Christianae Ignaris non Administrandis, Cap. I (Ad Baptismum nullus admittatur, nisi Doctrinam Christianam bene calleat), 20.

81. *Council of Trent*, ed. Waterworth, Twenty-Fourth Session, Decree on Reformation, chapter 7. The Nahuas coined the term "Chichimeca" ("barbarian") as a general concept to refer to indigenous communities that inhabited the area coinciding with present-day northern Mexico. See Karttunen, *Analytical Dictionary of Nahuatl.* See Operé, *Indian Captivity*, 139.

82. Operé, *Indian Captivity*, 139.

83. On the requirements for baptism, see *Concilio III provincial mexicano*, Titulus I (De Summa Trinitate, et Fide Catholica), De Sacramentis Doctrinae Christianae Ignaris non Administrandis, Cap. I (Ad Baptismum nullus admittatur, nisi Doctrinam Christianam bene calleat), 20. On singing approved songs, see *Concilio III provincial mexicano*, Titulus I (De Summa Trinitate, et Fide Catholica), De Impedimentis Propriae Salutis, ab Indis Removendis, Cap. I (Circa Indorum saltationes, ac ludos observanda), 23. On Arnaud de Bassac, see Mendieta, *Historia eclesiástica indiana*, 550.

84. *Concilio III provincial mexicano*, Titulus I (De Summa Trinitate, et Fide Catholica), De Doctrina Christiana Rudibus Tradenda, Cap. IV (Id etiam Ludi Magistri exequantur) and Cap. V (Parochi Scholarum erectionem promoveant), 17–18.

85. *Monumenta Mexicana*, vol. 1, doc. 62, Mexico, 31 December 1574. P'urhépecha (Tarascan) is a linguistic isolate, a language with no known relatives. Campbell, *American Indian Languages*, 166.

86. Lu Ann Homza's work on early modern Spain supports this suggestion. Homza, *Religious Authority.*

87. See, for instance, Christensen, *Nahua and Maya Catholicisms*, 8. For Peru, by contrast, Alan Durston has argued that Christian literature in Quechua lacks the degree of terminological and linguistic diversity seen in Mesoamerica. Durston, *Pastoral Quechua*, 303.

88. El Alaoui, *Jésuites, Morisques et indiens*, 22.

89. For example, see Schwaller, "The Expansion of Nahuatl," 675–76.

CHAPTER 5

1. For a copy of Charles III's decree, see Lorenzana y Buitrón, *Cartas pastorales y edictos*, 143–52. Toward the end of the decree, Charles indicated his desire that Castilian become the sole language of the Spanish Americas, to the exclusion of all other languages. For an English translation, see Heath, *Telling Tongues*, 215–20.

2. Charles III's comment has led to the misperception among contemporary scholars that the Spanish Crown repeatedly attempted to propagate Castilian at the expense of indigenous languages. See, for instance, Rospide, "Real cédula," 1415–48.

3. I use "multilingual" here in the simple sense of describing something that contains many languages.

4. See, for instance, Burkhart, *Slippery Earth*; and Schwaller, "Expansion of Nahuatl."

5. "Relación del distrito y pueblos," in *Epistolario de Nueva España*, vol. 14.

6. Heath, *Telling Tongues*, 5, 7, 36.

7. Seville, Archivo General de Indias (henceforth, AGI), Audiencia de Santa Fe, 533, L. 1, fol. 126v–27.

8. AGI, Indiferente General, L. 21, fol. 67v–69.

9. León-Portilla, *Bernardino de Sahagún.*

10. Ibid., 7–8, 132–33. The definitive modern edition of the *Historia general* is Sahagún, *Florentine Codex.*

11. Burkhart, *Slippery Earth*, 5.

12. Subordinate to the king, the Council of the Indies functioned as the highest governmental body for the Spanish Americas. See Gibson, *Spain in America*, 92. For Philip's response to the Sahagún case, see AGI, Patronato Real, 275, R. 79. For a full transcription of Philip's response, see Appendix 1 in García Icazbalceta, *Nueva colección.*

13. AGI, Indiferente General 427, L. 30, fol. 298v.

14. Ibid., fol. 299r.

15. Ibid.

16. "Relación del distrito y pueblos," in *Epistolario de Nueva España*, vol. 14. The report includes only minimal information regarding the many mendicant friars who served this diocese; twenty-nine towns were staffed by either Augustinian, Dominican, or Franciscan friars. The document includes neither the names of the religious nor their linguistic capabilities. Still, given that the overwhelming majority of sixteenth-century indigenous-language grammars, dictionaries, and catechisms identified a mendicant friar as the author, it seems reasonable to suggest that the linguistic capabilities of the friars probably matched—and perhaps exceeded—those of the secular priests.

17. For Tlaxcala, the rate may even exceed the percentage stated here because two of the forty-four secular priests had appointments to towns whose demographic makeup remains unclear. Juan Ruiz Flores, for instance, knew no indigenous language, but he served La Veracruz, which consisted of Spaniards. The record indicates that he served another town, La Rinconada, but it does not reveal explicitly whether this other location also was a town of Spaniards. Another secular priest, Francisco López de Rebolledo, also knew no indigenous language, and the record does not specify the ethnic background of the people whom he served.

18. While linguists today classify Nahuatl in the Uto-Aztecan family, they put Otomi and Popoloca in the Oto-manguean family, and they consider Totonac as a linguistic isolate. It is worth noting that Popoloca and Popoluca refer to different languages. Campbell and Mixco, *Glossary of Historical Linguistics.*

19. "Relación del distrito y pueblos," in *Epistolario de Nueva España*, vol. 14. The record reveals two cases in which a cleric described as *lengua mexicana* served Indians who spoke Nahuatl and some Indians who spoke Popoluca; one cleric with similar abilities had Nahuatl speakers and Yopi speakers as parishioners; several Nahuatl-speaking clerics served in areas that combined speakers of Nahuatl and Totonac.

20. "Carta al rey del arzobispo," in *Epistolario de Nueva España*, 10:206.

21. Ibid., 205.

22. Philip took a similar position in relation to the bishops who dealt with the Moriscos in Spain.

23. AGI, Indiferente General 744, n. 8 (1596).

24. Although it had been decided that such a position should be created in Mexico, it apparently did not come to fruition. Pérez Puente, "Creación de las cátedras públicas," 45–78.

25. AGI, Indiferente General 744, n. 8 (1596).

26. Ibid. In the sixteenth-century Spanish kingdoms, *mestizo* referred to a person with Amerindian and European ancestry. *Criollo* (creole) referred to an individual born in the Americas to European parents. What exactly motivated the members of the Council of the Indies to prefer European clerics over *mestizos* and creoles remains unclear in their letter. One might suggest that they simply used any reason

they could find in order to justify the increased usage of Castilian. Perhaps they believed that greater usage of Castilian would facilitate some other agenda, whether economic, political, or other.

27. AGI, Indiferente General 744, n. 8 (1596).

28. Ibid.

29. Ibid.

30. Perhaps Philip's position here was informed by his experience of the repercussions from prohibiting Granada's Moriscos from speaking or writing in Arabic. See chapter 2.

31. *Recopilación de leyes*, Lib. 1, Tit. 13, Ley 5. Interestingly, Philip IV promulgated this law on two occasions (March 1634 and November 1636), so his desire to propagate Castilian seems stronger than the position taken by Philip II.

32. *Ibid.*

33. The three texts are Alcalá, *Vocabulista arauigo en letra castellana*; Alcalá, *Arte para ligeramente saber*; and Pérez de Ayala, *Doctrina christiana, en lengua arauiga.* Alcalá's *Arte* included a substantial section of Christian doctrine. He would publish his *Vocabulista* and *Arte* together in 1506. Spanish Catholic clerics, of course, were not the only individuals who had published work on Arabic grammar. Other Arabic grammars circulated in Spain and in Europe, in general, during the early modern period. For example, see Muḥammad ibn Muḥammad al-Ṣanhāǧī Ibn Aǧurrūm (1273–1323), whose work on Arabic grammar (*Aljurrumía en árabe y traducida en romance*) continued to circulate in the early modern period. For a few other examples of early modern European work on Arabic grammar, see Erpenius, *Grammatica Arabica*; Guadagnoli, *Breues arabicae linguae institutiones*; and Aquila, *Arabicae lingvae novae.* The comparison between the indigenous-language texts and Arabic texts, of course, is an imperfect one. European Christians had centuries of contact with Muslims. Perhaps because sixteenth-century Europeans only recently had come into contact with the indigenous peoples of the Americas, one might suggest that the flurry of publications resulted from heightened early interest.

34. See the appendix for a list of sixteenth-century Franciscan friars who learned Mesoamerican languages. Gerónimo de Mendieta cited several indigenous-language texts that no longer survive. Mendieta, *Historia eclesiástica indiana*, 549–52. Mark Christensen has suggested three categories of indigenous-language religious texts: category 1 refers to printed texts that name a churchman as the author, aiming for a wide audience, including both churchmen and native readers; category 2 includes manuscript texts authored by a churchman and/or an indigenous writer for a more local audience; the final category consists of manuscripts written by native authors for native readers. See Christensen, *Nahua and Maya Catholicisms*, 51–95. See also Megged, review of *Nahua and Maya Catholicisms*, 208–9.

35. Sixteenth- and seventeenth-century western European authors frequently employed assistants to help in the production of their books. The assistants' work, however, did not grant them authorial status. Blair, "Information Flows."

36. On the Mixtecs, see Terraciano, *Mixtecs of Colonial Oaxaca.*

37. Alvarado, *Vocabulario en lengua misteca*, Prólogo al Lector.

38. Ibid., Aprobación de Fr. Antonio de los Reyes y Fr. Pablo Rodrigues.

39. Ibid., fol. 4r.

40. Ibid., Prólogo al Lector.

41. Ibid., fol. 4r.

42. On Vico's theology, see Sparks, *Americas' First Theologies*; Sparks, "Xalqat B'e"; and Sparks, "Use of Mayan Scripture," 396–429. On Vitoria's view of Vico, see Remesal, *Historia de la provincia*, 2:380.

Cited in *Popol Vuh*, ed., Goetz and Recinos, 31.

43. Quiché (or K'iché), part of the Mayan language family, today is the most widely spoken indigenous language in Guatemala. The Ayer Collection at Chicago's Newberry Library contains seventeen manuscript works attributed to Domingo de Vico. Of those texts, seven are believed to have been written during or around Vico's lifetime, with the others produced during the seventeenth and eighteenth centuries. The Newberry's Vico holdings are largely photographic reproductions, with most of the originals traced to the Bibliothèque Nationale de France and the Princeton University Library. Kaqchikel (or Cakchiquel) also forms part of the Mayan language family. For guidance regarding the Newberry's extensive indigenous-language materials (many of which are reproductions), I am indebted to two Newberry Library catalogues produced by Gabriel Angulo: "Colonial Spanish Sources for Indian Ethnohistory at the Newberry Library" and "Colonial Spanish Sources for Indian Linguistics at the Newberry Library."

44. For an extensive list of Nahuatl manuscripts, see Schwaller, *Guide to Nahuatl*. Chicago's Newberry Library, for instance, contains several similar texts. See, for example, Ayer MSS 1689 (Domingo de Ara, "Bocabulario en lengua tzeldal," ca. 1560, a Tzeltal-Spanish dictionary) and 1688 (Domingo de Ara, "Egregium opus fratris Dominici Dehara," ca. 1560, a Tzeltal-Spanish grammar, with parables and sermons). The Newberry holds the original of the grammar, parable, and sermon book, while the original dictionary is housed at Berkeley's Bancroft Library. Like Quiché and Kaqchikel, Tzeltal is another Mayan language. In 1616, Fray Alonso de Guzmán produced a manuscript copy of Ara's Tzeltal dictionary: Newberry Library, Ayer MS 1692, Domingo de Ara, "Bocabulario de lengua tzeldal segun el orden de Copanabastla." Several other indigenous-language catechetical manuscripts circulated well into the eighteenth century. See Newberry Library, Ayer MS 1548, Felix Solano, "Vocabulario en lengua castellana y guatemalteca que se llama Cak chi quel chi," ca. 1579. For a later copy of his sixteenth-century manuscript, see Ayer MS 1514.

45. Hernández, *Doctrina christiana*, fol. iii v.

46. Control of the doctrinal content may also have been a concern.

47. Coronel, *Doctrina christiana*. See also Peniche and González Cicero, *Historia de las bibliotecas*.

48. Mendieta, *Historia eclesiastica indiana*, 225.

49. Fray Juan Bautista, *A Iesv Christo S.N.*, Prólogo.

50. Though Molina died before the turn of the seventeenth century, his works continued to be printed well beyond his lifetime. He explicitly directed his brief confession manual to natives themselves, while acknowledging that it also would provide much help to churchmen. David Tavárez has noted that when authors like Molina wrote about native readers, they probably referred to indigenous elites, such as those educated at the Colegio de Tlatelolco. See Tavárez, "Naming the Trinity," 29.

51. Molina, *Aqui comiença vn vocabulario*, fol. a iii v.

52. One might suggest that teaching Castilian did not seem realistic because of staffing problems. Nonetheless, churchmen frequently complained about a lack of clergy throughout the sixteenth century, and they still persisted in their efforts to convert the Indians to Christianity. A large corpus of documentation indicates the need for more priests in the Americas. For a few examples, see the 1537 letter from the bishops of New Spain to Charles V in AHN, Diversos, Colección Documentos de

Indias, #22, n. 22; the 1573 letter from Pedro Sánchez, provincial of the Society of Jesus in New Spain, to Everard Mercurian, the Jesuit superior general, in *Monumenta Mexicana*, vol. 1, doc. 25, p. 74; the 1575 letter from Sánchez to Juan de Ovando, the president of the Council of the Indies, in *Monumenta Mexicana*, vol. 1, doc. 70, pp. 174–75; as well as the 1578 letter from Mercurian to Pedro Moya de Contreras, the archbishop of Mexico City, in *Monumenta Mexicana*, vol. 1, doc. 127, p. 360. Numbers, therefore, probably did not constitute the primary reason Molina stayed away from recommending Castilian-language instruction for Amerindians.

53. Molina, *Aqui comiença vn vocabulario*, fol. a iii.

54. Gilberti, *Dialogo de doctrina christiana*.

55. Ibid., a ii r.

56. Ibid., ii r.

57. Hernández, *Doctrina christiana*. That he appears less prolific than Molina and Gilberti may be less a result of his own abilities and perhaps a result of his location, distant from the printing capital of Mexico City.

58. Whether Hernández was making a general statement about the difficulty of evangelizing Native American communities or a comment about the Mixtecs, in particular, is not clear from the text. Hernández, *Doctrina christiana*, iii r.

59. Ibid., iii.

60. Ibid., iii v.

61. Ibid., iii v.

62. To take one example, in the endorsement of Gilberti's *doctrina*, the Augustinian friar Alonso de la Vera Cruz notes that "los naturales la entienden bien." See Gilberti, *Dialogo de doctrina christiana*, iii r.

63. Fray Juan de la Anunciación, *Sermonario en lengva mexicana*.

64. Ibid., Avisos del auctor al religioso lector.

65. The mendicant friars shared more than common attitudes toward indigenous languages. They also learned from one another in studying local tongues. For instance, the Dominicans credited the Franciscans with helping them to learn Nahuatl. Dávila Padilla, *Historia de la fundación*, 31.

66. Campbell and Mixco, *Glossary of Historical Linguistics*.

67. One should exercise care, however, in speaking about the "survival" of indigenous languages. Today, some Maya, for instance, claim that they do not speak "legitimate Maya." See Hanks, *Converting Words*, xvi.

68. In fact, the situation probably was even more complex. According to Gerónimo de Mendieta, the use of both languages led to the "corruption" of each one. He wrote, "The people's manner of speaking [Nahuatl] becomes corrupted each day because we, the Spaniards, frequently speak it as the blacks and other foreigners speak our language. The Indians take our own manner of speaking, and they forget how their fathers, grandfathers, and ancestors spoke. And the same thing happens here with our own Spanish language, which is half corrupt with words that stuck with our men during the conquest of the islands, as well as others that have been taken from the Mexican language." See Mendieta, *Historia eclesiástica indiana*, 552–53.

CONCLUSION

1. Apparently, due to jurisdictional tensions, no one actually held indigenous-language professorships until 1640. Pérez Puente, "Creación de las cátedras públicas," 45–78. On the assemblies related to the Moriscos, see London, British Library, MS Egerton 1511, fols. 111r and 249v. For a

detailed discussion of these assemblies, see chapter 3. Though the 1587 discussion in Valencia did not result in an Arabic chair, the result was different elsewhere in Spain. In 1593 Philip II approved a chair of Arabic for Diego de Urrea of the University of Alcalá. Rodríguez Mediano, "Fragmentos," 250.

2. Latin was not the liturgical language in all locations of the Catholic Church. The decrees of the Council of Trent do not state explicitly that the Mass must be in Latin. Instead, they support "the ancient usage of each church," which would have been Latin in the Spanish Crown and in Western Europe in general. But Eastern Catholics—such as Byzantine, Chaldean, and Maronite Catholics—had the right to use different languages. *Council of Trent*, ed. Waterworth. See the Twenty-Second Session, chapter 8.

3. Concilio Primero, 1555, Cap. LXIX.

4. Not until 1770 would the Spanish Crown officially attempt to prohibit indigenous languages. See Heath, *Telling Tongues*. On language policy in eighteenth-century Mexico, see Zakaib, "Built upon the Tower."

5. King Charles I, however, did link efforts to convert Amerindians with contemporary attempts among the Moriscos. See Zumárraga, *Don Fray Juan de Zumárraga*, 13–14.

6. For instance, in the late sixteenth century, the Jesuit José de Acosta wrote at length about the Andean natives among whom he lived. Aware that his audience probably would be well acquainted with Christian scripture but perhaps not with the Andean peoples, Acosta used biblical references to explain the religious situation of these Indians. Acosta, "On the Salvation of the Indians," 119. See also Fray Juan Bautista, *Advertencias para los confessores*, vol. 1, fol. 10v.

7. *Concilio III provincial mexicano*, 4.

8. Youssef El Alaoui, for instance, has highlighted the similarities between the 1554 Synod of Guadix and the 1583 Provincial Council of Lima. El Alaoui, *Jésuites, Morisques et Indiens*, 350–51.

9. *Council of Trent*, ed. Waterworth, Twenty-Fourth Session, Decree on Reformation, chapter 7. The decree recommends priestly explanations of the sacraments "in the vernacular tongue, if need be, and it can be conveniently done."

10. For a detailed reflection on this question, see Núñez Muley, *Memorandum*, 91–95. For the original text, see Garrad, "Memorial," 221–24. See also García-Arenal, "Religious Identity," 495–528.

11. On the Islamic conquest of Iberia, see Fletcher, *Moorish Spain*, 17–21. On Moriscos who apparently embraced Christianity, see García Pedraza, *Actitudes ante la muerte*. Some Moriscos assimilated so successfully that they lost their status as Moriscos and became known as Old Christians. Tueller, *Good and Faithful Christians*, 15. On concerns about Ottoman invasion and Morisco rebellion, see Coleman, *Creating Christian Granada*, 2.

12. For helpful overviews of Arabic as the sacred language of Islam, see Murata and Chittick, *Vision of Islam*, 175–80; and Sells, ed., *Approaching the Qur'an*, 1–12.

13. See chapter 2 for a discussion of the 1566–67 restriction of Arabic.

14. See, for example, Menocal, *Ornament of the World*.

15. See, for instance, Fernández-Morera, *Myth of the Andalusian Paradise*.

16. Columbus, *Select Letters*, 6.

17. Ibid., 7–8.

18. This view coincides with Heath's claim that the Habsburg monarchs favored Castilianization. Heath, *Telling Tongues*, 5. It also seems in line with Alan Durston's point that pastoral Quechua "was never intended to develop into a fully-fledged Christian language" since it "was restricted

to a range of functions." Durston, *Pastoral Quechua*, 312.

19. Elliott, *Spain, Europe, and the Wider World*, 176–77.

20. Mills and Grafton, *Conversion*, xii–xiii.

21. *Concilio III provincial mexicano*, 4.

22. The closest it came to an all-encompassing prohibition of a language was with Arabic in 1566–67 Granada. But even in that case, the decree focused on language use among Moriscos in only one region of Iberia. Old Christians theoretically could use Arabic; furthermore, Moriscos in the rest of Castile and Aragón did not fall under the decree's jurisdiction. Similarly, the Inquisition's suspicion of Castilian-language prayer books did not extend to delivering a sermon or administering the sacrament of confession in Castilian. Along the same lines, the Crown's confiscation of Bernardino de Sahagún's work in Nahuatl did not lead to any sort of restriction on using indigenous languages for preaching and catechisms.

23. *Apéndice á los concilios*, fol. 4. Similarly, for the French context, Dominique Deslandres has recognized that the example set by the missionary served as the most powerful tool of religious conversion—even more so than eloquence. Deslandres, "*Exemplo aeque ut verbo*," 264.

APPENDIX

1. Given that some of Mendieta's references are general (e.g., "supo la lengua"), one may wonder about the reliability of his claims. Still, his comments about linguistic ability seem reliable for at least two reasons: First, he did not attribute linguistic abilities to every churchman. For many, he remained silent about their knowledge of native tongues. In one notable anecdote, he candidly described how Fr. Martín de Valencia, the leader of the famous band of twelve Franciscans, learned very little Nahuatl. Second, when Mendieta did comment on linguistic ability, he often qualified it. For instance, he noted that the given churchman authored an indigenous-language text or that he knew it well enough to preach.

BIBLIOGRAPHY

COLLECTIONS CONSULTED

For the most part, the references in this section include only manuscripts. I have included references to specific printed materials in the next section, but the institutions that house them are listed here.

Alcalá de Henares (Spain)
Archivo de la Provincia de Toledo de la Compañía de Jesús
C-199

Berkeley
Bancroft Library, University of California–Berkeley
M-A 1, 5:2
M-M 101, 142, 170, 171, 268, 269, 436, 1717, 1737, 1756
Z-B 2
Z-C 217
Z-D 3, 121

Chicago
Newberry Library
MSS 1514, 1539, 1547, 1548, 1565, 1688, 1689, 1692

Espartinas (Spain)
Archivo de la Provincia Bética (O.F.M.)

Granada
Archivo de la Catedral de Granada
Reales Cédulas Carlos V, Libro II
Varios, Libro III
Biblioteca de la Facultad de Teología

Guadix (Spain)
Archivo Histórico Diocesano
Caja 83, legajo 11

London
British Library (BL)
MS Additional 10,238
MSS Egerton 444; 1,510; 1,511; 1,871

Madrid
Archivo Histórico Nacional (AHN)
Bca. 1464, 1524–28, 1530–32
Clero-Jesuitas Leg. 306, 312; Lib. 773
Consejos Leg. 41.248, 41.306, 43.780, 43.781, 50.722, 50.789, 50.805, 50.841; Lib. 1, 2, 640, 1529–31, 2220
Diversos (Colección Documentos de Indias) #22–26
Estado Lib. 743, 763
Inquisición Leg. 1864, 1930, 1953, 2075, 2942, 4426, 4427, 4435, 4436, 4443–45, 4462, 4474, 5353; Lib. 236, 352, 574–81, 914, 917, 936–38, 1047, 1064
Biblioteca Marqués de Valdecilla, Universidad Complutense de Madrid
BH DER 36 (3)
Biblioteca Nacional de España (BNE)
MSS 10388, 1210, 12179, 13019, VITR/26/9
Biblioteca Real
MSS II/555, II/2241, VIII/732
Instituto Valencia Don Juan
MS E45, C58, 245
Real Academia de la Historia
Salazar y Castro T. 22, sig. 9/586

Mexico City
Archivo General de la Nación (Instituciones Coloniales)
Gobierno Virreinal, Reales Cédulas Originales y Duplicados (100), Reales Cédulas Duplicadas, vol. D8
Indiferente Virreinal, Cajas 0141, 1432, 2467, 5232, 5307, 5413, 5591, 6486
Inquisición, Edictos de Inquisición (43), vol. III

Philadelphia
American Philosophical Society
Ruben Reina Papers

Princeton
Rare Books & Special Collections Library, Princeton University
Garrett-Gates Mesoamerican MS 1
William H. Scheide Library

Providence
John Carter Brown Library, Brown University
Codex Ind 4

Rome
Archivio Storico della Congregazione per l'Evangelizzazione dei Popoli
Congregazioni Particolari, vols. 1, 4, 6, 27, 28
Miscellanee Varie, vol. VIII
Archivum Romanum Societatis Iesu (ARSI)
Aragonia 2, 3, 4, 5, 6-I, 6-II
Bellarmine, Opp. N.N. 243
Castellae 7-I, 7-II
Fondo Gesuitico n. 720
Hispania 66, 67, 95–115, 117–27, 129–32, 134–39, 141
Historia Societatis Iesu 177

Salamanca
Biblioteca General Histórica
Biblioteca de la Universidad Pontificia de Salamanca

San Lorenzo del Escorial (Madrid)
Biblioteca de San Lorenzo del Escorial
MSS b. IV. 28; c. IV. 5; d. IV. 3; d. IV. 8; L. I. 12; O. III. 19; X. II. 21; &. II. 7

San Marino (Los Angeles)
Huntington Library

Seville
Archivo General de Indias (AGI)
Charcas 1
Filipinas 79, 84
Indiferente General 21, 424, 425, 427, 742, 744, 1092, 1962, 1964
Mexico 20, 1088
Patronato Real 275
Sante Fe 533
Biblioteca de la Universidad de Sevilla (Fondo Antiguo)

Simancas (Valladolid)
Archivo General de Simancas (AGS)
Cámara de Castilla, Libros de Relación 10, 12, 14
Estado, Legajos 72, 73, 84, 148, 149, 174, 175, 306, 892
Estado Castilla, Legajo 148
Patrimonio Real, Legajos 21, 22
Registro General del Sello, 1566 Nov

Toledo
Sección Nobleza del Archivo Histórico Nacional
Osuna C. 419, 1897, 1913, 4249

Valencia
Archivo del Real Colegio Seminario Corpus Christi
MSS Moriscos 178–84 (old reference: I-7-8, Moriscos)

Vatican City
Archivio Segreto Vaticano
Biblioteca Apostolica Vaticana
Congregatio Pro Doctrina Fidei
Index Librorum Prohibitorum, t. 1

Index Protocolli G; O; AA
Registrum Litterarum Vulgatarum et Latinarum Sacrae Congregationis Indicis, ab anno 1582 usque 1602; L. 7301

Washington, DC
Library of Congress
Kislak MS 091

PRINTED PRIMARY SOURCES

Acosta, José de. "José de Acosta on the Salvation of the Indians." In *Colonial Spanish America: A Documentary History*, edited by Kenneth Mills and William Taylor, 115–24. Lanham, MD: Rowman & Littlefield, 2006.

Alcalá, Pedro de. *Arte para ligeramente saber la lengua araviga*. Granada: Juan Varela, 1505.

———. *Vocabulista arauigo en letra castellana*. Granada: Juan Varela, 1505.

Aldrete, Bernardo de. *Del origen y principio de la lengva castellana ò romãce que oi se usa en España*. Rome: Carlo Vulliet, 1606.

———. *Varias antiguedades de España Africa y otras prouincias*. Antwerp: Iuan Hasrey, 1614.

Alva, Bartolomé de. *A Guide to Confession Large and Small in the Mexican Language, 1634*. Edited by Barry D. Sell and John Frederick Schwaller, with Lu Ann Homza. Norman: University of Oklahoma Press, 1999.

Alvarado, Francisco de. *Vocabulario en lengua misteca*. Mexico City: Pedro Balli, 1593.

Apéndice á los concilios primero y segundo mexicanos. S.l.: S.n., 1770.

Aquila, Antonio dell'. *Arabicae lingvae novae, et methodicae institutiones*. Rome: Propaganda Fide, 1650.

Austria, Jorge de, and Antonio Ramírez de Haro. *Les instructions e ordinacions perals nouament conuertits del regne de Valencia*. Valencia: Juan Mey, 1566.

Bertonio, Ludovico. *Arte de la lengua aymara*. Edited by Iván Tavel Torres. Cochabamba, Bolivia: PROEIB Andes: Ambassade van het Koninkrijk der Nederlanden, 2002.

Bleda, Jaime. *Defensio fidei cavsa neophytorvm siue morischorum regni Valentiae, totiusq[ue] Hispaniae*. Valencia: Juan Chrysóstomo Garriz, 1610.

Cano, Melchor. "Censura autógrafa de Fr. Melchor Cano y Fr. Domingo de Cuevas sobre los *Comentarios del Catecismo Cristiano* del Arzobispo de Toledo, D. Fr. Bartolomé Carranza." In *Vida del illmo. Sr. D. fray Melchor Cano del orden de Santo Domingo, obispo de Canarias, etc.*, by Fermin Caballero, 536–615. 1868. Reprint, Cuenca, Spain: Olcades, 1980.

———. *De locis theologicis*. Edited by Juan Belda Plans. Madrid: Biblioteca Autores Cristianos, 2006.

———. *De locis theologicis libri duodecim*. Salamanca: Mathias Gastius, 1563.

Capitulaciones para la entrega de Granada. 1492. Edited by Miguel Garrido Atienza. 1910. Reprint, Granada: Universidad de Granada, 1992.

Carochi, Horacio. *Grammar of the Mexican Language*. Edited by James Lockhart. Stanford: Stanford University Press, 2001.

Carranza, Bartolomé. *Comentarios sobre el catechismo christiano*. 2 vols. Edited by José Ignacio Tellechea Idígoras. Madrid: Editorial Católica, 1972.

———. *Controuersia de necessaria residentia personali episcoporu[m] & aliorum inferior[m] Pastorum*.

Salamanca: Andreas de Portonariis, 1550.

Catecismo de la doctrina christiana con las adiciones de las cosas necesarias del santo concilio tridentino. Mexico City: S.n., 158[?].

Catholic Church. *Concilio III provincial mexicano, celebrado en Mexico en el año de 1585, confirmado en Roma por el papa Sixto V, y mandado observar por el gobierno español, en diversas reales or ordenes*. Mexico City: E. Maillefert, 1859.

———. *Concilios provinciales. Primero, y segundo, celebrados en la muy noble, y muy leal ciudad de México, presidiendo el illmo y rmo señor don fr. Alonso de Montúfar: En los años de 1555, y 1565*. Mexico City: Joseph Antonio de Hogal, 1769.

Columbus, Christopher. *Select Letters of Christopher Columbus: With Other Original Documents Relating to His Four Voyages to the New World*. Edited by R. H. Major. Surrey, England: Ashgate, 2010.

Coronel, Juan. *Doctrina christiana, en lengua de maya*. Mexico City: Diego Garrido, 1620.

The Council of Trent: Canons and Decrees of the Sacred and Oecumenical Council of Trent. Edited by J. Waterworth. London: Dolman, 1848.

Covarrubias, Sebastián de. *Tesoro de la lengua castellana, o española*. Madrid: Luis Sánchez, 1611.

Dávila Padilla, Agustín. *Historia de la fundación y discurso de la provincia de Santiago de México: De la Orden de Predicadores por las vidas de sus varones insignes y casos notables de nueva España*. Brussels: Ivan de Meerbeque, 1625.

Díaz, Bernal. *The Conquest of New Spain*. Translated by John M. Cohen. New York: Penguin, 1963.

Disciplinary Decrees of the General Councils: Text, Translation, and Commentary. Edited by H. J. Schroeder. London: B. Herder, 1937.

Doctrina christiana, y catecismo para instrvccion de los indios, y de las de mas perionas, que han de ser enseñadas en nuestra sancta fé. Con vn confessionario, y otras cosas necessarias para los que doctrinan, que sc [sic] contienen en la pagina siguiente. Lima: Antonio Ricardo, 1584.

Domingo de la Anunciacion. *Doctrina xpiana breue y co[m]pendiosa por via de dialogo entre vn maestro y vn discipulo, sacada en le[n]gua castellana y mexicana*. Mexico City: Pedro Ocharte, 1565.

Eimeric, Nicolau. *Directorium Inquisitorum*. Venice: Simeonis Vasalini, 1585.

———. *Manuale dell'Inquisitore: A.D. 1376*. Edited by Rino Cammilleri. Casale Monferrato, Italy: Piemme, 2000.

———. *Le manuel des inquisiteurs*. 1376. Translated by Louis Sala-Molins. Paris: Mouton, 1973.

Eliano, Giovanni Battista. *Doctrina christiana nella quale si contengono li principali misteri della nostra fede rappresentati con figure per istrutione de gl'idioti et di quelli che non sano legere* [. . .]. Rome, 1587.

Epistolario de Nueva España: 1505–1818. 16 vols. Edited by Francisco del Paso y Troncoso. Mexico City: Antigua Librería Robredo, 1939–42.

Erasmus, Desiderius. *Ausgewählte Werke*. Edited by Hajo Holborn and Annemarie Holborn. Munich: Beck, 1933.

———. "The Paraclesis." In *Christian Humanism and the Reformation: Selected Writings of Erasmus*, edited by John C. Olin, 97–108. New York: Fordham University Press, 1975.

Erpenius, Thomas. *Grammatica Arabica.* Leiden: Officina Raphelengiana, 1613.

Francisca de los Apóstoles. *The Inquisition of Francisca: A Sixteenth-Century Visionary on Trial.* Edited by Gillian T. W. Ahlgren. Chicago: University of Chicago Press, 2005.

Gaona, Juan de. *Colloquios de la paz, y tranquilidad christiana en lengua mexicana.* Mexico City: Pedro Ocharte, 1582.

García-Arenal, Mercedes. *Los moriscos.* Madrid: Editorial Nacional, 1975.

Gilberti, Fray Maturino. *Dialogo de doctrina christiana en lengua de Mechuaca[n].* Mexico City: Juan Pablos Bressano, 1559.

———. *Thesoro Spiritual en lengua de Mechuacan.* Edited by Pedro Márquez Joaquín. Zamora, Mexico: El Colegio de Michoacán, 2004.

Gómez Adrin, Juan. *Memorial en defensa de la lengva castellana para qve se prediqve en ella en Cataluña.* S.l.: S.n., 1636.

Guadagnoli, Filippo. *Breues arabicae linguae institutiones.* Rome: Propaganda Fide, 1642.

Hernández, Fray Benito. *Doctrina christiana en lengua misteca.* Mexico City: Pedro Ocharte, 1568.

Historia del Colegio de San Pablo, Granada, 1554–1765: Archivo Histórico Nacional, Madrid, Ms. Jesuitas, libro 773. Edited by Joaquín de Béthencourt and Estanislao Olivares. Granada: Facultad de Teología, 1991.

Juan Bautista, Fray. *Advertencias para los confessores de los naturales.* 2 vols. Mexico City: Melchior Ocharte, 1600–1601.

———. *A Iesv Christo S.N. ofrece este sermonario en lengua mexicana.* Mexico City: Diego Lopez Dávalos, 1606.

Juan de Ávila, San. *Audi, filia.* 1556. Madrid: Editorial Católica, 1970.

Juan de la Anunciación, Fray. *Sermonario en lengva mexicana, donde contiene (por el orden del missal nvevo romano) dos sermones en todas las dominicas y festividades principales de todo el año: Y otro en las fiestas de los sanctos, con sus vidas, y comunes. Con un cathecismo en lengva mexicana y española, con el calendario.* Mexico City: Antonio Ricardo, 1577.

Juan de la Cruz, Augustinian. *Doctrina christiana en la lengua guasteca co[n] la lengua castellana.* Mexico City: Pedro Ocharte, 1571.

Ledesma, Diego de. *Tres catecismos de la doctrina cristiana.* Mexico City: Jerónimo Balli, 1609.

León, Martin de. *Camino del cielo en lengua mexicana: Con todos los requisitos necessarios para conseguir este fin, co[n] todo lo que vn [Christ]iano deue creer, saber, y obrar, desde el punto que tiene vso de razon, hasta que muere.* Mexico City: Diego López Dávalos, 1611.

———. *Manval breve y forma de administrar los santos sacramentos à los indios vniuersalmente, ex concessione SS.D.N. Pau. Pap[a]e III.* Mexico City: Maria de Espinosa, 1614.

———. *Primera parte del sermonario del tiempo de todo el año, duplicado, en lengua mexicana.* Mexico City: Viuda de Diego López Dávalos, 1614.

Lorenzana y Buitrón, Francisco Antonio. *Cartas pastorales y edictos.* Mexico City: Joseph Antonio de Hogal, 1770.

Luis, de Granada. *Libro de la oración y meditación.* 1554. In *Obras castellanas / Fray Luis de Granada*, edited by Cristobal Cuevas, vol. 2. Madrid: Biblioteca Castro; Turner, 1994.

Manuscritos del concilio tercero provincial mexicano. 1585. Edited by Alberto Carrillo Cázares. Mexico City: Universidad Pontificia de Mexico, 2006.

Mendieta, Gerónimo de. *Historia eclesiástica indiana.* Edited by Joaquín García Icazbalceta. Mexico City: Antigua librería, 1870.

Mijangos, Juan de. *Espeio divino en lengua mexicana: En que pueden verse los padres, y tomar documento para acertar a doctrinar bien a sus hijos, y aficionallos alas virtudes.* Mexico City: Diego López Dávalos, 1607.

———. *Primera parte del sermonario dominical, y sanctoral, en lengva Mexicana.* Mexico City: Juan de Alcazar, 1624.

Molina, Alonso de. *Aqui comiença vn vocabulario en la lengua castellana y mexicana.* Mexico City: Juan Pablos, 1555.

———. *Arte de la lengua mexicana y castellana.* Mexico City: Pedro Ocharte, 1571.

———. *Doctrina cristiana breve, en castellano y mexicano.* Guadalajara, Mexico: Universidad de Guadalajara, 1996.

———. *Doctrina cristiana traducida en lengua mexicana.* Mexico City: S.n., 1606.

———. *Vocabulario en lengua castellana y mexicana.* Mexico City: Antonio de Espinosa, 1571.

Monumenta Mexicana. 8 vols. Edited by Félix Zubillaga and Miguel Ángel Rodríguez. Rome: Monumenta Historica Societatis Iesu, 1956–91.

Nebrija, Antonio. *Gramática castellana.* Salamanca, 1492.

Núñez Muley, Francisco. *A Memorandum for the President of the Royal Audiencia and Chancery Court of the City and Kingdom of Granada.* Edited by Vincent Barletta. Chicago: University of Chicago Press, 2007.

Olmos, Andres de. *Arte de la lengua Mexicana.* Edited by Ascensión Hernández de León-Portilla and Miguel León-Portilla. Mexico City: Universidad Nacional Autónoma de México, 2002.

Pérez de Ayala, Martín. *Catechismo para instruccion de los nueuamente conuertidos de moros.* Valencia: Pedro Mey, 1599.

———. *De divinis, apostolicis atque ecclesiasticis traditionibus, deque authoritate ac vi earum sacrosanct, adsertiones ceu libri decem: In quibus ferè vniuersa ecclesiae antiquitas circa dogmata apostolica orthodoxè elucidantur.* Paris: Audoënum Paruum, 1549.

———. "Discurso de la vida." In *Autobiografías y memorias,* edited by Manuel Serrano y Sanz, 210–38. Madrid: Bailly/Bailliére, 1905.

———. *Doctrina christiana, en lengua arauiga y castellana.* Valencia: Juan Mey, 1566.

———. *Doctrina cristiana en lengua arábiga y castellana para instrucción de los moriscos.* 1566. Valencia: F. Vives Mora, 1911.

———. *Sínodo de la diócesis de Guadix y de Baza.* Granada: Servicio de Publicaciones de la Universidad de Granada, 1994.

———. *Synodus diocesana valentiae.* Valencia: Juan Mey, 1566.

Popol Vuh: The Sacred Book of the Ancient Quiche Maya. Edited by Delia Goetz and Adrián Recinos. Norman: University of Oklahoma Press, 1950.

El proceso romano del arzobispo Carranza, 1567–1576. Edited by José Ignacio Tellechea Idígoras. Rome: Iglesia Nacional Española, 1988.

Recopilación de leyes de los reynos de las Indias. Mandadas imprimir y publicar por la Magestad Católica del Rey Don Carlos II. 4 vols. 1681. Reprint, Madrid: Andrés Ortega, 1774.

Remesal, Antonio de. *Historia de la provincia de San Vicente de Chiapa y Guatemala de la orden de n[uest]ro glorioso Padre Santo Domingo.* Madrid: Francisco de Angulo, 1619.

Ribadeneira, Pedro de. *Obras escogidas del padre Rivadeneira.* Madrid: M. Rivadeneyra, 1868.

Rincón, Antonio del. *Arte mexicana.* Mexico City: Pedro Balli, 1595.

Roa, Martín de. *Historia de la Provincia de Andalucía de la Compañía de Jesús (1553–1662).* Edited by Antonio Martín Pradas and Inmaculada Carrasco Gómez. Écija, Spain: Asociación de Amigos de Écija, 2005.

Sahagún, Bernardino. *The Florentine Codex: General History of the Things of New Spain.* 12 vols. Edited by Charles E. Dibble and Arthur J. O. Anderson. Salt Lake City: University of Utah Press, 1950–82.

———. *Psalmodia Christiana, y Sermonario de los Sanctos del Año, en lengua Mexicana.* Mexico City: Pedro Ocharte, 1583.

Sandoval, Alonso de. *Treatise on Slavery.* Edited by Nicole von Germeten. Indianapolis: Hackett, 2008.

Talavera, Hernando de. *Cartilla y doctrina en romance del arçobispo de Granada para enseñar niños a leer.* Salamanca: Juan de Porras, 1505–8.

———. *Catholica impugnacion del heretico libello que en el año 1480 fue divulgado en la ciudad de Sevilla.* Salamanca: S.n., 1480.

Tercero cathecismo y exposicion de la doctrina christiana, por sermones. Lima: Antonio Ricardo, 1585.

Vargas, Melchor de, Fray. *Doctrina christiana, muy vtil, y necessaria en castellano, mexicano y otomí: Traduzida en lengua otomí.* Mexico City: Pedro Balli, 1576.

Vergara, Francisco. *Cartilla de la doctrina cristiana en lengua matlatzinga.* Mexico City: Diego López de Ávalos, 1602.

The Vulgate Bible: Douay-Rheims Translation. 6 vols. Edited by Swift Edgar and Angela M. Kinney. Cambridge: Harvard University Press, 2010–13.

Zumárraga, Juan de. *Breve y mas compendiosa doctrina christiana en lengua mexicana y castellana, que contiene las cosas mas necesarias de nuestra sancta fe catholica, para aprovechamiento destos indios naturales y salvacion de sus animas.* Mexico City: Juan Cromberger, 1539.

———. *Doctrina cristiana breve para enseñanza de los niños.* Mexico City: Juan Cromberger, 1543.

———. *Doctrina Cristiana: Mas cierta y v[er]dadera pa[ra] ge[n]te sin erudicio[n] y letras: En q[ue] se co[n] tiene el catecismo o informacio[n] pa[ra] indios co[n] todo lo principal y necessario q[ue] el xpiano deue saber y obrar.* Mexico City: Juan Pablos, 1546.

———. *Don Fray Juan de Zumárraga. Primer obispo y arzobispo de México: Documentos inéditos publicados.* Edited by Alberto María Carreño. Mexico City: J. Porrúa, 1941.

———. *Dotrina breue muy p[ro]uechosa delas cosas q[ue] p[er]tenecen ala fe catholica y a n[uest]ra cristiandad en estilo llano pa comu[n] intelige[n]cia.* Mexico City: Juan Cromberger, 1544.

SECONDARY SOURCES

Abé, Takao. *The Jesuit Mission to New France: A New Interpretation in the Light of the Earlier Jesuit Experience in Japan.* Boston: Brill, 2011.

Álvarez Rodríguez, J. Rosaura. "La Casa de la Doctrina del Albaicín: Labor apostólico de la Compañía de Jesús con los moriscos." *Cuadernos de la Alhambra* 19–20 (1983–84): 231–46.

Arigita y Lasa, Mariano. *El Ilmo. y Rvmo. Señor Don Francisco de Navarra, de la orden de San Agustín*. Pamplona, Spain: J. Ezquerro, 1899.

Arriaga, Gonzalo de. *Historia del colegio de San Gregorio de Valladolid*. Valladolid, Spain: Cuesta, 1928.

Azcona, Tarsicio de. *Isabel la Catolica: Estudio crítico de su vida y su reinado*. Madrid: Biblioteca de Autores Cristianos, 1964.

Back, Siegfried. *The Pelican: A Life of Saint Thomas of Villanova*. Villanova, PA: Augustinian Press, 1987.

Bailyn, Bernard. *Atlantic History: Concept and Contours*. Cambridge: Harvard University Press, 2005.

Bainton, Roland. *Here I Stand! A Life of Martin Luther*. 1950. Reprint, Peabody, MA: Hendrickson, 2009.

Balleriaux, Catherine. *Missionary Strategies in the New World, 1610–1690*. New York: Routledge, 2016.

Bataillon, Marcel. *Érasme et l'Espagne*. 1937. Reprint, Geneva: Librairie Droz, 1991.

Belda Plans, Juan. *Los lugares teológicos de Melchor Cano en los comentarios a la Suma*. Pamplona, Spain: Ediciones Universidad de Navarra, 1982.

Benítez Sánchez-Blanco, Rafael. *Heroicas decisiones: La monarquía católica y los moriscos valencianos*. Valencia: Institució Alfons el Magnànim, 2001.

Bernabé Pons, Luis Fernando, and María Jesús Rubiera Mata. "La lengua de mudéjares y moriscos. Estado de la cuestión." In *VII Simposio internacional de mudejarismo*, 599–632. Teruel, Spain: Centro de Estudios Mudéjares, 1999.

Bethencourt, Francisco. *L'Inquisition à l'époque moderne: Espagne, Portugal, Italie XVe–XIXe siècle*. Paris: Fayard, 1995.

Bilinkoff, Jodi. *The Ávila of Saint Teresa: Religious Reform in a Sixteenth-Century City*. Ithaca: Cornell University Press, 1989.

Blair, Ann. "Information Flows in a Global Renaissance: Through Orality, Manuscript, and Print." Paper presented at the annual meeting of the Renaissance Society of America. Washington, DC, March 22–25, 2012.

Boronat y Barrachina, Pascual. *Los moriscos españoles y su expulsión*. 2 vols. Valencia: Francisco Vives y Mora, 1901.

Brain, Cecilia. "Aprendizaje de lenguas indígenas por parte de españoles en Nueva España en los primeros cien años después de la conquista." *Colonial Latin American Review* 19, no. 2 (2010): 279–300.

Broggio, Paolo. *Evangelizzare il mondo: Le missioni della Compagnia di Gesù tra Europa e America: Secoli XVI–XVII*. Rome: Carocci, 2004.

———. "The Religious Orders and the Expulsion of the Moriscos: Doctrinal Controversies and Hispano-Papal Relations." In *The Expulsion of the Moriscos from Spain: A Mediterranean Diaspora*, edited by Mercedes García-Arenal and Gerard Wiegers, 156–78. Boston: Brill, 2014.

Burke, Peter. *Languages and Communities in Early Modern Europe*. New York: Cambridge University Press, 2004.

Burkhart, Louise M. "The 'Little Doctrine' and Indigenous Catechesis in New Spain." *Hispanic American Historical Review* 94, no. 2 (2014): 167–206.

———. *The Slippery Earth: Nahua-Christian Moral Dialogue in Sixteenth-Century Mexico*. Tucson: University of Arizona Press, 1989.

Burkhart, Louise M., and Barry D. Sell, eds. *Nahuatl Theater*. 4 vols. Norman: University of Oklahoma Press, 2004–9.

Caballero, Fermín. *Vida del illmo. Sr. D. fray Melchor Cano del orden de Santo Domingo, obispo de Canarias, etc.* 1868. Reprint, Cuenca, Spain: Olcades, 1980.

Cain, Andrew, and Josef Loessl, eds. *Jerome of Stridon: His Life, Writings and Legacy*. Burlington, VT: Ashgate, 2009.

Cameron, Euan. *The Sixteenth Century*. New York: Oxford University Press, 2006.

Campbell, Lyle. *American Indian Languages: The Historical Linguistics of Native America*. New York: Oxford University Press, 1997.

Campbell, Lyle, and Mauricio Mixco. *A Glossary of Historical Linguistics*. Salt Lake City: University of Utah Press, 2007.

Cañizares-Esguerra, Jorge, and Erik R. Seeman. *The Atlantic in Global History, 1500–2000*. Upper Saddle River, NJ: Pearson Prentice Hall, 2007.

Canny, Nicholas, and Philip D. Morgan. *The Oxford Handbook of the Atlantic World, 1450–1800*. New York: Oxford University Press, 2011.

Castro, Daniel. *Another Face of Empire: Bartolomé de las Casas, Indigenous Rights, and Ecclesiastical Imperialism*. Durham: Duke University Press, 2007.

The Catholic Encyclopedia. 15 vols. New York: Robert Appleton, 1907–12.

Cervantes, Fernando. *The Devil in the New World: The Impact of Diabolism in New Spain*. New Haven: Yale University Press, 1994.

Charles, John. *Allies at Odds: The Andean Church and Its Indigenous Agents, 1583–1671*. Albuquerque: University of New Mexico Press, 2010.

Christensen, Mark Z. *Nahua and Maya Catholicisms: Texts and Religion in Colonial Central Mexico and Yucatan*. Stanford: Stanford University Press, 2013.

———. "The Tales of Two Cultures: Ecclesiastical Texts and Nahua and Maya Catholicisms." *Americas* 66, no. 3 (2010): 353–77.

———. "The Use of Nahuatl in Evangelization and the Ministry of Sebastian." *Ethnohistory* 59, no. 4 (2012): 691–711.

Christian, William A. *Local Religion in Sixteenth-Century Spain*. Princeton: Princeton University Press, 1981.

Chuchiak, John F. *The Inquisition in New Spain, 1536–1820*. Baltimore: Johns Hopkins University Press, 2012.

———. "In Servitio Dei: Fray Diego de Landa, the Franciscan Order, and the Return of Extirpation Idolatry in the Colonial Diocese of Yucatan, 1573–1579." *Americas* 61, no. 4 (2005): 611–46.

Clendinnen, Inga. *Ambivalent Conquests: Maya and Spaniard in Yucatan, 1517–1570*. New York: Cambridge University Press, 1987.

———. *Aztecs: An Interpretation*. New York: Cambridge University Press, 1991.

Clossey, Luke Sean. *Salvation and Globalization in the Early Jesuit Missions*. New York: Cambridge University Press, 2008.

Coleman, David. *Creating Christian Granada: Society and Religious Culture in an Old-World Frontier City*. Ithaca: Cornell University Press, 2003.

Colombo, Emanuele. "La Compagnia de Gesù e l'evangelizzazione dei musulmani nella Spagna del seicento: Il caso González." *Revue Mabillon* 20 (2009): 203–27.

———. *Convertire i musulmani. L'esperienza di un gesuita spagnolo del Seicento.* Milan: Bruno Mondadori, 2007.

Dalmases, Cándido de. "San Francisco de Borja y la Inquisición Española, 1559–61." *Archivum Historicum Societatis Iesu* 41 (1972): 48–135.

Dedieu, Jean Pierre. *L'Administration de la foi: L'inquisition de Tolède, XVI–XVII siècle.* Madrid: Casa de Velázquez, 1989.

De la Costa, Horacio. *Jesuits in the Philippines: 1581–1768.* Cambridge: Harvard University Press, 1961.

Delumeau, Jean. *Catholicism Between Luther and Voltaire: A New View of the Counter-Reformation.* Translated by Jeremy Moiser. Philadelphia: Westminster, 1977.

———. *Le Catholicisme entre Luther et Voltaire.* Paris: Presses Universitaires de France, 1971.

Deslandres, Dominique. "*Exemplo aeque ut verbo*: The French Jesuits' Missionary World." In *The Jesuits: Cultures, Sciences, and the Arts, 1540–1773*, edited by John W. O'Malley, Gauvin Alexander Bailey, Steven J. Harris, and T. Frank Kennedy, 1:258–73. Toronto: University of Toronto Press, 1999.

Domínguez Ortiz, Antonio, and Bernard Vincent. *Historia de los moriscos: Vida y tragedia de una minoría.* Madrid: Revista de Occidente, 1978.

Don, Patricia Lopes. *Bonfires of Culture: Franciscans, Indigenous Leaders, and Inquisition in Early Mexico, 1524–1540.* Norman: University of Oklahoma Press, 2010.

Ducharme, Bernard. "De Talavera a Ramírez de Haro: Actores y representaciones de la evangelización de los mudéjares y moriscos en Granada, Zaragoza y Valencia (1492–1545)." In *De la tierra al cielo. Líneas recientes de investigación en historia moderna*, edited by Eliseo Serrano Martín, 39–52. Zaragoza, Spain: Institución Fernando el Católico, 2013.

Durston, Alan. "Indigenous Languages and the Historiography on Latin America." *Storia della Storiografia* 67, no. 1 (2015): 51–65.

———. *Pastoral Quechua: Christian Translation in Colonial Peru, 1550–1650.* Notre Dame: University of Notre Dame Press, 2007.

Edwards, John. *Torquemada and the Inquisitors.* Stroud, UK: Tempus, 2005.

Edwards, John, and Ronald Truman, eds. *Reforming Catholicism in the England of Mary Tudor: The Achievement of Friar Bartolomé Carranza.* Burlington, VT: Ashgate, 2005.

Ehlers, Benjamin. *Between Christians and Moriscos: Juan de Ribera and Religious Reform in Valencia, 1568–1614.* Baltimore: Johns Hopkins University Press, 2006.

Eire, Carlos M. N. *From Madrid to Purgatory: The Art and Craft of Dying in Sixteenth-Century Spain.* New York: Cambridge University Press, 1995.

El Alaoui, Youssef. "Ignacio de las Casas, jesuita y morisco." *Sharq al-Andalus* 14–15 (1997–98): 317–39.

———. *Jésuites, Morisques et Indiens: Étude comparative des méthodes d'évangelisation de la compagnie de Jésus d'après les traités de José de Acosta (1588) et Ignacio de las Casas (1605–1607).* Paris: Honoré Champion, 2006.

Elias, Norbert. *The Civilizing Process: The History of Manners and State Formation and Civilization.* Translated by Edmund Jephcott.

1939. Reprint, Oxford and Cambridge, MA: Blackwell, 1994.

Elliott, John H. *Imperial Spain, 1469–1716*. 1990. Reprint, New York: Penguin, 1963.

———. *The Revolt of the Catalans: A Study in the Decline of Spain, 1598–1640*. Cambridge: Cambridge University Press, 1963.

———. *Spain, Europe, and the Wider World, 1500–1800*. New Haven: Yale University Press, 2009.

Febvre, Lucien, and Henri-Jean Martin. *The Coming of the Book: The Impact of Printing, 1450–1800*. Translated by David Gerard. New York: Verso, 1997.

Fernández López, Sergio. *Lectura y prohibición de la Biblia en lengua vulgar. Defensores y detractores*. León, Spain: Universidad de León, Secretariado de Publicaciones y Medios Audiovisuales, 2003.

Fernández-Morera, Darío. *The Myth of the Andalusian Paradise: Muslims, Christians, and Jews Under Islamic Rule in Medieval Spain*. Wilmington, DE: ISI Books, 2015.

Fletcher, Richard. *Moorish Spain*. Berkeley: University of California Press, 2006.

Fowler, Jessica. "Illuminating the Empire: The Dissemination of the Spanish Inquisition and the Heresy of Alumbradismo, 1525–1600." PhD diss., University of California–Davis, 2015.

Gallego, María Ángeles. "The Languages of Medieval Iberia and Their Religious Dimension." *Medieval Encounters* 9, no. 1 (2003): 118–19.

Gallego y Burín, Antonio, and Alfonso Gámir Sandoval. *Los moriscos del reino de Granada según el sínodo de Guadix de 1554*. Granada: Universidad de Granada, 1996.

Galván Rodríguez, Eduardo. *El Inquisidor General*. Madrid: Dykinson, 2010.

García, Sebastián. "San Francisco de Asís y la Orden Franciscana en Extremadura." In *El culto a los santos: Cofradías, devoción, fiestas y arte*, edited by F. Javier Campos y Fernández de Sevilla, 759–80. El Escorial, Spain: Ediciones Escurialenses, 2008.

García-Arenal, Mercedes. "Moriscos e indios: Para un estudio comparado de métodos de conquista y evangelización." *Chronica Nova* 20 (1992): 153–75.

———. "Religious Dissent and Minorities: The Morisco Age." *Journal of Early Modern History* 81 (2009): 888–920.

———. "The Religious Identity of the Arabic Language and the Affair of the Lead Books of the Sacromonte of Granada." *Arabica* 56 (2009): 495–528.

García-Arenal, Mercedes, and Fernando Rodríguez Mediano. "Sacred History, Sacred Languages: The Question of Arabic in Early Modern Spain." In *The Teaching and Learning of Arabic in Early Modern Europe*, edited by Jan Loop, Alastair Hamilton, and Charles Burnett, 133–62. Boston: Brill, 2017.

García-Cárcel, Ricardo. "Estudio crítico del catecismo Ribera-Ayala." In *Les Morisques et leur temps*, 161–68. Paris: Editions du Centre national de la recherche scientifique, 1983.

———. *Herejía y sociedad en el siglo XVI: La Inquisición en Valencia, 1530–1609*. Barcelona: Ediciones Península, 1980.

García Icazbalceta, Joaquín. *Bibliografía mexicana del siglo XVI. Primera parte. Catálogo razonado de libros impresos en México de 1539 á 1600*. Mexico City: Andrade y Morales, 1884.

———. *Don Fray Juan de Zumárraga: Primer Obispo y Arzobispo de*

Mexico. Mexico City: Andrade y Morales, 1881.

———. *Nueva colección para la historia de Mexico*. Mexico City: Francisco Díaz de León, 1889.

García Oro, José. *Cisneros: Un cardenal reformista en el trono de España, 1436–1517*. Madrid: La Esfera de los Libros, 2005.

García Pedraza, Amalia. *Actitudes ante la muerte en la Granada del siglo XVI: Los moriscos que quisieron salvarse*. 2 vols. Granada: Universidad de Granada, 2002.

Garrad, Kenneth. "The Original Memorial of Don Francisco Núñez Muley." *Atlante* 2 (1954): 199–226.

Garrido Aranda, Antonio. *Moriscos e indios: Precedentes hispánicos de la evangelización en México*. 1980. Reprint, Mexico City: Universidad Nacional Autónoma de México, 2013.

———. *Organización de la Iglesia en el Reino de Granada y su proyección en Indias, siglo XVI*. Seville: Escuela de Estudios Hispano-Americanos, 1979.

Garrido García, Carlos Javier. "Guadix y su tierra durante el primer año de la rebelión de los moriscos (1569): Guerra y esclavitud." *Boletín del Centro de Estudios Pedro Suárez* 24 (2011): 73–108.

———. "El uso de la lengua árabe como medio de evangelización-represión de los moriscos del reino de Granada: Nuevos datos sobre Bartolomé Dorador, intérprete y traductor de Martín de Ayala, obispo de Guadix." *Miscelánea de Estudios Árabes y Hebraicos. Sección Árabe-Islam* 57 (2008): 123–37.

Gibson, Charles. *Spain in America*. New York: Harper, 1966.

Gil, Fernando. *Primeras doctrinas del nuevo mundo: Estudio histórico teológico de las obras de fray Juan de Zumárraga*. Buenos Aires: Universidad Católica Facultad de Teología, 1993.

Gilbert, Claire. "The Politics of Language in the Western Mediterranean, c.1492–c.1669: Multilingual Institutions and the Status of Arabic in Early Modern Spain." PhD diss., University of California: Los Angeles, 2014.

———. "Transmission, Translation, Legitimacy and Control: The Activities of a Multilingual Scribe in Morisco Granada." In *Multilingual and Multigraphic Documents and Manuscripts of East and West*, edited by Giuseppe Mandalà, Inmaculada Pérez Martín, and Alex Metcalfe, 425–62. Piscataway, NJ: Gorgias Press, 2015.

Giles, Mary E., ed. *Women in the Inquisition: Spain and the New World*. Baltimore: Johns Hopkins University Press, 1998.

Giménez-Eguibar, Patricia, and Daniel I. Wasserman-Soler. "*La mala algarabía*: Church, Monarchy, and the Arabic Language in 16th-Century Spain." *Medieval History Journal* 14, no. 2 (2011): 229–58.

Ginzburg, Carlo. *The Cheese and the Worms: The Cosmos of a Sixteenth-Century Miller*. 1980. Reprint, Baltimore: Johns Hopkins University Press, 1992.

———. *Formaggio e i vermi: Il cosmo di un mugnaio del '500*. Turin: G. Einaudi, 1976.

González de Cossío, Francisco. *La imprenta en México (1553–1820): 510 adiciones a la obra de don José Toribio Medina en homenaje al primer centenario de su nacimiento*. Mexico City: Universidad Nacional de México, 1952.

González Novalín, José Luis. *El inquisidor general Fernando de Valdés*. 2 vols.

Oviedo, Spain: Universidad de Oviedo, 1968.

Gormley, Joan Frances. "Introduction." In *John of Avila, Audi, Filia—Listen, O Daughter*, edited by Joan Frances Gormley, 1–31. New York: Paulist Press, 2006.

Greene, Jack P., and Philip D. Morgan. *Atlantic History: A Critical Reappraisal*. New York: Oxford University Press, 2008.

Greenleaf, Richard. *The Mexican Inquisition of the Sixteenth Century*. Albuquerque: University of New Mexico Press, 1969.

———. *Zumárraga and the Mexican Inquisition, 1536–1543*. Washington, DC: Academy of American Franciscan History, 1961.

Gruzinski, Serge. *La colonisation de l'imaginaire: Sociétés indigènes et occidentalisation dans le Mexique espagnol, XVIe–XVIIIe siècle*. Paris: Gallimard, 1988.

———. *The Conquest of Mexico: The Incorporation of Indian Societies into the Western World, 16th–18th Centuries*. Cambridge, MA: Blackwell, 1993.

Hamilton, Alastair. *Heresy and Mysticism in Sixteenth Century Spain: The Alumbrados*. Cambridge, UK: J. Clarke, 1992.

Hanks, William F. *Converting Words: Maya in the Age of the Cross*. Berkeley: University of California Press, 2010.

Harvey, L. P. *Islamic Spain, 1250–1500*. Chicago: University of Chicago Press, 1992.

———. *Muslims in Spain, 1500–1614*. Chicago: University of Chicago Press, 2005.

Heath, Shirley Brice. *La política del lenguaje en México: De la colonia a la nación*. Mexico City: SEP Instituto Nacional Indigenista, 1972.

———. *Telling Tongues: Language Policy in Mexico, Colony to Nation*. New York: Teachers College Press, 1972.

Herreros González, Carmen. *Pedro Guerrero, vida y obre de un ilustre riojano del siglo XVI*. Logroño, Spain: Instituto de Estudios Riojanos, 2012.

Homza, Lu Ann. *Religious Authority in the Spanish Renaissance*. Baltimore: Johns Hopkins University Press, 2000.

———, ed. *The Spanish Inquisition, 1478–1614: An Anthology of Sources*. Indianapolis, IN: Hackett, 2006.

Huerga, Álvaro. *Fray Luis de Granada: Una vida al servicio de la Iglesia*. Madrid: Editorial Católica, 1988.

———. *Historia de los alumbrados, 1570–1630*. 5 vols. Madrid: Fundación Universitaria Española, Seminario Cisneros, 1978–94.

Iannuzzi, Isabella. *El poder de la palabra en el siglo XV: Fray Hernando de Talavera*. Salamanca: Junta de Castilla y León, 2009.

Icaza Dufour, Francisco de. *Pedro Moya de Contreras*. Mexico City: Planeta DeAgostini, 2003.

Iranzo, Víctor Sebastián. *Las sinodales de Santo Tomás de Villanueva, exponente de la reforma pretridentina en Valencia*. Valencia: Vives Mora, 1959.

Jedin, Hubert. *A History of the Council of Trent*. 2 vols. Translated by Ernest Graf. London: T. Nelson, 1957–61.

Jericó Bermejo, Ignacio. *Bartolomé Carranza de Miranda: Seis circunstancias que marcaron una vida en el siglo XVI*. Salamanca: Editorial San Esteban, 2006.

Kagan, Richard. *Lucrecia's Dreams: Politics and Prophecy in Sixteenth-Century Spain*. Berkeley: University of California Press, 1995.

Kamen, Henry. *The Disinherited: Exile and the Making of Spanish Culture,*

1492–1975. New York: Harper Collins, 2007.

———. *Inquisition and Society in Spain in the Sixteenth and Seventeenth Centuries*. Bloomington: Indiana University Press, 1985.

———. *Philip of Spain*. New Haven: Yale University Press, 1997.

———. *The Spanish Inquisition: A Historical Revision*. New Haven: Yale University Press, 1997.

Karttunen, Frances. *An Analytical Dictionary of Nahuatl*. Norman: University of Oklahoma Press, 1992.

———. *Between Worlds: Interpreters, Guides, and Survivors*. New Brunswick: Rutgers University Press, 1994.

Kennedy, Hugh. *Muslim Spain and Portugal: A Political History of Al-Andalus*. New York: Longman, 1997.

King, Linda. *Roots of Identity: Language and Literacy in Mexico*. Stanford: Stanford University Press, 1994.

Kittelson, James M. *Luther the Reformer: The Story of the Man and His Career*. Minneapolis, MN: Augsburg, 1986.

Larkin, Brian. *The Very Nature of God: Baroque Catholicism and Religious Reform in Bourbon Mexico City*. Albuquerque: University of New Mexico Press, 2010.

Lea, Henry Charles. *A History of the Inquisition of Spain*. 4 vols. New York: Macmillan, 1906–7.

———. *The Moriscos of Spain: Their Conversion and Expulsion*. Philadelphia: Lea Brothers, 1901.

León, Nicolás. *Bibliografía mexicana*. Mexico City: Museo nacional de arqueología, historia y etnografía, 1923.

León-Portilla, Miguel. *Bernardino de Sahagun, First Anthropologist*. Translated by Mauricio J. Mixco. Norman: University of Oklahoma Press, 2002.

Li, Shenwen. *Stratégies missionnaires des jésuites français en Nouvelle-France et en Chine au XVIIe siècle*. Québec: Presses de l'Université Laval, 2001.

Lifshitz, Felice. *The Name of the Saint: The Martyrology of Jerome and Access to the Sacred in Francia, 627–827*. Notre Dame: University of Notre Dame Press, 2006.

Llin Cháfer, Arturo. *Santo Tomás de Villanueva: Pastor de la iglesia en tiempos recios*. Madrid: Agustiniana, 2010.

Lockhart, James. *The Nahuas After the Conquest: A Social and Cultural History of the Indians of Central Mexico, Sixteenth Through Eighteenth Centuries*. Stanford: Stanford University Press, 1992.

Lodares Marrodán, Juan R. "La contradictoria legislación lingüística americana (1500–1770)." In *Actas del VI Congreso Internacional de Historia de la Lengua española*, edited by J. L. Girón Alconchel and J. J. de Bustos Tovar, 2235–42. Madrid: Arco Libros, 2006.

López Martín, Juan. "El arzobispo de Granada D. Pedro Guerrero y la compañía de Jesús." *Anthologica Annua* 24–25 (1977–78): 453–98.

———. *La imagen del obispo en el pensamiento teológico—pastoral de don Pedro Guerrero en Trento*. Rome: Iglesia Nacional Española, 1971.

Lundberg, Magnus. *Unification and Conflict: The Church Politics of Alonso de Montúfar OP, Archbishop of Mexico, 1554–1572*. Uppsala, Sweden: Swedish Institute of Missionary Research, 2002.

———. *Unificación y conflicto: La gestión episcopal de Alonso de Montúfar, OP, arzobispo de México, 1554–1572*. Translated by Alberto Carrillo

Cázares. Zamora, Mexico: Colegio de Michoacán, 2009.

Luque Alcaide, Elisa, and Josep Ignasi Saranyana. "Los instrumentos pastorales del III concilio mexicano (1585)." *Scripta theologica* 23, no. 1 (1991): 185–96.

Lynn, Kimberly. *Between Court and Confessional: The Politics of Spanish Inquisitors*. New York: Cambridge University Press, 2013.

———. "Unraveling the Spanish Inquisition: Inquisitorial Studies in the Twenty-First Century." *History Compass* 5, no. 4 (2007): 1280–93.

———. "Was Adam the First Heretic? Diego de Simancas, Luis de Páramo, and the Origins of Inquisitorial Practice." *Archiv für Reformationsgeschichte* 97 (2006): 184–210.

MacCormack, Sabine. *Religion in the Andes: Vision and Imagination in Early Colonial Peru*. Princeton: Princeton University Press, 1991.

MacCulloch, Diarmaid. *The Reformation*. New York: Viking, 2004.

Magnier, Grace. *Pedro de Valencia and the Catholic Apologists of the Expulsion of the Moriscos: Visions of Christianity and Kingship*. Boston: Brill, 2010.

Marín Ocete, Antonio. *El arzobispo don Pedro Guerrero y la política conciliar española en el siglo XVI*. Madrid: Consejo Superior de Investigaciones Científicas, 1970.

———. "El concilio provincial de Granada en 1565." *Archivo teológico granadino* 25 (1962): 23–178.

Márquez, Antonio. *Los alumbrados: Orígenes y filosofía, 1525–1559*. Madrid: Taurus, 1972.

Martínez de Bujanda, Jesús, ed. *Index des livres interdits*. Vols. 5–6. Sherbrooke, Canada: Éditions de l'Université de Sherbrooke, 1984–93.

Martínez Millán, José. *Felipe II (1527–1598): La configuración de la monarquía hispana*. Valladolid, Spain: Junta de Castilla y León, Consejería de Educación y Cultura, 1998.

Matthew, Laura E. *Memories of Conquest: Becoming Mexicano in Colonial Guatemala*. Chapel Hill: University of North Carolina Press, 2012.

McQuown, Norman. "The Indigenous Languages of Latin America." *American Anthropologist* 57 (1955): 501–70.

Medina, Francisco de Borja. "La compañía de Jesús y la minoría morisca (1545–1614)." *Archivum Historicum Societatis Iesu* 57 (1988): 3–136.

Medina, José Toribio. *La imprenta en México, 1539–1810*. Sevilla: E. Rasco, 1893.

Megged, Amos. *Exporting the Catholic Reformation: Local Religion in Early Colonial Mexico*. New York: Brill, 1996.

———. Review of *Nahua and Maya Catholicisms: Texts and Religion in Colonial Central Mexico and Yucatan*, by Mark Christensen. *Catholic Historical Review* 102, no. 1 (2016): 208–9.

Menocal, María Rosa. *The Ornament of the World: How Muslims, Jews, and Christians Created a Culture of Tolerance in Medieval Spain*. Boston: Back Bay Books, 2003.

Mills, Kenneth, and Anthony Grafton, eds. *Conversion: Old Worlds and New*. Rochester: University of Rochester Press, 2003.

Mills, Kenneth, and William Taylor, eds. *Colonial Spanish America: A Documentary History*. Wilmington, DE: Scholarly Resources, 1998.

Ministerio de Cultura. *Los Moriscos: Españoles Trasterrados*. Madrid: Ministerio de Cultura, 2009.

Miralles, Antonio. *El concepto de tradición en Martín Pérez de Ayala*.

Pamplona, Spain: Ediciones Universidad de Pamplona, 1980.

Moreno, Doris. *La invención de la inquisición*. Madrid: Marcial Pons Historia, 2004.

Muir, Edward, and Guido Ruggiero. *Microhistory and the Lost Peoples of Europe*. Baltimore: Johns Hopkins University Press, 1991.

Murata, Sachiko, and William C. Chittick. *The Vision of Islam*. New York: Paragon House, 1994.

Nalle, Sara T. *God in La Mancha: Religious Reform and the People of Cuenca, 1500–1650*. Baltimore: Johns Hopkins University Press, 1992.

———. "Literacy and Culture in Early Modern Castile." *Past and Present* 125, no. 1 (1989): 65–96.

———. *Mad for God: Bartolomé Sánchez and the Secret Messiah of Cardenete*. Charlottesville: University of Virginia Press, 2000.

Nesvig, Martin. "The Epistemological Politics of Vernacular Scripture in Sixteenth-Century Mexico." *Americas* 70, no. 2 (2013): 165–201.

———. *Ideology and Inquisition: The World of the Censors in Early Mexico*. New Haven: Yale University Press, 2008.

Nichols, Deborah L., and Enrique Rodríguez-Alegría, eds. *The Oxford Handbook of the Aztecs*. New York: Oxford University Press, 2016.

Oberman, Heiko Augustinus. *The Harvest of Medieval Theology: Gabriel Biel and Late Medieval Nominalism*. 1963. Reprint, Durham, NC: Labyrinth Press, 1983.

———. *Luther: Man Between God and the Devil*. 1989. Reprint, New Haven: Yale University Press, 2006.

O'Callaghan, Joseph F. *Reconquest and Crusade in Medieval Spain*. Philadelphia: University of Pennsylvania Press, 2004.

Oliver Asín, Jaime. *Historia de la lengua española*. Madrid: Diana, Artes Gráficas, 1940.

O'Malley, John. *The First Jesuits*. Cambridge: Harvard University Press, 1993.

———. *Trent and All That: Renaming Catholicism in the Early Modern Era*. Cambridge: Harvard University Press, 2000.

———. *Trent: What Happened at the Council*. Cambridge: Harvard University Press, 2013.

Operé, Fernando. *Indian Captivity in Spanish America: Frontier Narratives*. Charlottesville: University of Virginia Press, 2008.

Padden, Robert C. "The Ordenanza del Patronazgo, 1574: An Interpretive Essay." *Americas* 12, no. 4 (1956): 333–54.

Pastor, José Francisco. *Las apologias de la lengua castellana en el siglo de oro*. Madrid: Compañía Ibero-Americana de Publicaciones, 1929.

Pastore, Stefania. *Il vangelo e la spada. L'inquisizione di Castiglia e i suoi critici (1460–1598)*. Rome: Edizioni di storia e letteratura, 2003.

Peniche, Surya, and Stella María González Cicero. *Historia de las bibliotecas en Yucatán*. Mexico City: SEP, Dirección General de Bibliotecas, 1987.

Peraita, Carmen. *Gobernar la república interior, enseñar a ser súbdito: Hagiografía y sociedad cortesana en Quevedo. Epítome a la vida de fray Tomás de Villanueva de Francisco de Quevedo*. Pamplona, Spain: Ediciones Universidad de Navarra, 2012.

Pérez Puente, Leticia. "La creación de las cátedras públicas de lenguas indígenas y la secularización parroquial." *Estudios de historia novohispana* 41 (2009): 45–78.

Pérez Villanueva, Joaquín, and Bartolomé Escandell Bonet, eds. *Historia de la Inquisición en España y América.* Madrid: Biblioteca de Autores Cristianos, 1984–2000.

Phelan, John Leddy. *The Hispanization of the Philippines: Spanish Aims and Filipino Responses, 1565–1700.* Madison: University of Wisconsin Press, 1959.

Pinto Crespo, Virgilio. *Inquisición y control ideológico en la España del siglo XVI.* Madrid: Taurus, 1983.

Pizzigoni, Caterina. *The Life Within: Local Indigenous Society in Mexico's Toluca Valley, 1650–1800.* Stanford: Stanford University Press, 2012.

Poole, Stafford. *Our Lady of Guadalupe: Origins and Sources of a Mexican National Symbol, 1531–1797.* Tucson: University of Arizona Press, 1995.

———. *Pedro Moya de Contreras: Catholic Reform and Royal Power in New Spain, 1571–1591.* 1987. Reprint, Norman: University of Oklahoma Press, 2011.

———. *Pedro Moya de Contreras: Reforma católica y poder real en la nueva España, 1571–1591.* Translated by Alberto Carrillo Cázares. Zamora, Mexico: Colegio de Michoacán, 2012.

Poska, Allyson. *Regulating the People: The Catholic Reformation in Seventeenth-Century Spain.* Boston: Brill, 1998.

Rafael, Vicente. *Contracting Colonialism: Translation and Christian Conversion in Tagalog Society Under Early Spanish Rule.* Ithaca: Cornell University Press, 1988.

Rawlings, Helen. *The Spanish Inquisition.* Malden, MA: Blackwell, 2006.

Resines, Luis. *Catecismos pictográficos de Pedro de Gante, Incompleto y Mucagua.* Madrid: Fundación Universitaria Española, 2007.

Restall, Matthew. "A History of the New Philology and the New Philology in History." *Latin American Research Review* 38, no. 1 (2003): 113–34.

———. *The Maya World: Yucatec Culture and Society, 1550–1850.* Stanford: Stanford University Press, 1997.

———. *Seven Myths of the Spanish Conquest.* New York: Oxford University Press, 2003.

Ricard, Robert. *La conquête spirituelle du Mexique.* Paris: Institut d'ethnologie, 1933.

———. *La conquista espiritual de México. Ensayo sobre el apostolado y los métodos misioneros de las órdenes mendicantes en la Nueva España de 1523–24 a 1572.* Translated by Ángel María Garibay K. Mexico City: Editorial Jus, 1947.

———. *The Spiritual Conquest of Mexico: An Essay on the Apostolate and the Evangelizing Methods of the Mendicant Orders in New Spain, 1523–1572.* Translated by Lesley Byrd Simpson. Berkeley: University of California Press, 1966, 1974.

Rico Callado, Francisco Luis. "Las misiones interiores en la España postridentina." *Hispania Sacra* 55 (2003): 109–29.

Robres Lluch. *San Juan de Ribera, patriarca de Antioquía, arzobispo y virrey de Valencia, 1532–1611; un obispo según el ideal de Trento.* Barcelona: J. Flors, 1960.

Rodríguez Besné, José Ramón. *El consejo de la Suprema Inquisición.* Madrid: Editorial Complutense, 2000.

Rodríguez Mediano, Fernando. "Fragmentos del orientalismo español del s. XVII." *Hispania* 66, no. 222 (2006): 243–76.

Roldán-Figueroa, Rady. *The Ascetic Spirituality of Juan de Ávila, 1499–1569.* Boston: Brill, 2010.

Román, Reinaldo, and Pamela Voekel. "Popular Religion in Latin American Historiography." In *The Oxford Handbook of Latin American History*, edited by José C. Moya, 454–88. New York: Oxford University Press, 2011.

Rospide, María Margarita. "La real cédula del 10 de mayo de 1770 y la enseñanza del castellano. Observaciones sobre su aplicación en el territorio altoperuano." In *Memoria del X Congreso del Instituto Internacional de Historia del Derecho Indiano*, 1415–48. Mexico City: Universidad Nacional Autónoma de México, 1995.

Ruiz Gutiérrez, Ana. *Fray Alonso de Montúfar: Loja y la formación de la iglesia indiana*. Granada, Spain: Fundación Ibn al-Jatib de Estudios de Cooperación Cultural, 2007.

Rummel, Erika. *Jiménez de Cisneros: On the Threshold of Spain's Golden Age*. Tempe: Arizona Center for Medieval and Renaissance Studies, 1999.

Ryan, María del Pilar. *El jesuita secreto: San Francisco de Borja*. Translated by Paz Fernández Cervera. Valencia: Biblioteca Valenciana, 2008.

Salomons, Carolyn. "1492 Reconsidered: Religious and Social Change in Fifteenth-Century Ávila." PhD diss., Johns Hopkins University, 2014.

Sánchez Albornoz, Claudio. *España: Un enigma histórico*. Buenos Aires: Editorial Sudamericana, 1956.

———. *Spain: A Historical Enigma*. Translated by Colette Joly Dees and David Sven Reher. Madrid: Fundación Universitaria Española, 1975.

Sánchez Rodríguez, Julio. *Pedro Moya de Contreras*. Las Palmas de Gran Canaria, Spain: JSP, 2006.

Sanz y Sanz, José. *Melchor Cano; cuestiones fundamentales de crítica histórica sobre su vida y sus escritos*. Monachil, Spain: Santa Rita, 1959.

Sarreal, Julia J. S. *The Guaraní and Their Missions: A Socioeconomic History*. Stanford: Stanford University Press, 2014.

Schwaller, John F. *The Church and Clergy in Sixteenth-Century Mexico*. Albuquerque: University of New Mexico Press, 1987.

———. "The Expansion of Nahuatl as a Lingua Franca Among Priests in Sixteenth-Century Mexico." *Ethnohistory* 59, no. 4 (2012): 675–90.

———. *A Guide to Nahuatl Language Manuscripts Held in United States Repositories*. Berkeley, CA: Academy of American Franciscan History, 2001.

———. *The History of the Catholic Church in Latin America*. New York: New York University Press, 2011.

———. "The Ordenanza del Patronazgo in New Spain, 1574–1600." *Americas* 42, no. 3 (1986): 253–74.

Schwaller, Robert C., ed. "A Language of Empire, a Quotidian Tongue: The Uses of Nahuatl in Colonial Mexico." Special issue, *Ethnohistory* 59, no. 4 (2012): 667–790.

Schwartz, Stuart. *All Can Be Saved: Religious Tolerance and Salvation in the Iberian Atlantic World*. New Haven: Yale University Press, 2008.

Sells, Michael, ed. *Approaching the Qur'an*. Ashland, OR: White Cloud Press, 1999.

Sigal, Pete. *The Flower and the Scorpion: Sexuality and Ritual in Early Nahua Culture*. Durham: Duke University Press, 2011.

SilverMoon. "The Imperial College of Tlatelolco and the Emergence of New Nahua Intellectual Elite in New Spain, 1500–1760." PhD diss., Duke University, 2007.

Smith, Michael E. "The Aztec Empire." In *The Aztec World*, edited by Elizabeth Brumfiel and Gary M. Feinman, 121–36. New York: Abrams, 2008.

Sparks, Garry. *The Americas' First Theologies: Early Sources of Post-contact Indigenous Religion*. New York: Oxford University Press, 2017.

———. "The Use of Mayan Scripture in the Americas' First Christian Theology." *Numen: International Review for the History of Religions* 61, no. 4 (2014): 396–429.

———. "Xalqat B'e and the Theologia Indorum: Crossroads Between Maya Spirituality and the Americas' First Theology." PhD diss., University of Chicago, 2011.

Steck, Francis Borgia. *El primer colegio de América, Santa Cruz de Tlaltelolco, con un estudio del códice de Tlaltelolco, por R. H. Barlow*. Mexico City: Centro de Estudios Franciscanos, 1944.

Suárez, Pedro. *Historia de el obispado de Guadix, y Baza*. Madrid: Antonio Román, 1696.

Tavárez, David. *The Invisible War: Indigenous Devotions, Discipline, and Dissent in Colonial Mexico*. Stanford: Stanford University Press, 2011.

———. "Naming the Trinity: From Ideologies of Translation to Dialectics of Reception in Colonial Nahua Texts, 1547–1771." *Colonial Latin American Review* 9, no. 1 (2000): 21–47.

Taylor, William B. *Magistrates of the Sacred: Priests and Parishioners in Eighteenth-Century Mexico*. Stanford: Stanford University Press, 1996.

Tellechea Idígoras, José Ignacio. *El arzobispo Carranza y su tiempo*. 2 vols. Madrid: Ediciones Guadarrama, 1968.

———. "Dos documentos inéditos para la historia de la Inquisición española en el siglo XVI." *Revista española de derecho canónico* 17, no. 50 (1962): 525–44.

———. *Fray Bartolomé Carranza: Documentos históricos*. 8 vols. Madrid: Real Academia de la Historia, 1962–94.

———. *El proceso romano del Arzobispo Carranza, 1567–1576*. Rome: Iglesia Nacional Española, 1988.

Terraciano, Kevin. *The Mixtecs of Colonial Oaxaca: Ñudzahui History, Sixteenth Through Eighteenth Centuries*. Stanford: Stanford University Press, 2003.

Thomas, Werner. *Los protestantes y la inquisición en España en tiempos de Reforma y Contrareforma*. Leuven: Leuven University Press, 2001.

———. *La represión del protestantismo en España, 1517–1648*. Leuven: Leuven University Press, 2001.

Thompson, Colin P. *The Strife of Tongues: Fray Luis de Leon and the Golden Age of Spain*. New York: Cambridge University Press, 1988.

Torres Palomo, María Paz. "Bartolomé Dorador y el árabe dialectal andaluz." PhD diss., Universidad de Granada, 1971.

———. "Don Martín de Ayala y la catequesis de los niños moriscos." In *Homenaje al prof. Darío Cabanelas Rodríguez, O.F.M., con motivo de su LXX aniversario*, 1:509–18. Granada: Universidad de Granada, 1987.

Townsend, Camilla. *Malintzin's Choices: An Indian Woman in the Conquest of Mexico*. Albuquerque: University of New Mexico Press, 2006.

Tueller, James B. *Good and Faithful Christians: Moriscos and Catholicism in Early Modern Spain*. New Orleans: University Press of the South, 2002.

Vinson, Ben. "Afro-Mexican History: Trends and Directions in

Scholarship." *History Compass* 3, no. 1 (2005): 1–14.

Vose, Robin J. E. *Dominicans, Muslims and Jews in the Medieval Crown of Aragon*. New York: Cambridge University Press, 2009.

Wagner, Henry Raup. *Nueva bibliografía mexicana del siglo xvi, suplemento a las bibliografías de don Joaquín García Icazbalceta, don José Toribio Medina y don Nicolás León.* Translated by Joaquín García Pimentel and Federico Gómez de Orozco. Mexico City: Editorial Polis, 1940.

Wasserman-Soler, Daniel I. "Language and Communication in the Spanish Conquest of America." *History Compass* 8, no. 6 (2010): 491–502.

———. "'*Lengua de los indios, lengua española*': Religious Conversion and the Languages of New Spain, c. 1520–1585." *Church History* 85, no. 4 (2016): 1–34.

———. "True Threat or Victim of Circumstance? Fray Luis de Granada's *Libro de la oración y meditación* and the Spanish Inquisition." *Hindsight Journal* 2 (2008): 1–26.

Weber, Alison. *Teresa of Avila and the Rhetoric of Femininity*. Princeton: Princeton University Press, 1990.

Whinnom, Keith. "The Problem of the Best-Seller in Spanish Golden-Age Literature." *Bulletin of Hispanic Studies* 57 (1980): 189–98.

Wiegers, Gerard. *Islamic Literature in Spanish and Aljamiado: Yça of Segovia (fl. 1450), His Antecendents and Successors*. New York: Brill, 1994.

Wilkinson, Alexander. *Iberian Books: Books Published in Spanish or Portuguese on the Iberian Peninsula Before 1601*. Leiden: Brill, 2010.

Williams, Megan Hale. *The Monk and the Book: Jerome and the Making of Christian Scholarship*. Chicago: University of Chicago Press, 2006.

Yannakakis, Yanna. *The Art of Being In-Between: Native Intermediaries, Indian Identity, and Local Rule in Colonial Oaxaca*. Durham: Duke University Press, 2008.

Zakaib, Susan B. "Built Upon the Tower of Babel: Language Policy and the Clergy in Bourbon Mexico." PhD diss., University of Texas at Austin, 2016.

Zavala, Vicente. *Fray Juan de Zumárraga*. Durango, Spain: S.n., 1985.

INDEX

Africans, Spanish, 5, 117, 125–26
Albotodo, Juan de (S.J.), 53–59, 62–63, 167
Alcalá, Pedro de (O.S.H.), 42–43
Aldrete, Bernardo de, 84
Almería (Spain), 46, 60, 62
alphabet, Roman, 108
Álvarez de Vozmediano, Melchior, 60–61
Alvarado, Francisco de (O.P.), 143–45
Alumbrados, 16–17, 19, 25–26
Ángeles, Francisco de los, 109–10
Angulo, Juan de, 32
Apostles, 28–29, 60, 105, 109, 115, 146
Apostles Creed, 74, 115, 124–26
Aquinas, Thomas (O.P.), 29, 33, 144
Arabic
  binary assessments of, 43–44
  churchmen lacking proficiency in, 4, 47, 50–51, 54–55, 64, 80–81, 90–97
  compared to use of Native American languages, 9–10
  as an interim/temporary language, 41, 52, 62–63, 67, 73–77, 80–97
  restrictions of language and customs, 1, 39–44, 45–46, 60–67, 69–80, 83–95
  as a secondary concern in catechesis, 83–90, 96–97
  university chair in, 85–88
  in Christian contexts, 41–44, 47–59, 72–81, 90–95
  in Spanish Islamic communities, 6, 66–67, 70–76, 83–87
Arias Montano, Benito, 34
Augustine, Order of St., 105, 133, 143, 152, 154
Austria, Jorge de, 73–77
Ávalos de la Cueva, Gaspar, 45–47, 52, 67
Ávila, John of, 14, 31, 52
Ayala, Martín Pérez de, 44, 47–53, 59–62, 65–68, 72–81, 85
Ayala-Ribera catechism, 88, 90–95

Aztecs. *See* Nahuas and Native Americans (Mesoamerica)

baptism, sacrament of, 43, 117, 125–26
Baptismal names, 51, 56, 76
Basacio, Arnaldo de (O.F.M.), 127
Baza (Spain), 48, 55
Bible
  Book of Job, 34
  lay reading of scripture (*see* Cano, Melchior; Carranza, Bartolomé)

Cano, Melchior (O.P.)
  De locis theologicis, 28–30
  lay reading of scripture and religious texts, 21–27, 28–30, 35–36
  on Carranza, 13, 19, 22–24
  on Louis of Granada, 17–18, 25–27
  reputation, 36–38
Carranza, Bartolomé (O.P.)
  Comentarios sobre el catechismo christiano, 13–14, 18–19, 21–24, 27–28
  critique of Spanish Inquisition, 18–19
  lay reading of scripture, 22–23, 28, 35–36
  reception of written work and reputation, 13–15, 35–38
  Inquisition trial, 18–20
Casillas, Tomás de (O.P.), 115
Castilian-Spanish
  absence of policy for, 1
  among Islamic communities, 41–42, 46–47, 51–68, 73–79, 83–85, 88–97
  among Native Americans, 98–100, 107–18, 125–33, 139–42, 145–48, 152, 155–56
  religious literature in, 13–15, 16, 22–25, 28–35, 118
  See also catechism
Castillo, Hernando de, 33
catechesis (religious instruction)

continuity and change in Granada, 39–40, 51–52, 59, 62–63, 67–68
of Amerindian children, 110, 113, 122, 127–28, 148
of Muslim and Morisco children, 41–42, 45, 51–61, 70–73, 85–88
on the necessity of clerical guidance, 23–24, 28–29, 35–36
catechism (book)
in Arabic and Castilian, 47–48, 73–74, 77–78
in Latin and Romance languages, 11, 14, 22, 84, 88–95
in Native American languages, 108, 118–19, 124–25, 145–46, 150–52, 158
Cavañas, Francisco de, 33–34
Çaybon, Diego, 66–67
censorship
Spanish religious texts, 13–16, 37–42
Charles I of Spain (Charles V of the Holy Roman Empire), 10, 45–47, 105, 109, 114, 133, 167
Charles II of Spain, 141–42
Charles III of Spain, 7, 131, 142, 156
Chichimecs, 125–26, 170
Church, Roman Catholic
conflicts within, 14–20, 84, 99–100, 106
enforcement of orthodoxy, 7–8
intransigence of churchmen, 7, 36–38, 101–2
flexibility/pragmatism of churchmen, 3–4, 7–8, 12, 36–38, 67–68, 95–103, 128–32
See also council, provincial; Inquisition, Spanish; and synod
confession, sacrament of, 50–51, 54–57, 70, 74, 108, 120–21, 135–36
conversion, religious. *See* catechesis
Conversos. *See* Jews, Sephardic
Coronel, Juan de, 145
Corrionero de Babilafuente, Antonio, 60–63
Cortés, Hernán, 103, 105, 107
Council of the Indies, 134, 139–41
council, provincial. *See* Granada; Guadix; Mexico, provincial councils of; synod; Valencia
cross, sign of the, 74, 116–17
Curiel, Juan Alonso del, 34

Deza, Pedro de, 39
Díaz, Bernal, 103–4
Doménech, Jerónimo (S.J.), 80–81, 84–85, 87
Dominicans. *See* Preachers, Order of
Dorador, Bartolomé, 47, 66–67, 94–95

encomenderos, 107, 126

Ferdinand II of Aragón, 9, 40, 43
Friars Minor, Order of (Franciscans), 105, 108–9, 133, 143, 146, 150, 154, 168–71
See also Basacio, Arnaldo de; Gante, Pedro de; Gilberti, Maturino; Jiménez de Cisneros, Francisco; Mendieta, Geronimo de; Molina, Alonso de; Sahagún, Bernardino de; Sarmiento de Osacastro (Hojacastro), Martín; Valencia, Martín de; Zumárraga, Juan de
Fuente, Alonso de la (O.P.), 31–32

Gante, Pedro de (O.F.M.), 108
García, Juan (S.J.), 56
Gilberti, Maturino (O.F.M.), 4, 148–54, 169
Granada
Albaicín, 53–58, 62–65
Alpujarras, 39, 42–43, 60, 73, 79, 81, 86
Capitulations of, 40, 43–44
compared to Valencia, 77–83, 86–87
demographics of, 44, 47
episcopal reform in, 45–53, 60–67
1526 Edict of, 45–47, 61
1565 Provincial Council of, 60–63
See also Ávalos, Gaspar de; Ayala, Martín Pérez de; Guerrero, Pedro; Talavera, Hernando de
Granada, Louis of (O.P.)
early life and work, 16–21
Libro de la oración y meditación, 13–17, 24–27
reputation, 13–15, 35–38
Guadix (Spain), 45–55, 60–62, 65–66, 72–76, 94–95, 160

Guerrero, Pedro, 19, 52–55, 60–63, 66
Guzmán, Hierónymo, 31–32
Guzmán Alarave, Juan, 70

Heath, Shirley Brice, 99, 130
Hebrew, 5
Hernández, Benito (O.P.), 145, 150–54
Holy Orders, sacrament of, 124
Holy Spirit, 17, 25, 33, 116–17, 146

Index of Prohibited Books. *See* Inquisition, Spanish
Indies, Laws of, 98, 129, 141
Inquisition, Spanish
 attitudes toward vernacular books, 14–18, 21–36
 conflict with papacy, 20
 Index of Prohibited Books, 15–17, 30–32, 37
 presence in Mexico, 106
 prosecution of Moriscos, 70–72, 78, 82, 87–89
 scholarly assessments of, 8–9, 13–16, 20, 35–38
 vigilance of Protestants, 14, 20, 24–26, 30
 See also Alumbrados; Carranza, Bartolomé; Quiroga, Gaspar de; Valdés, Fernando de
Interpreters/translators
 Amerindian languages, 104, 120–22, 138, 146, 163
 Arabic, 47, 50, 65–66, 91–97
Isabella I of Castile, 9, 40, 43, 99
Islam, 39–46, 66–67, 70–72, 80, 83, 97, 161
 See also Moriscos; Muslims

Jesuits. *See* Society of Jesus
Jews, Sephardic, 5–6
Jiménez de Cisneros, Francisco (O.F.M.), 43–44
Juan de la Anunciación, fray (O.S.A.), 152–54

Ladino, 5
Laínez, Diego (S.J.), 53–58
Luis, de Granada. *See* Granada, Louis of
language
 absence of policy, 3, 8, 99–100, 128–30
 accommodation vs. assimilation of, 3, 99–101, 159, 165
 diversity of, 1, 5–7, 10, 104, 129, 164
 See also Arabic; Castilian-Spanish; languages, Native American; Nahuatl; vernacular
languages, Native American (Mesoamerica)
 attempted elimination of, 131
 binary assessments of, 98–100, 128–30
 churchmen lacking proficiency in, 4, 109–12, 120–22, 132–38
 compared to use of Arabic, 9–10, 98–100, 114, 142–43, 157–64
 consequences for ignorance of, 115–16, 120
 diversity of, 6, 104
 range of approaches, 145–56
 suspicion of, 117–18, 134
 use/study by clergy, 1, 85, 98–102, 107–56
 See also Mixtec; Nahuatl; Otomi; P'urhépecha; Popoloca; Totonac
Las Casas, Ignacio de (S.J.), 84, 95–96
Latin
 among Native Americans, 110, 116–17, 122, 125–27
 as a biblical language, 11, 22, 158
 in Iberian religious literature, 6–7, 22, 32, 88, 164
 See also Castilian-Spanish
Leo X (pope), 109
León, Luis de (O.S.A.), 34
literacy, 20–21, 41, 127
Loaces, Fernando de (O.P.), 81
Luther, Martin (and Lutherans), 10–11, 21, 28, 30–31

Manrique, Alonso, 17, 25
Manrique, Antonio de Rojas, 44
Mass
 among Islamic communities, 41, 46, 61, 66, 74, 88–90
 among Amerindian communities, 117, 122, 125
 language use in, 36, 158

Mendieta, Gerónimo de (O.F.M.), 109, 168–71
Mexico (New Spain)
compared to Spain, 50, 85, 100, 114, 130, 157–63
episcopal reform in, 114–30
1524 *Primera junta apostólica*, 109–14
1574 *Ordenanza del patronazgo*, 123
mestizo cultures, 101–3
Spanish books in, 32, 118
Tenochtitlan, 103
Tlaxcala, 106, 135–36
See also languages, Native American (Mesoamerica)
Mexico, provincial councils of
as an under-studied topic, 102
First Provincial Council (1555), 114–19, 127
Second Provincial Council (1565), 119–22, 135
Third Provincial Council (1585), 5, 123–28
Mixtec (language), 136, 143–45, 150–51, 154
Molina, Alonso de (O.F.M.), 4, 146–54, 170
Montúfar, Alonso de (O.P.), 114–22, 138–42, 163
Moriscos
children, 56–61, 64, 70–73, 85–88, 95
definition of, 7, 43
enthusiasm or resistance to Christianity, 45, 53–57, 89, 95–97
expulsion of, 39–40, 62–64, 82, 90–92, 95–97
of Castile, 39, 96
of Granada, 39–40, 45–47, 54–57, 65–67
of Valencia, 69–72, 81–89
linguistic practices of, 7, 51–52
See also Arabic; Muslims
Moya de Contreras, Pedro, 123–28, 163
Mur, Jerónimo (S.J.), 81
Muslims
in Valencia, 6, 70–72
in Granada, 40–44
injunctions against names and customs, 46, 51, 59, 73, 76, 85
See also Moriscos

Nahuas, 101–5, 126, 133, 148
Nahuatl
as a standard tongue, 99, 103–4, 111, 130
in Christian evangelization, 117, 133, 146–54
spoken by Europeans and creoles, 110–12, 120–21, 136, 146
Native Americans (Mesoamerica)
encounter with Europeans, 8–9, 98–103, 107–9, 159, 162–63
as instructors of Christian doctrine, 107, 121–22
relationships with friars, 105–7
See also languages, Native American
Navarra y Hualde, Francisco de, 69
Navarro, Pedro (S.J.), 53–58
Núñez de Muley, Francisco, 41–44, 65–66

Otomi (language), 120–21, 136, 170

papacy, 60, 133
See also Leo X (pope); Paul III (pope); Paul IV (pope); and Pius IV (pope)
Paul III (pope), 114
Paul IV (pope), 20
Pérez de Ayala, Martín. *See* Ayala, Martín Pérez de
Philip II of Spain
on Arabic and Moriscos, 1, 10, 39–40, 46, 60–66, 72–73, 77–84, 87–94, 161
on Native American languages, 1, 10, 104, 131–42, 146, 151, 155
and Bartolomé Carranza, 18–21
and the Spanish Inquisition, 20, 32
and Louis of Granada, 17
response to Protestants, 30
Philip III of Spain, 96, 141
Philip IV of Spain, 141
Pius IV (pope), 14, 17
policy, language, 3–4, 99, 129, 158
Popoloca (language), 136, 171
Preachers, Order of, 10, 17, 35, 105, 133, 143, 154
See also Alvarado, Francisco de; Aquinas, Thomas; Cano, Melchior; Carranza, Bartolomé; Casillas, Tomás de; Granada, Louis of; Fuente, Alonso de la; Loaces, Fernando de; Hernández, Benito;Montúfar,

Alonso de; Tauler, Johannes; Vico, Domingo de
printing press, 11
P'urhépecha (language), 148–50

Quiroga, Gaspar de, 30–31, 37, 82–83
Quiroga, Vasco de, 115

Reconquista, 6, 12, 40, 161
Ramírez de Haro, Antonio, 73–77
Ribera, Juan de, 81–97, 157
Ricard, Robert, 98
Roa, Martín de (S.J.), 56–57
Rochet, Pedro, 72
Ruiz, Alfonso (S.J.), 53, 55

Salazar, Esteban de, 33
Sahagún, Bernardino de (O.F.M.), 133–34, 171
Sánchez, Francisco, 34
Santiago, Hernando de, 33
Sarmiento de Osacastro (Hojacastro), Martin (O.F.M.), 115
sermons
  in Amerindian languages, 112–13, 118, 128, 144, 150–55, 158, 168–71
  in Arabic, 48, 50, 53–59, 62–63, 95
in Castilian, 23, 31–32, 36, 82
songs, Native American, 118, 127
Serna, Juan de la, 123, 159, 165
Society of Jesus
  comparative study of missions, 9
  in Granada, 52–59, 62–65
  knowledge of Arabic, 53–59, 62–63
  in Mexico, 127–28
  in Valencia, 80–84
  See also García, Juan; Laínez, Diego; Las Casas, Ignacio de; Mur, Jerónimo; Navarro, Pedro; Roa, Martín de; Ruiz, Alfonso; Torre, Francisco de la
Spain. *See* Granada; Guadix; Valencia.
spiritual conquest thesis, 101
synod, 46, 160
  See also council, provincial; Granada; Guadix; Mexico, provincial councils of; Valencia

Talavera, Hernando de (O.S.H.), 7, 40–44, 53, 67–68, 114
Tarascan (P'urhépecha), 148–50
Tauler, Johann (O.P.), 31–32
Terrazas, Francisco de, 136
Toral, Francisco del (O.F.M.), 133
Torre, Francisco de la (S.J.), 53, 56–57
Totonac (language), 136, 169–70
Trinity, 33, 117
Trent, Council of
  nature of leadership at, 7–8
  relationship to other councils and synods, 48–50, 115, 119, 123–25, 158–60
  Spanish delegates at, 18, 48, 60
  on translation of scripture, 10–11, 22

Valdés, Fernando de
  absenteeism, 18
  careerism, 20
  compared to later inquisitors, 30–31, 37
  prohibition of religious literature, 13–15, 17, 24
Valencia
  Arabic speakers in, 83–84
  episcopal reform in, 72–78, 81–95
  fear of Morisco rebellion, 72–73, 81
  1548 synod, 75
  1561 assembly, 69–70
  1566 synod, 75–76
  1573 assembly, 87–88
  1587 assemblies, 81–87
  1595 assembly, 87–90
Valencia, Martín de (O.F.M.), 109–19, 129, 140, 163
Valencian language, 4, 6, 67, 73–80, 83–89, 94, 97
vernacular
  significance in fostering conversion, 4–5, 12, 50, 53–54, 109–10, 122–23
  use in the Middle Ages, 10–11
  See also Arabic; Castilian-Spanish; language
Vico, Domingo de (O.P.), 144
Villanueva, Tomás de (O.S.A.), 75
Vulgate, 10–11

Zumárraga, Juan de (O.F.M.), 105, 114

www.ingramcontent.com/pod-product-compliance
Lightning Source LLC
LaVergne TN
LVHW091131080826
845145LV00008B/2115

* 9 7 8 0 2 7 1 0 8 6 0 0 2 *